Walking a Winding Road

A Study of the Book of Judges

Christy Voelkel

Copyright © 2021 by Christy Voelkel

Scripture taken from the New King James Version®. Copyright © 1982 by Thomas Nelson. Used by permission. All rights reserved. Unless otherwise noted, all Scripture cited in this study is from the NKJV.

Scriptures passages have been copied from the online Bible reference source, Blue Letter Bible (www.blueletterbible.org) using its copy feature.

Strong's Hebrew Lexicon definitions from Blue Letter Bible. Web. 11 December, 2020.

Table of Contents

Introduction: How to Use This Study — iii

Part 1: Overview

    Lesson 1: Pursuing the Inheritance: Gains and Losses — 13

    Lesson 2: Another Generation — 29

    Lesson 3: The Solution to All Oppressions — 43

Part 2: The Judges

    Lesson 4: Oppression #1: Othniel — 77

    Lesson 5: Oppression #2: Ehud and Shamgar — 87

    Lesson 6: Oppression #3: Deborah and Barak — 97

    Lesson 7: Oppression #4: Gideon — 131

    Lesson 8: Abimelech — 173

    Lesson 9: Oppression #5: Tola and Jair — 189

    Lesson 10: Oppression #6: Jephthah, Ibzan, Elon, and Abdon — 199

    Lesson 11: Oppression #7: Samson — 219

Part 3: A Nation Without a King

    Lesson 12: Micah and the Danites — 271

    Lesson 13: The Redemption of Benjamin — 289

Conclusion — 313

How to Use This Study

The objective of this study is to work through the book of Judges in an expository manner and find in it application that is relevant to us as believers in this age. It is very easy to write off Old Testament books such as this as being little more than the sad history of Israel slipping further and further away from her relationship with God; but then, isn't that a description of our world today?

While the book of Judges is a historical narrative, it is written for future generations, namely us, as 1 Corinthians says:

> *"Now all these things happened to them* [Israel] *as examples, and they were written for our admonition, upon whom the ends of the ages have come."* —1 Corinthians 10:11

For this reason, we cannot dismiss the book of Judges as being without application in our day and age. It is a history we were meant to learn from, and that is how we will approach the book in this study.

Studying the Old Testament Pictures

Before we begin, I want to explain a little bit about studying the Old Testament. The Old Testament books have to be approached a little differently from the way we are used to studying the New Testament. The New Testament explains what the Old Testament describes. You will never find a clear explanation of anything in the Old Testament the way you do in the New Testament. You must derive that understanding and application from what you see being modeled or described in the pictures of people and events.

Identifying the picture is key.

So, how do you do that? It's pretty simple, really. You just work through the text asking who, what, when, where, why, and how until you have gathered the big picture. So that is what we will do.

In addition to the basic questions, we will **expand the picture with some Hebrew word studies.** The Old Testament Hebrew is made up of big, often complex, picture words that bring additional context to the passage, but we lose the nuances in the text when we do not study it in its original language. For this reason we will be incorporating into the picture the meanings of names, specifically people and places. Not all names in the Old Testament lend themselves to their narratives, but when God calls certain people to certain places as He does with the judges, names become important. I will also be highlighting key words that will develop a better understanding of the picture.

So, how do you study Hebrew words if you don't know Hebrew? Using a concordance or lexicon to look up the meanings of words is the simplest way and can render a very rich picture. I use the online version of *Strong's Hebrew Lexicon* found online at *www.blueletterbible.org*, and the definitions I use in this study will be taken from that source.

For this study, we will be investigating:

- The meanings behind Hebrew names (people and places).
- The words and root words they spring from (etymology).
- How the same words are used elsewhere in the Old Testament. This is important because some words are always used in the same context. For instance, the word *lechi* is the Hebrew word for "cheek"; but almost every place that word crops up in the Old Testament, it involves someone getting a slap in the face. When we find the word *lechi* in the narrative of Samson, we might consider what kind of slap in the face he is being given and by whom. And so, we will incorporate the mini pictures behind these words into the greater narrative. (Just a note: I will try to transliterate the Hebrew letters into the equivalent English sounds as closely as I can, but it will be an estimate at best. Please don't think my transliteration is the way the words are actually spelled.)

About Hebrew Words

Since we are delving into the world of Hebrew and English translations, there are a few things you should know about Hebrew words in general to get the right picture out of the text.

1) **English words are not always translated as the same Hebrew word. There can be multiple Hebrew words for each English word.**

For example: The word "rest" can be any one of these Hebrew words: *shabbath, nuach, shaqat,* or *shalal*. Each Hebrew word has a different picture behind it. You have to know which Hebrew word is being used for good interpretation of the picture.

2) **One Hebrew word may be translated as a number of different English words or phrases, so we don't make the connections we are supposed to make.**

    For example: The Hebrew word *chomer* is translated into English as "clay," "mortar," a unit of measure called a "homer," or "heap." Hebrew readers would read the same word in all those instances where we see different words. As a result, they would connect these passages and see a picture in it that we don't.

3) **Hebrew words are keywords used to connect different passages.**

    For example: the Hebrew word *shamir* means thorn or brier and is found in Judges 10:1, Isaiah 9:18, Isaiah 32:13, and Ezekiel 3:9. When we study the word across the Isaiah and Ezekiel passages, we find commonalities in the overall picture that give us an understanding of how to interpret our picture in Judges.

    There are times, however, when the context we are studying will be in stark contrast to the other usages. For instance, the proper name Heber springs from the common word *heber* which means "association" or "fellowship," but doesn't necessarily tell us whether the association is a good or bad one. It is most often used in a negative application—to be in league with sorcerers, murderers, robbers, etc. But we can see from Deborah's narrative that Heber is a good associate or comrade for Israel, not a bad one. For this reason, I give you this warning: **You must always keep the context you are studying foremost and let it drive your understanding of the usage of the Hebrew words. The uses of these words in other contexts may be helpful in gaining an overall sense of the word, but the specific application may differ from the one you are studying.**

4) **Hebrew words are picture words that get their flavor from their root words.**

    It is necessary to consider the root words and even their "family" words (derivatives like nouns, adjectives, and verbs) because they are part of the picture.

For example: We will be studying a place called Seirah, which comes from the common word *seirah* meaning bristly (like a goat in the sense of having rough, bristling hair). Seirah comes from the root verb *sa'ar* meaning "to storm, shiver, dread, bristle with horror," or "to storm away, sweep away, whirl away." The picture behind the verb *sa'ar* is that of a person whose hair is standing on end, bristling with horror at the sight of a whirlwind (of judgment) coming at him. It carries intense negative emotion paired with an experience of violence. What happens at the place Seirah is reflected in its root word *sa'ar* which is part of the picture you would miss if you just stopped at the meaning "bristly." You have to ask: bristly *in what sense?*

Another example: Caleb means "dog," but not a dog. It means dog-like in a sense of aggressiveness and forcefulness, like a dog straining at a leash to be let go. You have to pay attention to the *sense* of the word—what qualities are being expressed. It's part of the picture.

As we work through the text, I will show you more examples of how the Hebrew words work out, but you should be aware of these things before you delve into the pictures.

Working Through the Text

Each lesson will begin with a passage for reading along with overview notes where applicable. Read through the passage and see how much of the picture you can grasp. Ask the who, what, when, where, why, and how questions for yourself and look up the meanings of words using a concordance/lexicon like the one found at blueletterbible.org. For instructions on how to use the BlueLetterBible for this task, see the Appendix at the end of the book.

Following the reading, we will work through the text in chunks, first building the picture and then applying it. The applications include discussions of what is being modeled, how it translates into something we experience, and how the picture is explained, applied, or clarified in New Testament teachings.

I have written out the who-what-when-where questions that I asked as I worked through the text myself and added the conclusions I came to in studying the text and applying it. The answers and applications reflect my personal experience and perspective and may have different expressions for you based on your experiences. That's okay. The behaviors and profiles being modeled in the text are wide-ranging and work themselves out at national, community, and personal levels.

I have also included some "Questions for Reflection" in places where I want you to consider how these picture models work out in your personal life. Israel gives us not just the behavior model but an understanding of how certain behaviors play out and their consequences. Not every model is a good model to follow. If you have gone down a similar winding path in your own life, perhaps this study will help you get back on track.

I hope you find the lessons as rich and relevant as they have been to me.

—Christy Voelkel

About the Book of Judges

It is always good to start with a brief overview of the whole book, so let me begin with some general information.

The authorship of the book of Judges is attributed to the prophet Samuel, and records the time of the judges from the death of Joshua to the death of Samson—twelve judges in all. It is a historical narrative, although Jewish texts classify it among the Nevi'im or prophetic books. (Have you ever thought of the book of Judges as being prophetic? It is.)

While scholars differ on the date of the book's official writing, it was most certainly written after the death of Joshua since the opening chapter details the campaigns recorded in the book of Joshua, as well as Joshua's death. In regards to an end date, it is assumed that the book was written before the time of the kings on such evidence as Sidon being mentioned without Tyre. Tyre and Sidon are paired in later books, with Tyre being the more dominant of the two cities, but Tyre is never once mentioned in the Judges text. Therefore, it is surmised that the book was written before Tyre's rise to prominence in the age of the kings. There are other indications beside this, but let's not get bogged down in those explanations. Moving on . . .

In structure, the book of Judges is divided into three narrative sections:

Part 1: Judges 1:1–3:6
This section gives us a sweeping overview looking back at Joshua's work and then forward as another generation rises afterward. The narrative turns at Judges 2:10. This section sets us up for where we are in the timeline and explains Israel's general condition going into this time as well as the role of the judges to come.

Part 2: Judges 3:7–16:31
This section highlights the cycles of Israel's oppressions and wars with the Canaanites and other external enemies, and details the narratives of the twelve judges, Othniel through Samson.

Part 3: Judges 17:1–21:25
This section focuses on the internal problems of corruption, idolatry, and civil war within the congregation of Israel.

Parts 2 and 3 happen concurrently.
A parenthetical note in Judges 20:27-28 gives us the timeline benchmark of Phinehas, the son of Eleazar, the son of Aaron, standing at the Tabernacle in these days. Phinehas succeeds his father, Eleazar, as high priest at Eleazar's death, which is noted at the end of the book of Joshua (Joshua 24:33). So we know that Part 2 begins with Phinehas as high priest. Phinehas is also standing as high priest in Part 3 as noted in Judges 20:27-28, so the events of Part 3 are also placed at the beginning of the judges' timeline and not the end.

> *Note: this Phinehas is not to be confused with the wicked son of Eli who comes much later. Eli's son never attained the position of high priest as did Phinehas, the son of Eleazar, son of Aaron.*

This detail has a significant implication. As we go through the days of the judges, we see Israel's descent into degradation, and it is logical to think that Part 3 is simply a continuation of the Part 2 timeline because Israel seems so very debased in those closing chapters. But if Part 2 and 3 are concurrent, then Israel's debasement is not where they ended, but where they began. This was Israel's condition from the beginning.

The mountains of Ephraim are central to the narrative, and become the seat of rebellion and cultic practices. This is the beginning of what would become the idolatrous northern Kingdom of Israel. Even though the Tabernacle of the LORD stood at Shiloh in the mountains of Ephraim, there is no mention of the Tabernacle until the closing chapters.

Other points of interest will be discussed in the lessons to come.

Let's begin.

JUDGES, PART 1: OVERVIEW

Judges 1:1–3:7

Judges	cf. Joshua	Narrative
❶ Jdg 1:1	Jos 24:29-31	"Now after the death of Joshua, it came to pass . . ."
❷ Jdg 1:2-7		Bezek campaign (Judah & Simeon)
Jdg 1:8-10	Jos 11:16-23	Jerusalem, South & Lowland campaigns (Judah & Simeon)
Jdg 1:11-13	Jos 15:13-17	Debir campaign (Judah & Simeon)
Jdg 1:14-15	Jos 15:18-19	Achsah's blessing of springs of water
Jdg 1:16		The Kenites settling the land
Jdg 1:17		Zephath/Hormah campaign (Judah & Simeon)
Jdg 1:18		Gaza, Ashkelon, Ekron campaign (Judah & Simeon)
Jdg 1:19		Assessment of the Lowland campaign: The Lord was with them, yet they failed to take the lowlands
Jdg 1:20	Jos 15:14	Assessment of Debir campaign: Caleb succeeds in driving out the Anakim
Jdg 1:21	Jos 15:63*	Assessment of Jerusalem campaign: Benjamin's failure to drive Jebusites out
❸ Jdg 1:22-26		Bethel campaign: The Lord was with the house of Joseph
Jdg 1:27-28	Jos 17:12-13	Manasseh's failure to drive Canaanites out
Jdg 1:29	Jos 16:10	Ephraim's failure to drive Canaanites out of Gezer
❹ Jdg 1:30		Zebulun's failure to drive Canaanites out; put under tribute
Jdg 1:31		Asher's failure to drive Canaanites out
Jdg 1:33		Naphtali's failure to drive Canaanites out; put under tribute
Jdg 1:34-36	Jos 19:47**	Dan's failure to drive Amorites out; Amorites later put under tribute by the house of Joseph
❺ Jdg 2:1-5		Judgment of Israel by the Angel of the LORD at Bochim
Jdg 2:6		Joshua dismisses the people and they go to their inheritance
❶ Jdg 2:7-9	Jos 24:29-31	Death of Joshua

*In the book of Joshua, the failure to drive out the Jebusites is attributed to Judah, not Benjamin.
** Joshua 19:47 varies widely in translations. The Hebrew basically says that the land of Dan "went out from them" and so they took Leshem. (Leshem is assumed to be Laish of Judges 18.) Jewish texts render "went out from them" as "slipped from their grasp."

LESSON 1

Pursuing the Inheritance: Gains & Losses

READ

Judges 1:1–2:9

OVERVIEW

There is a lot of detail in this first section, so it will be helpful if we work through it systematically in chunks using the chart on page 12.

About the chart: In the first column, I have listed the verses we will be covering. In the second column, I have included cross-references to where the same events are found in the book of Joshua, several of which are repeated word for word as if the author took the passage straight out of the Joshua narrative. In the third column, I have summarized the gist of the verse or set of verses.

We will begin with section ❶ (Judges 1:1 and 2:7-9), which bookends the selection and focuses on the death of Joshua.

Then we will work our way down through ❷, ❸, and ❹, which are the campaigns and assessments of the tribes' efforts to claim their inheritance in the Land.

> Section ❷ details the campaigns of Judah and Simeon.
>
> Section ❸ details the campaigns of the house of Joseph (namely Ephraim and Manasseh).
>
> Section ❹ details the assessment of the rest of the tribes. This brings us to the end of chapter 1.

Chapter 2 focuses on the Angel of the LORD's judgment of Israel's effort at a place called Bochim (section ❺), which brings us back to Joshua again.

Lesson 1: Walking a Winding Road | 13

BUILD THE PICTURE

Death of Joshua, Judges 1:1, 2:7–9

1. **Why begin with a reference to the death of Joshua in verse 1?**

   Judges 1:1 connects us back to the previous book of Joshua, and establishes the continuum of that timeline. Overall, the events of the book of Judges occur after Joshua's death, as the text explains in Judges 2:9-10, but the narrative flow of the book of Judges does not follow a linear timeline, per se. Judges 1:1–2:6 are actually a review of events that happened during the days of Joshua, as evidenced by the fact that entire verses are duplicated between Joshua and Judges (see the number of cross-referenced verses in the chart on page 2). If you were to begin reading the book of Judges without knowing the events in the book of Joshua, you might be misled into thinking these events actually happen after the death of Joshua. They don't.

2. **If all these campaigns happened during the days of Joshua, why list them after the statement "Now after the death of Joshua . . ."?**

   In terms of the overall book, the narrative events will pick up the historical timeline from Joshua's death going forward through the time of the judges. That is the first and foremost function of the verse.

   In terms of the immediate passage, the death of Joshua is not used as a timeline marker so much as a literary device for structuring the passage. There are different ways to structure information within a text. These are some basic narrative structures used in the Scriptures:

   - **Linear progression (timeline).** This lays out events in the order in which they happen. Even though the text element may include a timeline point, that doesn't mean the information that follows is necessarily in timeline order.

   - **Inclusio.** This is where repeated phrases at the beginning and end of a passage become bookends that encapsulate a particular picture. The inclusio phrases reflect the picture's theme.

   - **Chiasm or chiastic structure.** The author may build the narrative to a point (point A, then point B, then point C), then resolve the statements in reverse order (C-B-A). So you get an ABBA structure.

BOOKEND	Joshua 24:29-30	*"Now it came to pass after these things that Joshua the son of Nun, the servant of the LORD, died, being one hundred and ten years old. And they buried him within the border of his inheritance at Timnath Serah, which is in the mountains of Ephraim, on the north side of Mount Gaash."*	A
	Joshua 24:31	*"Israel served the LORD all the days of Joshua, and all the days of the elders who outlived Joshua, who had known all the works of the LORD which He had done for Israel."*	B

PICTURE	**Judges 1:1–2:6**
	The decision Israel makes to claim the full inheritance or not, considering all that has already been accomplished for them by Joshua's death.

BOOKEND	Judges 2:7	*"So the people served the LORD all the days of Joshua, and all the days of the elders who outlived Joshua, who had seen all the great works of the LORD which He had done for Israel."*	B
	Judges 2:8-9	*"Now Joshua the son of Nun, the servant of the LORD, died when he was one hundred and ten years old. And they buried him within the border of his inheritance at Timnath Heres, in the mountains of Ephraim, on the north side of Mount Gaash."*	A

Judges 1:1 and 2:8 both have repeated statements of Joshua's death. Thus, they form an inclusio that bookends the description of Israel's campaigns and accomplishments up to the day of Joshua's death.

Judges 1:1 points us back specifically to Joshua 24:29-31. Judges 2:7-9 also points to Joshua 24:29-31. In fact, Judges 2:7-9 is an exact repeat of those verses in Joshua, except they are presented in a chiastic or ABBA order (see the chart above). Even the name of Joshua's burial place is presented in chiastic structure: S-R-H—H-R-S.[1] Whenever you find such a tightly knit structure in the Scripture, it is important to consider the verses that fall between the bookends as a singular cohesive picture.

There is the surface picture that we understand from a literal observation of the passage, but there is also a prophetic picture

---

1 Remember, there are no vowels in the original Hebrew text. Vowel points were only added later to help with pronunciation.

described within these bookends that we will discuss at the end of this lesson after we have worked through the verses.

So, let's begin working our way through the picture.

The Bezek Campaign, Judges 1:2-7

3. **Why did Judah and Simeon team up for these campaigns?**

   Judah and Simeon teamed up for these campaigns because Simeon's territory was within Judah's territory (Joshua 19:1). Inheritance was based on the size of the tribe, and at the time of the second census, Simeon was the least of all the tribes in number, whereas Judah was the greatest. Joshua 19:9 says:

   > "The inheritance of the children of Simeon was included in the share of the children of Judah, for the share of the children of Judah was too much for them. Therefore the children of Simeon had their inheritance within the inheritance of that people." —Joshua 19:9

   So, Judah and Simeon teamed up and launched out of Gilgal to tackle the strongest Canaanite king in Judah's territory, namely Adoni-Bezek.

4. **What do we know about Adoni-bezek?**

   About the Canaanites: Canaanite nations in Israel at this time were organized like city-states. A powerful landowner would capture a certain territory and rule it. Adoni-Bezek had conquered seventy kings from the lands around him (Judges 1:3-7), which made him a significant ruler over a large territory. This is perhaps why Judah and Simeon tackled him first. He was also known for his brutality from his infamous treatment of the vanquished kings in cutting off their thumbs and big toes, which reduced them to slaves who were fed from the scraps that fell from his table.

   Adoni-Bezek means Lord of Bezek. Adoni is the lesser version of Adonai which is the name for the LORD. Bezek comes from the root word *bazak* meaning "lightning." So Adoni-Bezek could be called "Lord of Lightning."

   Another Hebrew word for lightning is *barak*. The *barak* lightning is almost exclusively used of God coming in judgment with lightning and a glittering sword. God is Adonai-Barak—LORD of Lightning.

Adoni-Bezek went head-to-head with Adonai-Barak and was dealt an eye-for-eye type of justice. He was captured, and his thumbs and big toes were cut off. He himself admitted that "as I have done, so God has repaid me."

The Bezek campaign was a victory for Judah. From there Judah and Simeon move south to tackle Jerusalem, the southern desert and lowlands. I will pass over Jerusalem for the moment because we will return to it farther down in the text.

The Jerusalem, South & Lowland Campaigns, Judges 1:8-10

5. Judah fought against Hebron, aka Kirjath Arba. Kirjath Arba means "city of Arba." Who was Arba? (Joshua 21:11)

Arba was the father of Anak and the Anakim, the greatest among the giants. Arba actually means "four" in the sense of being a totality (like the four corners of the earth). Arba represented a totality of this kind of enemy. When we get to the assessment of the campaigns, it will be noted that Caleb was the one who expelled the Anakim out of the area and was given Hebron as a reward.

The name Hebron means "associations" or "joinings," taken from the common word *heber* or association. When *heber* is used in other places in Scripture, the associations are always bad ones—associations with charmers, mediums, robbers, murderers, etc. The old associations should have been removed with Israel's taking of this place, but we will find the men of Judah are still in bad company when we revisit this place in the narrative of Samson.

The Debir Campaign, Judges 1:11-16

6. What do we know about Caleb and his family from their names?

Caleb means "dog" in the sense of forcefulness and aggression, like a dog straining at the master's leash to be set free to pursue the prey.

Kenaz means the "hunter."

Othniel means "lion of God." Othni means "lion," and El means "God." There are five different words for "lion" used in the Old Testament Scripture, but *othni* is a singular use of the word. It is only ever

Lesson 1: Walking a Winding Road | 17

used as a proper name, not a common word, and the name is only recorded twice among the Old Testament Hebrew names. (There is one other Othni mentioned in 1 Chronicles 27:15 and that is all.) This is a singular "lion," and this word for "lion" indicates a sense of forcefulness. Kind of like the *caleb*, only bigger and fiercer.

Do you get a sense of the character of this family based on their names? They are aggressive hunters and fighting men. No wonder God sent them out first.

Achsah means anklet, either as a bridal adornment or shackle (funny how that word serves that dual purpose).

Debir was formerly known as Kirjath Sepher. Kirjath Sepher meant "city of the book," but it was changed to Debir which means "sanctuary," from the root word *debir* meaning "innermost recess of the sanctuary." It is a name given to the Holy of Holies in Solomon's Temple. *Debir* comes from the root verb *dabar* which means "to speak or declare." The Holy of Holies was the place from which the LORD declared, commanded, warned, and otherwise spoke to Israel.

So, we have some picture elements of fierce fighting men (the second generation more fierce than the first), a bride, and a place that is deep within the territory being claimed.

7. **What was Othniel's reward for taking Debir?**

   Othniel received Achsah for a bride and the desert lands. The dry lands were of no use without water, and so he had Achsah ask for the upper and lower springs of water. The renewable springs were most desired for water sources because they did not dry up as rivers did or become stagnant and polluted as pools of water did.

8. **Who were the Kenites?**

   Kenites were Midianites by nationality, and the Midianites had historically been an adversary of Israel. This sect, however, broke away from Midian to be associated with Moses and Israel. As Israel was on their way to the Promised Land, Moses made a promise to his brother-in-law Hobab that if he would come with Israel, then the family would be given a share of the good that the LORD promised Israel (Numbers 10:29-32).

There was no further mention of the Kenites in the Numbers narrative, nor were they mentioned in the campaigns of Joshua, but they reappear now in Judges 1. They were with Israel at the City of Palms (aka Jericho, Deuteronomy 34:3) and moved to settle in the southern deserts of Judah. They were the only Gentiles granted a place in the Land. Since they were not Canaanite, they were not on the list of those to be thrown out.

We have gathered our picture elements of the Debir campaign. Now put them together.

PICTURE SUMMARY

Othniel, prince of Judah, cleared the way and conquered Debir so that the children of Israel might enter into their inheritance. As a reward he was given Caleb's daughter and received a dowry of a field with the upper and lower springs of water as part of the blessing. The Kenites came in after him and were given a place in his territory.

In other words (substitute the meaning of the words):

The Lion of God, prince of Judah, cleared a way to the Holy of Holies, so that the children of Israel might enter into their inheritance. He claimed the Bride as a reward and was granted an inheritance of a kingdom from which springs of living water flow. (Actually, it is the Bride who asked for the living waters.) The Gentiles were also brought in and given a place in his kingdom.

APPLY THE PICTURE

9. Of whom is Othniel a picture?

He is a picture of Jesus Christ in His first coming.

Knowing what we know of Christ from the book of Hebrews, we see this as a prophetic picture of Christ and the work He did on the cross for us in His role as our high priest, but it is a picture of the Messiah that would have been dismissed in Old Testament times. Under Old Testament law, a prince of Judah would never be allowed to enter the Holy of Holies. That is a role reserved for the priesthood. For this reason, this picture of the coming Messiah needed clarification, which the New Testament provides. The writer of the book of Hebrews explains at length how a prince of Judah could enter the Holy of Holies and why it had to be that way. He clarifies this doctrinal picture for us:

> *"This hope we have as an anchor of the soul, both sure and steadfast, and which enters the Presence behind the veil, where the forerunner has entered for us, even Jesus, having become High Priest forever according to the order of Melchizedek."* —Hebrews 6:19-20

> *"For it is evident that our Lord arose from Judah, of which tribe Moses spoke nothing concerning priesthood . . . For if He were on earth, He would not be a priest, since there are priests who offer the gifts according to the law;"* —Hebrews 7:14, 8:4

> *"Not with the blood of goats and calves, but with His own blood He entered the Most Holy Place once for all, having obtained eternal redemption."* —Hebrews 9:12

> *"Therefore, brethren, having boldness to enter the Holiest by the blood of Jesus, by a new and living way which He consecrated for us, through the veil, that is, His flesh, and having a High Priest over the house of God,"* —Hebrews 10:19-21

10. Who are Achsah and the Kenites a picture of?

Achsah is a veiled picture of the Church (Bride), and the Kenites are the Gentiles who are also given a place in the Kingdom.

BUILD THE PICTURE

The Hormah Campaign, Judges 1:17

11. In whose territory was Zephath and why rename it Hormah?

Zephath (meaning "the watchtower") was in Simeon's territory, and it was utterly destroyed. Therefore, it was given the name Hormah meaning "devotion" in the sense of devoting it to God for utter destruction. It creates an interesting minor note in the picture.

The Assessment of Judah and Simeon, Judges 1:18-21

12. What was the overall assessment of these campaigns?

Overall, Judah and Simeon were successful. Judah was the only tribe to take its border towns (Gaza, Ashkelon, and Ekron mentioned in verse 18). The text says that Judah failed to take the lowlands because the enemy had chariots of iron. They took the mountain regions, but were at a loss in dealing with the enemy on the plains where horses and chariots could be implemented.

13. Were chariots of iron a reason to fail?

No, they shouldn't have been—not if the LORD was with them as it says in verse 19, and not if they had their brethren fighting alongside them. We will see in the narrative of Deborah that Barak went up against nine hundred chariots of iron and prevailed. I suggest that the reason for the failure was purely a lack of faith.

14. If Judah and Simeon took Jerusalem and set it on fire (1:8), why does the text point out that Benjamin failed to drive the Jebusites out of Jerusalem?

This question brings up the broader question of why there were still enemies in the land if Joshua "took" the land and put the enemy to the sword. We will discuss this at greater length in the next lesson, but for a simple answer, we need to understand what Joshua's work entailed.

Joshua's campaigns were meant to break the back of the enemies who had the power to displace Israel again once they were in the land. He took out major seats of power, the kings, and their armies, but left the general population for Israel to deal with. The general population did not have the ability to establish reign over Israel—unless Israel allowed it.

In regards to Benjamin mentioned in verse 21, the Judges' account differs from the cross-reference in Joshua. In Judges, the fault for not removing the Jebusites from Jerusalem was laid against Benjamin, whereas in the Joshua account, the failure was laid against Judah (Joshua 15:63). Jerusalem is a border town between Judah and Benjamin, but it is officially allocated to the tribe of Benjamin (per Joshua 18:28). I do not know why there is this difference in accounts except to say that the account of Joshua and Judges have different focuses, and the Judges account is not so much about Joshua's work as it is the follow-on work of the tribes after Joshua has taken the area. Ultimately, it was Benjamin's responsibility, and their failure is pointedly noted.

Overall, Judah was the largest tribe given the greatest amount of land and they took most of it with only a failure in the lowlands. Included in this picture is a blessing which the other tribes will not have.

The Campaigns of the House of Joseph, Judges 1:22-29

15. What do we know about Bethel and what does Bethel mean?

Bethel's name was originally Luz, meaning "almond tree," probably because almonds were grown in this area. It was apparently a fortified city with a hidden entrance. The men of Ephraim and Joseph surrounded it but had to wait for someone to come out in order to find a way inside.

Bethel means "house of God," not to be confused with the Tabernacle that was the house of God and stood at Shiloh in these days.

16. How did this campaign resemble Joshua's taking of Jericho?

In the Jericho campaign, Joshua sent in the spies to assess it first, and Rahab and her family were spared because she helped the spies. In a similar way, the men of Israel spied out Bethel and spared the man who showed them the way into the city. Manasseh and Ephraim took a tactic out of Joshua's play book in their approach to Bethel.

17. What is the final assessment of Ephraim and Manasseh's effort?

They campaigned as one house, but each was assessed individually. Manasseh did not take its border towns, and Ephraim did not take Gezer. They were given the second largest section of land west of the Jordan, and they made one significant gain, but not as much as they should have made.

The Campaigns of the Remainder of Israel, Judges 1:30-36

18. Did the other tribes make any gains?

There are no other gains mentioned for the rest of Israel. The author only mentions their failures. They took the land that Joshua had given them and sat on it. Curiously, Issachar is not mentioned at all, and I can find no reason for the omission.

Judgment at Bochim, Judges 2:1-6

19. How does the Angel of the LORD identify Himself? Who is he?

The Angel of the LORD makes a series of statements that give us a clue as to His identity. Consider who did the following:

"I led you up from Egypt..." Who led them up from Egypt? God and Moses. (The Angel of the LORD is not Moses.)

"[I] brought you to the land of which I swore to your fathers; and I said, 'I will never break My covenant with you.'" Who made that covenant with Israel? God.

These statements point to the Angel of the LORD as being God, and yet He is a manifest form of God. No man could see the LORD and live, and yet here He appeared in visible form. For this reason, we consider the Angel of the LORD as a Christophany—an Old Testament appearance of Christ.

The LORD gave Israel directions concerning the Angel in Exodus 23:

> *"Behold, I send an Angel before you to keep you in the way and to bring you into the place which I have prepared. Beware of Him and obey His voice; do not provoke Him, for He will not pardon your transgressions; for My name is in Him. But if you indeed obey His voice and do all that I speak, then I will be an enemy to your enemies and an adversary to your adversaries. For My Angel will go before you and bring you in to the Amorites and the Hittites and the Perizzites and the Canaanites and the Hivites and the Jebusites; and I will cut them off. You shall not bow down to their gods, nor serve them, nor do according to their works; but you shall utterly overthrow them and completely break down their sacred pillars."* — Exodus 23:20-24

20. What charge does the Angel of the LORD bring against Israel?

"But you have not obeyed My voice." The authority was given to Him by the Father Himself, and the Angel was given the right to judge Israel if they do not obey.

21. What is the punishment?

"Therefore I also said, 'I will not drive them out before you; but they shall be thorns in your side, and their gods shall be a snare to you.'"
—Judges 2:3

This comes from Numbers 33:55-56:

"But if you do not drive out the inhabitants of the land from before you, then it shall be that those whom you let remain shall be irritants in your eyes and thorns in your sides, and they shall harass you in the land where you dwell. Moreover it shall be that I will do to you as I thought to do to them."— Numbers 33:55-56

Note: The Angel did not send Israel out of the Land for her failure. She did not lose her inheritance. But her experience in the Land would be significantly different for not having obtained the full inheritance.

22. What does Bochim mean?

Bochim means "weeping." It shares this character with Bethel where the children of Israel come weeping before the LORD in Judges 20 and 21. Bochim and Bethel may be the same place.

We have come to the end of the inclusio, and now we need to talk about the big, big picture within the inclusio . . .

PICTURE SUMMARY

I am going to present this exactly as the author writes it in literal order:

Joshua dies (1:1) and disappears from the narrative for a time. After that, the children of Israel set about the task of claiming their inheritance. Some are given a large inheritance and make the most of it. Some are given less but make some gain. The rest take what Joshua gave them and sit on it without gain. (1:2-36). On a later day of judgment, the Angel of the LORD assesses Israel's effort (2:1-5), and Joshua reappears in the narrative to dismiss them to their inheritance (2:6). And there is weeping.

Joshua is a type of Christ, as is the Angel of the LORD. So let's plug Christ into the picture for them.

In other words . . .

Christ dies and disappears from the narrative for a while. After that, God's children set about the task of claiming their inheritance. Some are given more inheritance; some are given less, according to their abilities. On Judgment Day, Christ returns to administer the judgment and dismiss them to their inheritance, and there is weeping (and gnashing of teeth).

What is the main point of the inclusio?

The picture revolves around the decision God's people make to pursue their full inheritance or not, considering what has already been accomplished for them at Joshua's death.

APPLY THE PICTURE

The Parable of the Talents (Matthew 25:14-30) Comparison

There is a very strong parallel between Jesus' Parable of the Talents and the picture presented in the Judges' passage. Let's compare the two accounts and see how the Old Testament picture is reinforced and even clarified in the New Testament parable.

26. Both passages begin with someone "going away." Who?
The Landowner/Joshua.

27. In the parable, the servants are left with various allotments.
One was given five talents, one was given two, and one was given one. The one who was given the most also made the most. The one who was given some made some, and the one who was given the least did nothing with it.

In Judges 1:3-35:

- **Which tribe received the most and gained the most with minimal failure?**

    Judah. Judah was given the largest area to conquer and took the most territory with significant victories at Hebron and Debir. Their account includes the awarding of an inheritance and a reward.

Lesson 1: Walking a Winding Road | 25

- **Which tribe(s) received some and gained some, but with more failure?**

    Ephraim/Manasseh were given the next largest area to conquer (they actually negotiated with Joshua to get two lots instead of one, in Joshua 17:14-18). They took some of it with a significant victory at Bethel, but did not gain as much as they could have made.

- **Which tribes received the least and did nothing with it?**

    The rest of Israel took what Joshua had conquered for them and sat on it without any gains.

28. **Both passages end with someone returning. Who?**

    The Landowner/Joshua, paired with the Angel of the Lord.

29. **How do the parable and the Judges' narrative both end?**

    With judgment and weeping by the servants who failed.

30. **In the Judges' narrative, those who failed to claim their inheritance didn't lose their place in the Land, but their experience was very different going forward. If the parable compares to Judges, then to what does the "outer darkness" equate?**

    If the pictures equate to one another in all other aspects, then I assume the outer darkness does not represent being sent "out of the Land," that is, losing your place in the Kingdom or your salvation. The judgment rendered against Israel is that their experience in the Land would be very different going forward.

    This pairing of pictures lends credence to the Doctrine of Rewards that some teach. They believe that salvation is assured at the point of belief, and failure to pursue the full reward in the journey does not garner a punishment of losing one's salvation and being sent out of the Kingdom. But the experience in the Kingdom to come will be very different for those who choose not to pursue the full inheritance.

    This particular picture is complete for Israel at the initial taking of the Land. For us as believers today, we are still in the midst of this timeline, figuratively speaking. Our Joshua (Jesus) has not yet returned, and our judgment day is still to come. We are still battling to claim our full inheritance in the kingdom.

Is the Parable of the Talents applicable to us? Yes, of course. Then so is the book of Judges.

The Parable of the Talents ends at the judgment, but the book of Judges goes on. From here out, the narrative will focus on the experience of those who made the decision not to pursue the reward of their full inheritance. The problems Israel encountered will be the same problems we encounter in this life when we get off the straight highway that is God's way and begin walking the winding roads of coping and compromise. Israel will model this for us.

Questions for Reflection:

- At the day of judgment, the Angel asks Israel, "Why have you done this?" Let's answer His question. What reasons might Israel give for letting the Canaanites stay instead of driving them out of the Land? Why didn't they push on to claim the full inheritance?

- Why don't we pursue the inheritance? Do we have a clear picture of the inheritance for which we are striving?

LESSON 2

Another Generation . . .

READ

Judges 2:10–3:6

BUILD THE PICTURE

Israel's Unfaithfulness, Judges 2:10-15

1. Which generation is the narrative focused on? (Judges 2:10)

Judges 2:10 presents us with a turning point in the narrative. Where Judges 1:1-2:9 looks back at the work done under Joshua and the elders who outlived him, now we are looking forward with "another" generation.

"Generations" are relative to their relationship with God, not their actual calendar years or ages, and are often benchmarked to Israel's coming out of Egypt, which was the start of that relationship.

The first generation saw the works of the Lord and yet became faithless and died in the wilderness.

The second generation experienced the fulfillment of God's covenant promise to bring them into the Land. That was another benchmark moment in Israel's corporate relationship with God. The second census taken in the wilderness shows that some families had already reached the fifth generation in terms of fathers begetting sons and daughters, but these generations have a commonality of experience in that they were "the generation" who came into the Land.

Now "another" generation is going to rise who are in the Land but know nothing of the Lord's work first hand. That generation is not capped. It is left open-ended as if to imply that it is a continuing condition.

Think of this in a New Testament context. There were those of the first generation who knew Christ personally and saw His work on earth. These became the elders who outlived Jesus. When these eyewitnesses died, they left only a written account of what they had seen. Then there was "another" generation who rose after them, of which we ourselves are a part, who live by faith in the written record.

2. **What characterized the lives of this new generation?**

   They lacked an experiential knowledge of God. They had only heard the stories without actually witnessing His works. And they slipped into serving the Baals and Ashtoreth.

3. **What are two other characteristics of the times from Judges 17:6?**

   First, there was no king in Israel—no physical, human king. Israel at this point was a theocracy, where God was king and the priesthood ruled as His ministers, except the priesthood were notably dysfunctional as a ruling class in the Judges' narrative. The only mention of a high priest standing before the Lord at the Tabernacle will be Phinehas in Judges 20:28. Even then it is only a parenthetical phrase.

   Secondly, this generation did what was right in their own eyes. "Doing right in your own eyes" is associated with Israel's time in the wilderness, as Moses warns them:

   > "You shall not at all do as we are doing here today—every man doing whatever is right in his own eyes—for as yet you have not come to the rest and the inheritance which the LORD your God is giving you."—Deuteronomy 12:8-9

4. **What was the wilderness experience like?**

   Israel wandered. An entire generation drifted through life aimlessly, going in circle and cycles, having no rest, no fruit, and no goals. They had to learn that man does not live by bread alone, but by what comes from the word of the LORD; they lived with what God gave them but stumbled often in their faith. All that was supposed to come to an end when they entered the Land. In the Land, they were supposed to experience rest, stability, and fruitfulness.

   Doing what is right in your own eyes leads to a wilderness-like existence. Every time Israel returned to doing what was right in their own eyes, they experienced drifting, going in circles/cycles, hiding and following winding roads to skirt obstacles and enemies. They suffered leanness physically and spiritually.

What is true of Israel is true of us. God has established a path that is described as a straight highway. When we get off the path, we end up on winding roads of coping and compromise that take us into a rootless, fruitless, wilderness-like existence just as it did with Israel.

Serving Baal and Ashtoreth

The Baals and Ashtoreth present us with a picture of a way of life. You don't necessarily need to have physical Baal and Ashtoreth idols in your house to be pursuing this way of life. We will look at the literal, physical model of Israel first, and then discuss how this model translates into our context.

5. What was Baal? What does its root word *ba'al* mean?

Baal is a proper name for an idolatrous deity, but not a singular deity. The Baalim (plural) represent a class of cultic deities of similar nature. Baal means "lord" and is often combined with a place name, such as Baal-Berith or Lord of Berith (Judges 8:33). Baal can also mean "husband." Baal worship was a fertility cult that incorporated illicit sexual acts and child sacrifice into their worship.

Ashtoreth (Judges 2:13) and Asherah (Judges 3:7) were both the same class of goddess. In general, they were the Canaanite fertility goddesses for fortune and happiness and the supposed consorts of Baal. There is a little variation in the meaning of the names, but they are essentially the same.

6. What picture do we get of the Ashtoreth/Asherahs?

Ashtoreth is the plural of **ashterah**, meaning a "flock" in the sense of prosperity from increasing offspring.
Its root verb, **ashar** (beginning with the Hebrew letter *ayin*), means "to be or become rich, pretend to be rich."

Asherah is from the common word **asherah** meaning "groves" (carved wooden idols).
Its root verb, **ashar** (beginning with the Hebrew letter *aleph*), means "to go straight, advance, progress toward being happy and blessed."

7. **How does the worship of Baal and Ashtoreth mimic God?**

    God promised Israel He would be Lord and Husband to them and give them prosperity and increase of flocks and wealth in the Land where He established them (Deuteronomy 28:3-6). The Baals mimic God as lord and husband of the people, and the Ashtoreth/Asherah celebrated prosperity and gain of "flocks." The concepts sound the same but in practice they are radically different.

    When God promises an increase of flocks and harvest, it is in terms of animal flocks and fruit of the earth. God's people are a "flock" only in a figurative sense. In Baal and Ashtoreth worship, the people are the literal flock. They focus on sexual acts and prostitution as a means of increasing the flock of people, and children, therefore, were the fruit.

    God demanded a tithe of increase from animal flocks and harvest. The tithe was not completely wasted but went to feed the priesthood and needy in the community. The Baals and Ashtoreth demanded the sacrifice of increase in terms of children (the product of a human flock), and it was a complete, fruitless sacrifice. Sacrifice of family was a way of pursuing happiness and blessedness with the ultimate goal of becoming wealthy or having the appearance of wealth. It was, in essence, a prosperity cult.

    The Baals and Ashtoreth play to man's carnal nature—the lust of his eyes and flesh, and the pride of life.

8. **How did Israel slip into Baal worship?**

    They fashioned themselves idols and shrines, set up their household gods, consecrated a son as priest, and then did what was right in their own eyes. They gathered all the trappings of what felt like a religious experience, and then made up their own rules.

    In effect, Israel threw off God's headship and pursued other masters who promised them gain. This is where the model crosses into something to which we can relate.

APPLY THE PICTURE
---

9. **How do we slip into our own form of Baal and Ashtoreth worship (i.e., throwing off a master to pursue gain in some form)?**

   The spiritual decamping begins with coveting. The person wants to pursue something that is right in their eyes, but being under the master does not give them that freedom. The coveting then produces the desire to throw off the yoke of the physical master. Accepting God's headship over us includes accepting the headship He has placed over us in the form of physical masters, so the rebellion isn't just against the physical master but God, by extension.

   We may join the "flock" of a different master, or we may simply slip into the pursuit of something that then takes over our life. We begin to redefine and pursue "prosperity," but it will be more focused on physical rather than spiritual prosperity. Such pursuit is often at the cost of our families, particularly our children.

   Paul presents us with a similar picture of throwing off the yoke of a master in pursuit of prosperity or gain. **Read 1 Timothy 6.**

   1 Timothy 6:1–2 gives instructions concerning masters to whom we are slaves—those from whom we get our livelihood and our gain. The masters may be believers or unbelievers, but it really doesn't matter. The point is that they are masters over us.

10. **How does the pursuit of freedom and prosperity play out?**

    - **First, there is a change of attitude toward the master. What is the attitude (6:2, 4)?**

      They begin to despise the master, convince themselves of what seems right in their own eyes, and become arrogant and combative.

    - **How does the conflict progress?**

      The rebels become obsessed with disputes over words—a verbal attack. They will begin to fight *with* words. They will fight *over* words.

      They will fight the physical master, but also the teaching of God's Word because the authority of masters is established by God in

His Word. There are passages in the Bible they would just as soon ignore. When they are taught those passages, they will dispute them.

They argue over technicalities and definitions. They look for loopholes for casting doubt. They will try to redefine the truth of God's Word and tell you it doesn't mean what you think it means. They will cast doubt on the masters based on evil suspicions (as opposed to the truth).

- **How does envy or covetousness escalate to fighting (strife)?**

The desire to decamp began with wanting some freedom the master was denying them. The rebels feel they have a right to do whatever they see as right in their own eyes, and that their right is being denied.

Coveting leads to a victim mentality, and victims need support. They seek to sway others to their cause. They will begin to build a "flock" by enlisting others' help in gaining their "freedom."

Their words will be angled to produce covetousness in you. They want you to identify with them and make you feel like you are being victimized and denied. Then they will demand that you take up the cause and fight. Whether you support them or fight them, they will bring you into the strife.

- **What is the effect of "useless wrangling" on the congregation?**

Their "useless wrangling" becomes a constant friction in the congregation. From such people, turn away. They are only seeking "gain," not godliness (1 Timothy 6:5). They may cloak their arguments in talk of godliness, but it is only a mimicry of godliness. We know this by the path and tactics they use to achieve their goal.

- **What is gain by God's definition?**

Godliness with contentment. The things of this world are temporary. Pursue only as much of this physical world as is needed for living, but then focus on the spiritual pursuit of a relationship with God.

- **What is gain by the worldly (Baal and Ashtoreth) definition?**

Earthly riches and prosperity; "freedom" to pursue our own way of thinking—doing what is right in your own eyes; "freedom" to pursue carnal lusts. Sadly, these people may actually think they are pursuing something godly or a form of godliness when, in fact, it is merely a cloak for what they really want.

- **What does Paul instruct Timothy to do (v11-12, 20)?**

    "From such withdraw yourself... But you, O man of God, flee these things and pursue righteousness, godliness, faith, love, patience, gentleness. Fight the good fight of faith, lay hold on eternal life... O Timothy! Guard what was committed to your trust, avoiding the profane and idle babblings and contradictions of what is falsely called knowledge" —1 Timothy 6:5, 11-12, 20

As you can see, even though we don't have literal Baals and Ashtoreth that we worship, we can follow the same process of slipping into the idolatry of carnal pursuits as Israel did.

Back to Judges... Israel is unfaithful to their covenant with God, but God is faithful in keeping up His part of the covenant (Judges 2:15).

BUILD THE PICTURE

11. What were the cycles of judgment God promised to visit on Israel if they didn't keep His ways? (Leviticus 26:16-22)

He said He would appoint terror over them and wasting diseases (like the punishment for unfaithful wives in Numbers 5). Their enemies would take the produce of their fields and reign over them. The land would experience famine, wild beasts would come among them (animals or possibly bestial men), and their highways would be deserted because of the predators that haunt them.

The Judges, Judges 2:16-19

12. Who were the judges and what tribe(s) did they come from?

There are fourteen judges named in Scripture, but only twelve in the book of Judges.[1] The judges we will be studying are: Othniel, Ehud,

---

1 Eli and Samuel were also judges of Israel, but they are not included in the Judges

Shamgar, Deborah, Gideon, Tola, Jair, Jephthah, Ibzan, Elon, Abdon, and Samson.

Unlike priests who came from one tribe, the judges in the book of Judges came from many tribes, including Judah, Benjamin, Manasseh, Issachar, Zebulun, Ephraim, and Dan. Othniel is the only judge from the southern kingdom (Judah). The rest are all from the northern tribes of Israel.

The only Levite priest who was also a judge was Eli (1 Samuel 4:18), not mentioned as part of the Judges narrative. There is a notable absence of the levitical priesthood among the judges and saviors in the book of Judges.

13. What were the roles of the judges?

There were three types of judges mentioned in the Old Testament: the *dayan*, the *paleel*, and the *shofet*. The *dayan* and *paleel* had purely judicial roles, but the *shofet* was a judge with the added distinction of governing at a civic level. The word *shofet* is often rendered "chieftain" in the Hebrew. They were not kings, but they had a rulership over the people. **All the judges in the book of Judges were shofet**, which was why the name of the book in the Hebrew is *Shofetim* (plural of *shofet*).

Some judges had a secondary role as deliverers or *moshia*. The word *moshia* comes from the word *yasha* meaning "to save or deliver." Other Hebrew words in this family include Joshua, Yeshua, Moshia, Moshiach, and Messiah. There is a Messianic element in the pictures of those judges who were also deliverers.

Seven judges have specific years noted for their rule; seven have the task of *yasha*-ing or delivering God's people (but not the same seven); and four give rest.

The judge represented a restraining presence in the Land. So long as the judge lived, there was a restraint of the enemies that plagued Israel as well as a measure of restraint within Israel as a people. Israel's heart didn't change, however, which was why the sin and oppression returned when the judge died.

The LORD was with all the judges in general, but the narrative notes

---

narrative. Eli was the thirteenth judge as mentioned in 1 Samuel 4:18, and Samuel was the fourteenth and final judge noted in Israel's history, as understood from 1 Samuel 8:1.

Years in Oppression	Judge	Judges' Roles		
		Judged	Delivered	Gave Rest
8	**Othniel**	?	✓	40 years
18	**Ehud**	?	✓	80 years
	Shamgar	?	✓	
20	**Deborah (Barak)**	?		40 years
7	**Gideon**	?	✓	40 years
	Tola	23 years	✓	
	Jair	22 years		
18	**Jephthah**	6 years	✓	
	Ibzan	7 years		
	Elon	10 years		
	Abdon	8 years		
40	**Samson**	20 years	✓	

that the Spirit of the Lord came specifically upon four—Othniel, Gideon, Jephthah, and Samson—and empowered them. So there is a subtle inclusion of the Holy Spirit's work meshed with the picture of the work of the judges.

14. Were the judges a solution to Israel's unfaithfulness and idolatry?

No. While the judges represented a restraining presence, they could only prompt the people toward faithfulness and righteous living, and render judgment when necessary. But they warred continually against the eroding influence of the Canaanites who lived side by side with the people. The book of Judges ends with the critical comment, *"In those days there was no king in Israel .."*, suggesting that the judges were ineffective and that the only solution to Israel's heart issue would be found in a coming king.

Why God Left the Canaanites in the Land, Judges 2:20-3:6

15. Why did God leave the Canaanites in the Land?

Israel drove the LORD to fury with her idolatry and unfaithfulness, so the LORD refused to drive out the Canaanites before Israel. Israel on her own was not capable of driving them out without the LORD's help. The Canaanites became the LORD's tool in testing future generations of Israel and teaching them how to wage war.

APPLY THE PICTURE

16. Who is the restraining force in the lives of believers in this age?

The indwelling Holy Spirit is the empowering and restraining influence for us as believers in this age. He is our internal Helper in overcoming our carnal side, and yet, even with the presence of a Spirit, we still fall short of ridding ourselves of our "Canaanite" tendencies. In the same way, the judges provided restraint, but did not change the heart of Israel.

The Holy Spirit is also described as the restrainer of lawlessness in this age. 2 Thessalonians 2:6-8 says:

> *"And now you know what is restraining, that he may be revealed in his own time. For the mystery of lawlessness is already at work; only He who now restrains will do so until He is taken out of the way. And then the lawless one will be revealed, whom the Lord will consume with the breath of His mouth and destroy with the brightness of His coming."*—2 Thessalonians 2:6-8

17. Is the Holy Spirit a solution to our unfaithfulness?

No. The Holy Spirit is no more a solution to our unfaithfulness than the judges were. While we have the Holy Spirit within us to prompt us to faithfulness and holiness, that Spirit wars with the carnal body in which it is housed and a will that drives our choices.

18. What form do our Canaanites take?

In an external sense, the Canaanites represent the secular world with whom we live and engage on a day-to-day basis. They do not walk according to God's ways and have enslaved themselves to a way of life that involves the pursuit of self-centered fulfillment and worldly wealth, often with the sacrifice of family. They become an eroding factor in our lives that we must battle. They may engage us in physical battle, but the nature of the battle remains at heart a spiritual one, as we are reminded:

> *"For we do not wrestle against flesh and blood, but against principalities, against powers, against the rulers of the darkness of this age, against spiritual hosts of wickedness in the heavenly places."*
> —Ephesians 6:12

> *"For though we walk in the flesh, we do not war according to the flesh. For the weapons of our warfare are not carnal but mighty in God for pulling down strongholds, casting down arguments and every high thing that exalts itself against the knowledge of God, bringing every thought into captivity to the obedience of Christ,"*
> —2 Corinthians 10:3-5

Our battle is not of an earthly nature against an earthly enemy, but a spiritual battle against a spiritual enemy. However, the spiritual fight can have a physical face and can involve us in physical warfare.

The Canaanites also represent the internal, spiritual struggle. Think of the Land as a human body and Israel as the spiritual "new man" that comes to live in the Land. The "new man" has been given a positional place in the Land, but finds himself having to contend with the preexisting carnal "Canaanite" inhabitants and their way of life. The new man is commanded to rid the Land of these carnal enemies which will enslave him to lusts and pursuits of wealth, and the new man battles—to an extent. More often than not, the new man succumbs and even embraces the carnal way of life (the ways of Baal and Ashtoreth).

The Land becomes a picture of a body in which two natures are at war. The battle that Israel faces in terms of a Canaanite enemy in the Land is the same battle we face in being spiritual new men living in carnal Canaanite bodies.

Joshua fought the battles that broke those enemies who could displace Israel from its kingdom, but left the Canaanites with whom Israel must contend.

Jesus fought the battle that broke the reign of sin and death that would disqualify us from the heavenly Kingdom, but there remains this carnal body with which we must contend.

The carnal Canaanite nature no longer reigns over us (unless we give it reign), but it remains in our body to influence and tempt us continually. It draws us into a pursuit of lusts and worldly wealth down paths that take us away from God and eventually may bring us into bondage. Just as the judges intervened to bring Israel out of times of bondage and oppression, so our Savior and Helper intervene to bring us out of our enslavement to Canaanite masters. Like Israel, we must battle and overcome our Canaanites to gain the full inheritance.

We share Israel's experience in living with Canaanites. Israel came into this condition because of disobedience, while we come to this condition by obedience to the mandate to go out into the world and mingle with it as salt and light. Whichever way we came, we both share a common experience of living side by side with Canaanites. Israel will go through the experience first, and we will see from her example what are the pitfalls and stumbling points in the relationship dynamic. These will be the same problems we, too, will experience through living in our world and in our own carnal bodies. So we will take a lesson from that.

It should be noted that the structure of the book of Judges reflects both the internal and external aspects of this struggle:

- **Part 1** sets up the focus on believers who are positionally in the Kingdom, but have not pressed on to claim the full inheritance and put away the enemy.

- **Part 2** unpacks the **external** warfare aspect—the continuing cycle of occupation, oppression, and war with external enemies that Israel has allowed to remain in their lives.

- **Part 3** unpacks the **internal** warfare aspect—dealing with sin in the (congregational) body.

In Parts 2 and 3 we are shown the trail of events that spin off of Israel's decision to stop pursuing the full inheritance and live with the Canaanites.

This is the author's intent in the book of Judges: To show us what happens as a result of failing to press on for the final reward and inheritance and letting our carnal Canaanite side dominate us.

Overview Summary: Fighting the Good Fight, 1 Timothy 6

- **Know God as King**—His power and eternality. Confess Christ's kingship and Godhead.
- **Know what is right in God's eyes and the truth of His Word.**
- **Know how (and when and who) to fight:**
  - Know the enemy and his tactics.
  - Know how to equip yourself by a study of God's Word. When you give up a study of God's Word, at some point you are going to lose the old knowledge you once had.
  - Understand the dynamics of oppression and what is needed to deal with it.
  - Know how to strengthen yourself with the right mindset when you are under oppression.
  - Understand what role the judge/deliverer/helper plays.
- **Hold the borders in the spiritual battles.**
  - Know what "gain" you are pursuing—what is God's definition of freedom, wealth, and where contentment lies. Hold material wealth lightly.
  - Maintain the borders in your personal life, family, and sphere of authority or influence where the world seeks entrance and control.
  - Resist the eroding presence of the world around us.
  - Guard the places where spiritual battles have already been fought and won.
- **Live the faith openly and fruitfully.**

Questions for Reflection:

We studied the process of throwing off a master in pursuit of gain.

- What forms do masters take in your life and what gain are you pursuing?

> The victim mentality is promoted relentlessly by our culture. It is one thing to be a victim, but it is another thing to let that experience define you perpetually and become your identity. God does not want us to see ourselves as perpetual victims.
>
> - What "freedoms" or "rights" do people with a victim mentality hope to gain by throwing off authority?
> - If they succeed in achieving freedom or justice, do they quit agitating over the issue?
> - How do they go about recruiting for their cause?
> - How can they become oppressors?

LESSON 3

The Solution to All Oppressions

READ

Selections from Isaiah 40–63 *(See list on page 45)*

OVERVIEW

Oppressions are coming—for Israel in the narrative, but also for us in real time. So, before we get into the oppressions, I want to talk about the mindset we need to have going into these times that will keep us from floundering in our faith. There will be some key stumbling blocks we run into when we begin our battles to return to the Lord after getting off the path, and we will discuss some strategies for dealing with them.

Recap: What was the purpose of God sending oppressors to Israel and leaving Canaanites in the Land?

- As punishment for unfaithfulness and idolatry
- To teach them how to wage war
- To drive them back to Himself when they get off the path

Solution to All Oppressions

All the oppressions in the Judges' narrative begin with people doing what is right in their own eyes and walking away from God to pursue other roads in life. These winding roads lead Israel into an existence of coping, compromise, and eventually oppression as she loses sight of God and give up pursuit of the her inheritance in the Kingdom.

All the oppressions end with the people returning to God. The battles don't happen when Israel goes into the oppression. The enemy never puts up a fight when God's children are getting off the path. The battles begin only when Israel decides to return to God's straight highway. The *mecillah*, the "highway," is where the battle rages.

Just as it was for Israel, so it is for us. Enduring trials and tribulations is part of the Christian walk. Oppressions can play out at all levels of human relationship, whether within our personal lives, family lives, community or congregational lives, or even on a national scale. They can come as a result of sin in our lives when we get off a godly path and become the catalysts that God uses to drive us back to Him. God also allows various trials in our lives for the purpose of testing and refining our faith.

But those are just the day-to-day trials. There are even greater oppressions on the horizon for us. Christians everywhere are facing greater and greater attacks on our faith and values from an increasingly hostile world.

How do we endure and respond to the trials and tribulations that are already in our lives? How do we prepare for an even greater oppression on the horizon without stumbling in our faith?

It all depends on our mindset. How we prepare ourselves mentally and strengthen ourselves from day to day with the renewing of that mindset will determine if we fall away from God or grow closer to Him in difficult times. So, what is the mindset?

We should ask Isaiah. As God was preparing His people for the Babylonian captivity, He described for them through the words of Isaiah the mindset they needed to have going into that oppression if their faith was to survive that testing. His words were words of comfort but also conviction.

When oppression happens as a result of sin in our lives, the first step to remedying the oppression is to deal with the sin. We need to right our relationship with God and adjust our thinking along godly lines, and help other strugglers do the same. This requires a certain amount of self-reflection, self-correction, and often repentance. The act of repentance may be all that is needed to relieve the oppression, although the consequences at times may generate a new battle which we then must work through. Other times, the oppression may need to be endured until it has run its course. That is part of our refining.

Not surprisingly, the relationship with God is often the last thing we are focused on when we are in the midst of difficulties. Let's face it. When we are already struggling, we don't want to add more conviction to that struggle. All we really want is for the experience to end—and *then* we can focus on our relationship with God. And so we seek ways to get out of the oppression instead of letting the oppression serve its purpose in us.

We need to remember that the oppression may be physical in its outworkings, but the cause is spiritual. Therefore, the spiritual must be addressed before the oppression can be relieved. We can get caught up in a physical battle with the physical combatant in front of us instead of righting our minds and hearts spiritually. But if the relationship with God is right, then even if the oppression remains, it becomes endurable and even transformative.

Oppression can be sometimes caused by sin in our lives, but not always. Sometimes sin in other people's lives impacts us to the extent that they draw us into their oppressive circumstances. Regardless of how it happens, once we are in oppressive circumstances, we must respond in the day-to-day battle. The objective of the battle is a return to God, either on our part or in helping another. That is where the solution to all oppression lies. Success in the battle will require navigating a number of stumbling blocks in the path of return, and we will keep them in mind as we work our way through the Judges narrative.

Seven Stumbling Blocks in the Way of Return

These stumbling blocks are pictured in the book of Isaiah, and they were given at a time when the Babylonian captivity was looming on Israel's horizon. God wanted to prepare His people mentally for facing the time they would spend under that oppressor, and having this preparation beforehand is meant to be a comfort. These passages are very convicting because the first step in preparing any people for oppression is to get them right in their relationship with Him and adjust their thinking. But there will be comfort in the long run for having been prepared. We will use these passages to prepare ourselves for our study of the oppressions to come.

Preparing the Way

There is a three-fold command in Isaiah to "prepare the way" for the return of God's people out of oppression. It is the theme of the inclusio that bookends Isaiah 40 thru 63 (Isaiah 40:3 and 62:10):

> "The voice of one crying in the wilderness: '*Prepare the way* of the LORD; make straight in the desert a highway for our God.'" —Isaiah 40:3 (emphasis added)

> *"Go through, Go through the gates! <u>Prepare the way</u> for the people; Build up, Build up the highway! Take out the stones, Lift up a banner for the peoples!"* —Isaiah 62:10 (emphasis added)

The third instance of this phrase is in Isaiah 57:14 where God commands His people to help each other by removing the stumbling blocks in the way:

> *"Heap it up! Heap it up! <u>Prepare the way</u>, take the stumbling block out of the way of My people."* —Isaiah 57:14 (emphasis added)

So, what are these stumbling blocks? The seven we will focus on are:

1. Seeking comfort in transient things and failing to cling to God's power (Isaiah 40:1-31)
2. Experiencing despair and self-pity, and rejecting God's love (Isaiah 49:14–51:3)
3. Pursuing heavenly blessings versus earthly gains (the Baal and Ashtoreth way) (Isaiah 54:11–55:5)
4. Feeling fearful (Isaiah 51:12–52:12)
5. Feeling shame and humiliation (Isaiah 54:1–10)
6. Letting our dark side overcome us and losing sight of being children of light (Isaiah 60:1–22)
7. Remaining silent and acting with destructive anger (Isaiah 61:10–63:9)

We are going to work through these one at a time and flesh out the picture they present. Then we will reflect on them with some application questions.

#1 Seeking comfort in transient things

Read Isaiah 40:1-31.

When life gets difficult, where do you seek comfort? Think of all the myraid ways we find escape in life. If home life is oppressive, we may turn to work or activities that take us out of the house. If work is oppressive, we may seek comfort at home. If our marriage has become oppressive, we seek other relationships—wrong relationships—for comfort and acceptance. If we are having a bad day, we may seek solace in a pan of brownies, sports, or online shopping. I had a friend who cleaned house whenever she was upset (definitely not my first choice, but it worked for her). We've all got our go-to things that give us comfort and distraction. In worst-case scenarios, there is the oblivion of alcohol, drugs, and other addicting pursuits that offer fleeting relief, but end up bringing us into a new kind of bondage.

All these are like grass, the Lord says.

Isaiah 40 opens with the Lord commanding His prophet to comfort His people and the voice in the wilderness asks, "What shall I tell them?"

God replies:

> *". . . All flesh is grass, and all its loveliness is like the flower of the field. The grass withers, the flower fades, because the breath of the LORD blows upon it; surely the people are grass. The grass withers, the flower fades, but the word of our God stands forever."* —Isaiah 40:6-8

Is that comforting? When we are facing trials and tribulations, do we want to dwell on our own fragility and mortality? No, of course not!

Isaiah gives us three appropriately brief verses of man's fragility, mortality, and ultimate insufficiency, but then goes on for twenty-three verses to extol God's power, wisdom, sovereignty, and eternality with the opening command, *"Behold your God!"* (Isaiah 40:9-31).

Isaiah 40:26 pauses to pose a question. *"Why do you say, O Jacob, and speak, O Israel: 'My way is hidden from the LORD, and my just claim is passed over by my God'?"* Israel asks: Why doesn't God see my plight and do something about it?

Having been given such a grand view of God, why does Israel still question it? Because, when it comes to comfort—let's face it—we want the tangible things we can see and feel. We look for what is right in our own eyes. It is the same for us as it was for Israel.

When we get into oppressions, the picture can get reversed. The picture of God's greatness is reduced to three verses while the power of our oppressors grows to twenty-three verses. The world seeks to convince us that we can empower ourselves and throw off our oppressors by our own will or with the support of other equally transient and ultimately insufficient people. They try to make us think that we can overcome our oppression with more education, awareness, support groups, self-help books, and charitable foundations. The reality is that those who seek empowerment ultimately become oppressors themselves. They want power, and they take power by sheer force if need be. And so it becomes a battle between tyrants, us against "them" (whoever is the oppressor of the day by their definition).

The world's message of empowerment is a lie that flies in the face of God. God says, "You are grass." We are weak, fragile, and mortal. But in our weakness, God is strong for us. It is not about *our* empowerment and glory; it's about God's empowerment and glory.

We stumble when we think we can free ourselves of oppression by our own power and seek comfort in that which is transient and fragile, whether in material things or human relationships. We fall if we let our oppressors become more powerful than God in our minds. God's power is something you must grasp and cling to in times of oppression.

> ## Questions for Reflection:
>
> - Where do you seek comfort/distraction/escape when you feel oppressed?
> - Why does God begin with a picture of His power and not His love? Isn't love more comforting?
> - Why would the understanding of our own mortality to God's eternity be the first thing God establishes in our mindset in preparing us for adversity?
> - How do we take comfort in God's power?
> - What do you know of God's power from past experience? Has He been faithful to you in the past?
> - If you give your situation over to Him, do you believe He has the power to deal with it?
> - If He has the power to deal with your circumstances, do you trust Him to deal with it? Are you willing to let go of your own control and empowerment and give Him control?
> - Do you trust Him enough to be at peace with His handling of the situation?

#2 Experiencing despair and self-pity; rejecting God's love

Read Isaiah 49:14–51:3

The passage opens with this cry of despair from Israel:

> *"But Zion said, 'The LORD has forsaken me, and my Lord has forgotten me.'"* —Isaiah 49:14

The Lord responds with an outpouring of love for Israel in two pictures.

First, in Isaiah 49:15-26, God gives them a verbal three-fold reassurance that He has not forgotten His people.

Secondly, in Isaiah 50:1-11, God expresses His love by sending a comforter who has suffered as they have and can identify with them (50:4-51:3). The comforter is a helper and an advocate against the adversary.

The verbal three-fold reassurance (Isaiah 49:15-26)

The first reassurance (49:15-8) is that He remembers His people in their current generation. He reminds them that while people may forget them, He will not. The fact is, people do forget. We get prayer lists all the time, and while we may remember to pray for the needs in the moment, we rarely keep praying for an extended length of time until it is resolved. We may sympathize deeply, but fleetingly. God doesn't. He is there with us the whole time until He sees us restored to peace and health. And when we see our world beginning to crumble around us and feel powerless to do anything, He reassures us that this is not the end. The destroyers are but for a time, but a future generation will return and rebuild.

In the second reassurance (49:19-24), God promises a return of future generations to a renewed land. Though we suffer loss now, it is not a permanent loss. A new kingdom is coming. When we see dark days ahead of us, do we worry about our children and grandchildren and what life will be like for them? Greater persecutions are in store for them than anything we have experienced. Will they remain faithful when the persecutions begin in earnest? Will they resist the world's bombardment or will they walk away from the faith and be lost to us? These are genuine worries, and they can bring us into despair when we realize how little power we have to protect or even prepare our children for what is coming. In a future kingdom, the Lord promises that not only will we have our children returned to us, they will be restored in abundance. We should not despair over this.

Finally, God remembers us, but He also remembers our persecutors. He sees our plight—the abuse, humiliation, and need—and assures us that justice will be done. He promises to contend with those who contend with us, and avenge us. Think about what it means to have God contend with our adversaries. He is our advocate, and deliverance is coming. We cannot let ourselves despair. Part of dealing with despair is overcoming the sense that there is no hope in sight. We have hope, if we will only believe.

The Comforter

Isaiah 50:1-3 opens with a reminder of God's power and sovereignty. Israel got herself into this mess, and there was no human agent who could save her from her situation. When our world is deteriorating as a result of generations of sin for which we are now reaping the consequences, to whom do we look for solutions? God looked down on Israel and said, "No one's calling for Me. Do you think I have so little power to save you?" This brings us back to our view of God's power that we studied in the previous stumbling block. Only God can redeem the situation and only because of His power and sovereignty over both heaven and earth. He particularly notes His power over the seas, which is an allusion to the ungodly nations who are persecuting His people.

Into this desperate situation God sends a second form of comfort. He sends "Me" in Isaiah 50:4-9.

1. **Who is the "Me" in the passage?**

    "Me" is a picture of a person who goes through trials like us, endures the same affliction, and gives us comfort and a model for enduring the trial ourselves. In context with the previous verses, "Me" is an extension of God Himself, that is, Christ, who sympathizes with our weakness, was tempted even as we are tempted, endured being struck and beaten, spit upon and shamed, and finally crucified. Having endured that trial and persevered through that lesson, He is able to comfort us because He has been there.

2. **Did "Me" enter into that suffering willingly?**

    Yes. He entered into that experience willingly and did not rebel or turn away from it.

3. **How did "Me" respond to being unjustly wronged?**

   He took his grievance to a higher court. He challenged his oppressors to stand with him before God and give an account.

4. **To whom did "Me" look for his justification and validation?**

   He stood before His accusers boldly—set His face like flint—because He was assured of God's promise to help and justify Him.

While we see Christ as "Me" in the big picture, when we read this in the first person, it is hard not to envision "Me" as ourselves in this role. God sends *me* into trials for the purpose of helping others in those same trials. So, how do we model Christ in this passage? Change the "Me" to "I."

Questions for Reflection:

- Have I endured suffering in life that has made me uniquely able to comfort others, offer timely words, or serve as a role model?

- Did I enter into that suffering willingly?

- How did I respond to being unjustly wronged?

- To whom do I look for my justification and validation?

Validation and justification are forms of comfort and can become stumbling blocks if we look for them in this world and not from God.

Isaiah 50 ends with a comparison of those who walk in light versus those who walk in darkness, which is like comparing the one who walks with God's understanding versus man's understanding. Remember, from the last stumbling block, we compared the transience and short-lived nature of man to God's overpowering sovereignty and longevity. There is a similar comparison here.

People who walk in darkness must walk by the light of their own fire—they encircle themselves with sparks. How long do sparks last? How far does their light reach? They float up to the heaven and—poof!—are gone. Such is the wisdom of man and the enlightenment that he makes for himself. The comforter offers true light. Those who reject his comfort for comfort of their own understanding will sink into torment and fear.

We are challenged to take the higher view of our circumstances in light of what God is trying to accomplish in us. Sending us into trials is needed for our refining, but also for our equipping. The words of the Servant were meant for our enlightenment, and we are called to model the servant as an expression of God's love to others, to bring them out of the darkness in which they suffer from torment, fear, and despair.

1 John 4:17-18 says:

> "Love has been perfected among us in this: that we may have boldness in the day of judgment; because as He is, so are we in this world. There is no fear in love; but perfect love casts out fear, because fear involves torment. But he who fears has not been made perfect in love." —1 John 4:17-18

We are not called to fear but to love.

So, with all these reassurances, why would Israel still believe God has forsaken her? Why would she reject God's love?

There are two reasons that a person might refuse comfort. One is if the comforter hasn't "been there." We can sympathize deeply with a person going through a particular trial, and yet our effort to comfort them will fall flat despite our best intentions because of our lack of identification with their exact circumstances. Only a person who has had cancer can truly identify with someone with cancer. Only a person who has lost a young child can truly identify and offer comfort to a couple who have lost a child. The identification aspect is necessary for us to give effective comfort.

When we go through trials and tribulations, does it help to think that something good might come out of all the bad—that somehow this experience might be repurposed or used to equip us for helping another person somewhere down the road? Being others-focused in these times can keep us from becoming overly focused on ourselves and sinking into despair and self-pity.

A second reason a person might succumb to self-pity and refuse to be comforted is because they don't want to acknowledge that their sin has caused their oppression. It is easier to turn the blame on others and make it someone else's problem to fix rather than acknowledge a personal failing. Some people don't want to take responsibility for their actions or change their ways, and so they choose to remain in their oppression. **Self-pity is a point of stumbling.** This is why God says that if His people refuse the comfort of the Servant—the one whom He has uniquely prepared to help them in their trial—they will lie down in torment.

Paul reminds us:

> *"But we have this treasure in earthen vessels, that the excellence of the power may be of God and not of us. We are hard-pressed on every side, yet not crushed; we are perplexed, but not in despair; persecuted, but not forsaken..."* — 2 Corinthians 4:7-9

When we despair, we deny the power of God within us.

Questions for Reflection:

- Has there ever been a time in your life when you refused to be comforted because of weariness or despair? If so, why?

- Have you ever tried to offer comfort, but your comfort was refused? If so, why was it refused?

#3 Pursuing heavenly blessings or earthly gains

Read Isaiah 54:11–55:9

The passage opens with God's response to Israel's despair. He casts her vision toward this future reward of a kingdom. God's kingdom is gorgeous and glorious in its appearance, built upon a wealth that the nations of this earth, even Satan himself, covet. But more than its physical wealth, it embodies an intangible wealth of enlightenment, peace, and righteousness. There will be no oppression because there will be no fear. Think about that. Fear is a source of oppression. When you free yourself of fear, you rid yourself of oppression, to a large extent. We will talk about fear in the next stumbling block.

The LORD goes on to assure His people that if there are any combatants to face, it will not be because the He has sent them (as He will do with the Babylonians). Once the judgment is over, whatever power these combatants had over God's children to hurt them or condemn them will be broken.

Isaiah 54:16-17 says that every tongue that rises against us in judgment will be condemned. This is our right as servants of God, and our righteousness is from Him. There is an important premise here. This passage in Isaiah 54 is a follow-on picture to Isaiah 53, where the Suffering Servant, Jesus Christ, took the people's affliction and sin upon Himself, faced that judgment, and died in their place that they might enter this kingdom. There is, therefore, no condemnation for those who are in Christ Jesus and have been given a place in His kingdom.

This is the first and most important truth to embrace. This kingdom is not achieved by our own power or righteousness. Our righteousness is not our own but a heritage gifted to us by Christ. Because our righteousness is not our own, when the world rises up to judge and condemn us, it is not us that they condemn but Christ. For this reason, we can stand strong in defiance of their condemnation and not be made to stumble over feelings of fear, guilt, shame, or humiliation that will keep us in oppression.

Isaiah 55 opens with an invitation to abundant life in this kingdom.

> *"Ho! Everyone who thirsts, come to the waters; and you who have no money, come, buy and eat. Yes, come, buy wine and milk without money and without price. Why do you spend money for what is not bread, and your wages for what does not satisfy? Listen carefully to Me, and eat what is good, and let your soul delight itself in abundance. Incline your ear, and come to Me. Hear, and your soul shall live . . ."* —Isaiah 55:1-3a

This kingdom offers a rich abundance of good living—wine and milk, water and bread. These things are needful things, and therefore, things on which this world places a price. The world sends us in relentless pursuit of transient things—things which pass through us and through our hands with only fleeting satisfaction. Even though we eat and drink, we are still hungry and thirsty.

The LORD challenges us to redefine our values. Why spend money for what is not bread? What is bread? Bread feeds the body, but does not satisfy the soul. If the things you are pursuing are not satisfying, why pursue them? The abundance of the kingdom is not achieved in the pursuit of what satisfies the body, but what satisfies the soul. We take in that nourishment, not by the mouth but by the ear. Hear, and you shall have all that is needful for living.

But it is not enough to listen. We have to consider the source that is speaking to us. The world promotes the pursuit of the kind of wealth and abundance that God's kingdom offers, but it does so by its own wisdom and its own definition. It craves the riches of God's kingdom but will try to achieve them by unrighteous means, fear, and oppressive tyranny. It tries to convince us that it is pursuing a kingdom of peace and safety and enlightenment, but it is a kingdom achieved by oppression.

Even in the Christian world, we find prosperity cults that twist the definition of abundant living into a worldly pursuit of wealth. Believers can stumble when they do not have a clear picture of the kingdom, its blessings, and how those blessings are achieved.

The LORD reminds us through Isaiah:

> "'For My thoughts are not your thoughts, nor are your ways My ways,' says the LORD. 'For as the heavens are higher than the earth, so are My ways higher than your ways, and My thoughts than your thoughts.'"— Isaiah 55:8-9

Our Isaiah passage ends with God's promise to make an everlasting covenant with His people according to the sure mercies of David. While God promises to honor the Davidic covenant by establishing the Messianic king on his throne, Isaiah's words indicate that He now extends royal status to all the people in His kingdom as part of our glorification, and all of humanity will benefit as a result of our redemption. This democratization of the kingship is likened to the democratization of the priesthood in Isaiah 61:6, such that all of God's people in the kingdom will become a royal priesthood. This combined picture is the picture Peter is referencing in 1 Peter 2:4-10:

> "Coming to Him as to a living stone, rejected indeed by men, but chosen by God and precious, you also, as living stones, are being built up a spiritual house, a holy priesthood, to offer up spiritual sacrifices acceptable to God through Jesus Christ. Therefore it is also contained in the Scripture, 'Behold, I lay in Zion a chief cornerstone, elect, precious, and he who believes on Him will by no means be put to shame.'
>
> "Therefore, to you who believe, He is precious; but to those who are disobedient, 'The stone which the builders rejected Has become the chief cornerstone,' and 'a stone of stumbling and a rock of offense.' They stumble, being disobedient to the word, to which they also were appointed.
>
> "But you are a chosen generation, a royal priesthood, a holy nation, His own special people, that you may proclaim the praises of Him who called you out of darkness into His marvelous light; who once were not a people but are now the people of God, who had not obtained mercy but now have obtained mercy." —1 Peter 2:4-10

God's people are the precious stones on which His kingdom is built, the chief cornerstone being Christ Himself. The wealth of God's kingdom is embodied in His people.

Christ is the ultimate stumbling stone, because without Him, this kingdom could never be realized. Israel sought a kingdom of righteousness by works, not through a relationship with the Messiah. The world seeks a likeness of the kingdom in its wealth and peace and enlightenment, but it tries to take it by force and fraud instead of receiving it by the inheritance of righteousness that comes through relationship with Christ.

How do you define abundant life—God's way or the Baal/Ashtoreth way? By spiritual riches or earthly riches?

How do you pursue this kingdom—God's way or the Baal/Ashtoreth way? Where are your values?

We as believers can stumble when we lose touch with this vision of the kingdom. Its values are not based on earthly values. It cannot be pursued by earthly wisdom and ways. It is up to us to listen to the word and understand what is the inheritance and reward in the kingdom we are pursuing.

Understanding our identity with Christ is key in avoiding this stumbling block of pursuing an earthly kingdom and earthly riches. When we build an identity based on transient, earthly things, and that identity collapses—and it will—we lose our identity and stumble back into despair. Despair and self-pity then establish a new identity for us—the victim identity, which drives us away from God instead of toward Him. The victim identity is also something the world promotes to keep us in its oppression.

Lift your head and keep your eyes fixed on this vision of the kingdom. You cannot afford to stumble at this point.

Question for Reflection:

- God casts this vision of a future kingdom for the comfort and strengthening of a people sunk in despair over the darkness looming on their horizon. How is it a comfort to us?

- Beyond the need for basics, to what extent do money and material things offer comfort and security or contribute to anxiety and fear in your life?

#4 Feeling fearful

Read Isaiah 51:12–52:12

This passage deals with fear and ties together the first three stumbling blocks we just studied. They talked about the need for a firm grasp on God's power, His love, and the picture of His kingdom, including His values and our identification with Christ. If we can anchor ourselves in these three—power, love, and a sound mind—then we will be able to overcome the stumbling block of fear, or at least not let its oppression rule us.

In Isaiah 51:12, God confronts fear head on. He begins by reminding us of His power and who we are to Him.

> *"I, even I, am He who comforts you. Who are you that you should be afraid of a man who will die, and of the son of a man who will be made like grass? And you forget the LORD your Maker, Who stretched out the heavens and laid the foundations of the earth; You have feared continually every day because of the fury of the oppressor, when he has prepared to destroy. And where is the fury of the oppressor?"*
> —Isaiah 51:12-13

We are like grass, but so are our oppressors. That abusive, overbearing person in your life can seem so strong and hold such power over you, but they are just as fragile as you, and they are going to die the same as you. They are nothing. They are grass. When trials and persecutions strike us, we have to remind ourselves that this is how God sees them. While they may persecute us now, that persecution will end. While they may contend with us now, there will come a day when they contend with our God, and their fury will be nothing compared to His fury. And when their day is over, they will lose a kingdom where we will gain one.

Isaiah goes on to say:

> *"The captive exile hastens, that he may be loosed, that he should not die in the pit, and that his bread should not fail."* — Isaiah 51:14

Fear robs a person of a sound mind, and the behavior of a fearful person is marked by haste. He moves hastily. He makes decisions hastily based on the need for self-preservation. He thinks that by pleasing the oppressor he will be set free, which is a vain hope. Oppressors do not readily set their prisoners free. Even so, the captive quickly bows and bears the burden because he believes if he doesn't that he will be abandoned to die. It is a curious thing how posture communicates what is in the mind and heart. A man who bows has his eyes fixed on the earth and contemplates the grave. His vision and understanding become short-sighted.

The captive is quick to please for the sake of having such basic necessities as food to eat. But in the end, he is like a vessel poured out and left empty. The Hebrew word for captive exile is *sa'ah* which means to be stooped or bent under a burden or one who bows. Jeremiah uses the word figuratively to described a man as a vessel used by wine-workers—transient laborers—who tip him over, poured him out, and leave him empty and broken. These oppressors are transient—they come and go in a season—and yet this is the state in which they leave the man.

We can find ourselves at the mercy of oppressors and abusers—at home, at work, even as citizens of a nation. When we have to rely on our abusers for basic daily needs such as food and shelter, then life quickly becomes one of pleasing those masters and, thus, we empower them. And yet for all our effort to please them, it lightens our burden so little.

Where is God in our circumstances? Where is the sense of His power over our abusers? Where is the sense of His purpose in sending us into these circumstances? As I said earlier, the picture of God's power can be reduced to three verses while the abuser's power expands to 23 verses, instead of the other way around. When we let go of God's power, we bow to fear. Lift your head!

God says:

> *"But I am the LORD your God, who divided the sea whose waves roared—The LORD of hosts is His name. And I have put My words in your mouth; I have covered you with the shadow of My hand, that I may plant the heavens, lay the foundations of the earth, and say to Zion, 'You are My people.'"* —Isaiah 51:15-16

God presents us first with the picture of His power; next, the picture of His love. Picking up with Isaiah 51:17, we read:

> *"Awake, awake! Stand up, O Jerusalem, you who have drunk at the hand of the LORD the cup of His fury; You have drunk the dregs of the cup of trembling, and drained it out. There is no one to guide her among all the sons she has brought forth; nor is there any who takes her by the hand among all the sons she has brought up. These two things have come to you; Who will be sorry for you?—Desolation and destruction, famine and sword—By whom will I comfort you? Your sons have fainted, they*

> *lie at the head of all the streets, like an antelope in a net; They are full of the fury of the LORD, the rebuke of your God."* —Isaiah 51:17-20

This part of the picture echoes Isaiah 50 where God began with some tough love in reminding Israel that their oppression was a consequence of their sin, and they were powerless apart from Him to escape their bondage. But He goes on to challenge His people's understanding of how and by whom He comforts them in His love.

Verses 17-23 speak about a cup of judgment that must be drunk to the dregs—a cup that is taken from Israel and given to the oppressor so that Israel may be delivered. When Jesus the Messiah made His triumphal entry into Jerusalem, Israel expected Him to fulfill this prophecy. They waited in anticipation for Him to hand the cup of judgment to the Roman oppressors of the day, as Isaiah 51:23 seemed to indicate would happen.

But Jesus didn't do that. He took the cup Himself. As He prayed in the garden of Gethsemane on the night before His crucifixion, Jesus asked the Father to take from Him this cup of judgment described in Isaiah 51:22. As He died on that cross, He was taunted for His powerlessness to deliver Himself, just like this picture of the sons of Israel here in Isaiah who have fainted and been ensnared by the enemy, and who are filled full of the fury and rebuke of the LORD.

Israel wanted a Messiah who would deliver them from the physical oppressor, but they did not realize that so much of their oppression came from within them and their broken relationship with God. The Roman oppressors with their brutal adherence to iron-clad laws were merely the reflection of Israel's leadership who ruled brutally over the people in adherence to their own laws (Mosaic Laws). As we will see in the Judges narrative, God picks oppressors who are deliberate reflections of Israel to challenge His people to consider their ways. The deliverance from outside oppressors could not happen until the internal affliction had been dealt with so that the people could be reconciled in their relationship with God.

Isaiah 51:12-16 recalls God in His power. Isaiah 51:13-23 details His act of love in taking the cup of judgment from us. Having dealt with the judgment, we now come to the "good news" in Isaiah 52 as we see the awakening of a new, purified Jerusalem. The kingdom has been accomplished, and God takes back His people from their oppressors with a vengeance. His people were taken by the oppressor without payment; they are redeemed from the oppressor without payment.

> "How beautiful upon the mountains are the feet of him who brings good news, who proclaims peace, who brings glad tidings of good things, who proclaims salvation, who says to Zion, 'Your God reigns!'" —Isaiah 52:7

Isaiah 52:1-12 exhorts us to rejoice even as suffering and trials loom on the horizon and proclaim the good news of our deliverance. Can you be joyful when faced with trials? James says:

> "My brethren, count it all joy when you fall into various trials, knowing that the testing of your faith produces patience. But let patience have its perfect work, that you may be perfect and complete, lacking nothing." —James 1:2-4

Fear is oppressive, and fear is a tool that oppressors use to overpower us. **We stumble when we let fear rule us.**

Paul reminds us:

> "For God has not given us a spirit of fear, but of power and of love and of a sound mind." —2 Timothy 1:7

If you can root yourself in an understanding of God's power, His love, and a sound view of the purpose of your trials and the reward you are pursuing, then you will be able to overcome the fear associated with oppression.

We have talked about how fear affects us personally. Now let's talk about how fear works through us to affect others.

Fear is socially contagious. It is hard not to be afraid when the entire world is running around in a panic and demanding we act upon their fear. But this is exactly when God's people cannot show fear. When we give in to fear, we deny the power of God, the love of God, and our belief in the coming kingdom. It is a three-fold denial.

In regards to the power . . . When we let the world's fear rule us, we deny the power of our God and His sovereignty over us. To the unbelieving world, we are saying our God isn't big enough, strong enough, resourceful enough, or even faithful enough to deal with our circumstances. When we fear, we take God's power from Him, and we lose the opportunity to show the unbelieving world God's power in action. We lose the battle on that front.

Without God's power, we must find ways to empower ourselves—in which case, we can become controlling tyrants—or we submit, withdraw, and concede power to the oppressor. And so we lose the battle on that front as well.

Fear is a stumbling block especially in battle. Did you know that, according to the Law, fear is a reason to be exempted from battle?

Deuteronomy 20:8 says:

> *"The officers shall speak further to the people, and say, 'What man is there who is fearful and fainthearted? Let him go and return to his house, lest the heart of his brethren faint like his heart.'"*
> — Deuteronomy 20:8

God doesn't want fearful people fighting for Him, because fearful people will bail in the middle of the fight, and they will take others with them. God has a purpose for sending us into persecutions and trials. He has an objective. When we are in the midst of that battle, the natural reactions of fight or flight will kick in but without the control needed for a believer to accomplish God's objective in the circumstances. God needs His people to identify with His power and act with control according to His direction. We have to embrace the bigger picture of God working with us through these trials if we are going to prevail in the spiritual battle. Fear should never exempt a believer from the battle.

In regards to love . . . Fear can twist and poison love with jealousy and possessiveness. This happens when we objectify the people we love and transform them into earthly things to be possessed. As a result, they become things we can lose, and fear enters into the relationship. We can even objectify God's love. We can give it a value based on earthly works and make it something that must be earned or lost. And so fear enters into our relationship with God and denies us the comfort that the assurance was meant to bring—the assurance purchased with Christ's death on the cross. Can you truly love someone if you are afraid of losing them? Can we love God if we are afraid of losing our relationship with Him?

John tells us:

> *"There is no fear in love; but perfect love casts out fear, because fear involves torment. But he who fears has not been made perfect in love. We love Him because He first loved us."* —1 John 4:18-19

There is torment in fear, but not in love. Perfect love casts out fear. We cannot lose God's love because He is the one holding onto us, not us holding onto Him. Even if we stumble and let go, He does not let go of us. If we continue to fear, having such a great reassurance, then we deny that Christ's death was sufficient. If Christ's death was insufficient, then what is?

When we fear, we deny God's power and His love, and we also deny the reality of the coming kingdom. The unbelieving world has no promise of another kingdom as we have, and so they grip onto earthly possessions, kingdoms, and even their own lives with a vengeance borne of desperation. When we let their fear cause us to bow to a pursuit of earthly things, we are agreeing with them that these earthly things are all we have to hope for in life. We lose our witness to them of a more glorious kingdom, and with it, their need for a relationship with Christ.

Questions for Reflection:

- Has fear ever robbed you of power, love, and a sound mind in life? If so, how?
    - Are you afraid of losing your relationship with God? If so, how does this passage help you combat that fear?
    - Are you afraid of other people in life? If so, how does this passage help you combat that fear?
- Do you believe that God is more powerful than the things you fear? Do you trust Him to deal with your oppressors in His time?
- How does fear affect your decision-making?
    - Has fear ever kept you from speaking the truth or doing something that you know you should do?
    - Has fear ever caused you to do something you know you shouldn't?
    - Has fear led you into a life of coping and compromise? (Coping doesn't relieve the oppression. It just perpetuates it.)
- What happens when a fearful person or group of people are also the ones in power? (For example, what is life like for a child living with fearful parents, or citizens living in a nation run by fearful leaders? How do those scenarios play out—what does life become under the leadership of fearful people?)

#5 Feeling shame and humiliation

Read Isaiah 54:1-10

This fifth stumbling block addresses the aspects of shame and humiliation that we suffer as a consequence of sin. They are weapons an oppressor can wield against us, but they can also keep us in oppression even after the oppressor has been dealt with. And so, they become stumbling blocks that prevent our healing and the restoration of our relationships with others and with God.

Because of our relationship to Christ and our identification with Him, we have been given a place by His side in the kingdom. In verses 2-3, the Lord commands us to sing and enlarge our tents in preparation for the fruitfulness to come after the days of leanness are over. But most of all, He commands us not to fear, but forget. Forget the shame and disgrace and reproach of your past and focus on the future.

Note the specific command not to fear in verse 4. There is a fear factor that comes into play when we step out in our identity with God through Jesus, because we have this past full of failings that can continue to be our current failings. When Jesus died on the cross, He paid for the sin and took away the dishonor, shame, and guilt associated with our sins. He rolled back the stumbling stone of reproach so that, in God's eyes, we have no reason to stand ashamed before Him or anyone—not for our past failings, and certainly not for our identity with Him. When we let go of that identity with Him, we stumble back into shame and humiliation over sin, and with it, fear and despair over not being loved by God.

God tells Israel that the oppression was needed to drive them back to that relationship with Him, but that doesn't mean the relationship was broken on His end. The fact that He puts them through these trials is proof of His love for them, that He wants that relationship restored and will do what it takes to restore it.

The passage finishes with these words of comfort in verses 9-10:

> *"For this is like the waters of Noah to Me; for as I have sworn that the waters of Noah would no longer cover the earth, so have I sworn that I would not be angry with you, nor rebuke you. For the mountains shall depart and the hills be removed, but My kindness shall not depart from you, nor shall My covenant of peace be removed,' says the LORD, who has mercy on you."* —Isaiah 54:9-10

God promises not to be angry and punishing to His people forever. Think about that. What is it like to live with someone who has been angry with you over something for years and still holds the remembrance of that failing over your head? Or are you the one who has decided to hold onto the anger and punish them forever? This is not a godly behavior. God promises not to let His anger and judgment rule the relationship with His people permanently. His mercy and kindness toward them will always be there, and He desires to be at peace with them.

God forgets, but people don't. People in our lives—and that includes other believers—can wield shame and humiliation as a way of having power or control over us. They can also use these tools for lifting themselves up by putting others down.

Social media has become the perfect platform for these kinds of oppressors who delight in shame and humiliation. Every mistake and ill-spoken word can be captured and broadcasted before the world in the blink of an eye. *And people like it.* They support it and encourage it. But it's humiliating. It's a form of public shaming that can shatter a person emotionally and ruin their lives. And that is just over the stupid stuff we do and say. Heaven forbid they catch us taking a stand for our faith. Have you ever had someone post something humiliating about you on Facebook or Twitter? Have you ever done this to someone else?

Shame and humiliation are closely tied to guilt. Guilt is an oppression that takes us from behind. Issues that we have battled in the past become weak spots where the enemy can attack us and bring us into oppression. People or circumstances from our past may show up again in our lives to remind us of that old failing which might also be our current failing. Time and again, Israel slipped into old habits, and so do we. When that happens, we can become swamped with guilt over past failings and succumb to shame.

There may be a physical person in our lives who uses guilt to control us. People who wield guilt may not be people we consider our enemies, but they are. They can use guilt to bind us to them through obligation, and they can assume a place and a power over us that they have no right to have—unless we give it to them. And once they have achieved that foothold, they make us pay and pay and pay.

Humiliation and guilt are ways that people in our lives punish us. They can be a parent's alternative to spanking and physical punishments. But should these be part of punishment in the case of wrongdoing?

Consider what Deuteronomy 25:2-3 says:

> *"[T]hen it shall be, if the wicked man deserves to be beaten, that the judge will cause him to lie down and be beaten in his presence, according to his guilt, with a certain number of blows. Forty blows he may give him and no more, lest he should exceed this and beat him with many blows above these, and your brother be humiliated in your sight."*—Deuteronomy 25:2-3

If we are guilty of wrongdoing, it should be a cut-and-dried matter. The guilty party takes the prescribed punishment and makes restitution as befits the sin, but then the issue is finished as far as God is concerned. Whatever goes beyond beneficial correction becomes nothing more than a gratuitous tearing-down for someone's pleasure.

The reason God tells us not to humiliate one another is because shame and humiliation rob a person of self-worth and dignity and prevent them from returning to fellowship even if they repent. When we suffer humiliation at someone's hand, it becomes very hard to face them again because every time we see them we are reminded of the sin but also the hurt we experienced at their hands. The constant reminder prevents reconciliation and healing and often makes us throw up barriers to keep the person away. And so, it becomes an ongoing battle for us not to let ourselves fall back under the tyranny of shame and guilt.

It is God's desire to see a person restored to fellowship. That is why He asked His Son to go through that crucifixion so that shame and guilt would no longer oppress us. Judgment is like the waters of Noah to Him. When He made that covenant of peace with us through Christ's death on the cross, He promised not to be angry with us or rebuke us forever or withhold His kindness from us. Once the judgment is over, it is over and we will be restored. The Lord commands us to see ourselves as children of grace and honor and not to fear people who wield guilt and shame. If we fear them, we give them power over us, and we deny Christ's death was sufficient.

Never lift yourself above a fellow believer when dealing out humiliation as a punishment. If you resort to humiliation, you undo the good that the punishment should have effected and make it impossible for the person to be reconciled to fellowship. If Christ took away your shame with His death on the cross, what right do you have to hold guilt and shame over anyone? If you do this, then you have become an oppressor, and God will contend with you for it.

We stumble when we become swamped with guilt over past failings or fall victim to shame and humiliation. We stumble when we use these tools to oppress one another.

God is our Husband, and He is the one who has taken away our guilt and shame out of His great love for us. He has promised to contend with those who contend with us, and He is more powerful than an oppressor. Cleave to Him!

Questions for Reflection:

- Have you ever felt shame or humiliation in your relationship with another person? What would it take to remove that shame and humiliation?

- Have you shamed people in how you speak to them or about them? Are you given to criticism, belittling people, or patronizing people? If so, why? What do you get out of it?

- Do you use humiliation as a punishment?

- We are commanded to comfort one another even as God comforts us. How do you restore a person's self-worth and dignity after you have humiliated them?

#6   Letting our dark side (Canaanite side) overcome us

Read Isaiah 60:1–22

In this sixth passage, we find the stumbling block of letting our dark side overcome us and losing sight of being children of light. Light and darkness are themes in this passage, but there is also a second theme of glorification that runs through the picture. How you define your glorification and the means by which you strive to attain it can be an outworking of your dark side and, therefore, a stumbling block in your relationship with God and others.

In the opening verses, we see the theme of light and dark being played against one another.

> "Arise, shine; for your light has come! And the glory of the LORD is risen upon you. For behold, the darkness shall cover the earth, and deep

darkness the people; But the LORD will arise over you, and His glory will be seen upon you. The Gentiles shall come to your light, and kings to the brightness of your rising." —Isaiah 60:1-3

The Glory of the Lord has risen upon us in the form of Jesus Christ, our risen Lord, who declared Himself to be the Light of His people. He has enlightened and glorified us as His people, and we now stand in contrast to the darkness of the world. The risen Light brings into His kingdom of light this great ingathering of enlightened people to whom the world comes bringing gifts in worship and praise.

"The sons of foreigners shall build up your walls, and their kings shall minister to you; For in My wrath I struck you, but in My favor I have had mercy on you. Therefore your gates shall be open continually; They shall not be shut day or night, that men may bring to you the wealth of the Gentiles, and their kings in procession. For the nation and kingdom which will not serve you shall perish, and those nations shall be utterly ruined." —Isaiah 60:10-12

Not only do the Gentiles bring an enormous wealth into the kingdom, they build its walls, minister at the altar, and are given as servants to God's people. This reversal of fortune is the outworking of God's mercy on His exiled people. Verse 11 talks about the kingdom's gates being open continually. Gates were always closed at dark and only reopened again with the morning light for security reasons. The security of this kingdom with its indwelling light is so great that the gates stay open continually.

Verses 13-14 describe the glorification of God's Tabernacle and His people.

"The glory of Lebanon shall come to you, the cypress, the pine, and the box tree together, to beautify the place of My sanctuary; and I will make the place of My feet glorious. Also the sons of those who afflicted you shall come bowing to you, and all those who despised you shall fall prostrate at the soles of your feet; and they shall call you the City of the LORD, Zion of the Holy One of Israel." —Isaiah 60:13-14

God's people are called the City of the LORD. The city is not made of mere buildings in which people live. It is made of living stones—the people themselves.

Verses 17-18 present a series of contrasting pictures. In these verses we have a reminder of the darkness from which we came and the inferiority of the kingdom for which we once labored in bondage.

> *"Whereas you have been forsaken and hated, so that no one went through you, I will make you an eternal excellence, a joy of many generations. You shall drink the milk of the Gentiles, and milk the breast of kings; You shall know that I, the LORD, am your Savior and your Redeemer, the Mighty One of Jacob. Instead of bronze I will bring gold, instead of iron I will bring silver, instead of wood, bronze, and instead of stones, iron. I will also make your officers peace, and your magistrates righteousness. Violence shall no longer be heard in your land, neither wasting nor destruction within your borders; but you shall call your walls Salvation, and your gates Praise."*
> —Isaiah 60:17-18

The passage ends with a picture of God's glory:

> *"The sun shall no longer be your light by day, nor for brightness shall the moon give light to you; But the LORD will be to you an everlasting light, and your God your glory. Your sun shall no longer go down, nor shall your moon withdraw itself; for the LORD will be your everlasting light, and the days of your mourning shall be ended. Also your people shall all be righteous; They shall inherit the land forever, the branch of My planting, the work of My hands, that I may be glorified. A little one shall become a thousand, and a small one a strong nation. I, the LORD, will hasten it in its time."* —Isaiah 60:19-22

Overall, we are given a picture of a kingdom of light inhabited by the children of light, yet there remains a memory of the darkness from which we have come. We should be children of light in a darkened world, but when the darkness of our world surrounds us, it can darken our vision of the kingdom of light that we should be pursuing and our identity as children of light.

This kingdom is possessed of all the wealth and glorification that the followers of Baals and Ashteroth worship and pursue by their own means. Just as gold, silver, bronze, and iron can be replaced by inferior materials, spiritual wealth can become redefined as earthly wealth, and heavenly enlightenment degraded by what the world considers knowledge. We can be lulled into a pursuit of our own glorification that we seek by our own means instead of glorifying God and letting Him glorify us.

When God gives us these pictures, He often presents them in a way that creates a gut reaction in us. Imagine it for a moment. How do you feel about people from all over the world coming to you, bowing down at your feet to praise you and serve you, and giving all their wealth to you as tribute to your royal status? What kind of gut reaction does that spur? Do you feel any warfare between your light and dark sides? If so, why?

Having the kind of glory and wealth portrayed in this passage handed to us can easily go to our head. It can engage our dark side by making us arrogant, pompous, self-righteous, and entitled. We are not in this kingdom yet. While we look to this future glorification, we are still in the process of being sanctified. **We stumble when we lose sight of our vision and mission to become children of light in a kingdom of light. We can also stumble into self-glorification and let the world derail us into pursuing a less glorious facsimile of this kingdom today.**

Questions for Reflection:

This passage uses the themes of light and darkness figuratively. Being children of light is also a theme that runs throughout the New Testament.

- Paul references this Isaiah passage in Ephesians 5:8-14. How does Paul apply it?
- John also uses the light and dark theme heavily in 1 John 2. How does John apply it?
- What are some signs that our dark side is at work in us? (Consider John 3:20-21, 1 John 1:5-7, 2 Corinthians 4:5-9, 2 Corinthians 6:14.)

Glorification is another theme in this picture. In regards to glorification . . .

- How does the world define glorification and how does it strive to achieve it?
- How do we as believers define our glorification and how is it achieved?
- Where do you seek praise and validation?
- Is the light in you for your glorification or God's glorification? (Consider Matthew 5:16, 2 Corinthians 4:5-7.)
- Are you willing to be broken so that God's light might shine through you and your circumstances?
- As believers we instinctively shy away from embracing pictures like this because we know we are called to walk in humility and set our sights on heavenly gain. This picture seems like something

> a prosperity cult would appropriate as a way of validating their pursuit of earthly wealth. So why would God expect us to consider ourselves in this setting?
>
> **John 3:20-21** says: *"For everyone practicing evil hates the light and does not come to the light, lest his deeds should be exposed. But he who does the truth comes to the light, that his deeds may be clearly seen, that they have been done in God."*
>
> - Do you live your life in such a way that it can bear being brought to light (even on social media)?
> - How well do you handle the truth of God's Word?

#7 Remaining silent and acting with destructive anger

Read Isaiah 62:1–63:14

Remaining silent

This passage has a dual picture, and yet the two pictures are intertwined. It opens with God modeling something and then calling His people—His watchmen—to follow His example:

> *"For Zion's sake I will not hold My peace [remain silent], and for Jerusalem's sake I will not rest, until her righteousness goes forth as brightness, and her salvation as a lamp that burns."* —Isaiah 62:1

God then calls His watchmen to follow His model:

> *"I have set watchmen on your walls, O Jerusalem; They shall never hold their peace [not be silent] day or night. You who make mention of the LORD, do not keep silent,"* —Isaiah 62:6

The watchmen are explained in Ezekiel 33:1-11 and begin with the literal picture of a watchman's job. When the Lord brings the sword of judgment on the Land, it is the watchman's job to blow the trumpet and warn the people. If people don't take the warning, then the watchman is not held responsible in God's eyes (Ezekiel 33:3-4). But if the watchman does not warn the people that the sword is coming, and the sword takes the people because of their iniquity, their blood is on their head, but also on the head of the watchman who didn't warn them when he should have (Ezekiel 33:6).

Ezekiel 33:8-9 summarizes the responsibility God places on the watchman in helping his fellow man:

> *"When I say to the wicked, 'O wicked man, you shall surely die!' and you do not speak to warn the wicked from his way, that wicked man shall die in his iniquity; but his blood I will require at your hand. Nevertheless if you warn the wicked to turn from his way, and he does not turn from his way, he shall die in his iniquity; but you have delivered your soul."* —Ezekiel 33:8-9

Isaiah 62 ends with a final command in verse 10:

> *"Go through, Go through the gates! Prepare the way for the people; Build up, Build up the highway! Take out the stones, Lift up a banner for the peoples!"* —Isaiah 62:10

We are commanded to remove the stones—to warn of judgment and help one another return to God when we drift from the path. We are not to keep silent. We are to be light-bearers to a darkened world, to a world that does not know God but also to fellow believers who are heading back into that darkness. God charges us with this task.

Acting with destructive anger

In Chapter 63, we are given a second picture. God holds Himself up as a model of destructive anger:

> *"I have trodden the winepress alone, and from the peoples no one was with Me. For I have trodden them in My anger, and trampled them in My fury; their blood is sprinkled upon My garments, and I have stained all My robes. For the day of vengeance is in My heart, and the year of My redeemed has come. I looked, but there was no one to help, and I wondered that there was no one to uphold; therefore My own arm brought salvation for Me; and My own fury, it sustained Me. I have trodden down the peoples in My anger, made them drunk in My fury, and brought down their strength to the earth."* —Isaiah 63:3-6

We talked about the cup of affliction that the Lord gave to Israel, and how Jesus drank that cup to the dregs on our behalf. We look back at that and see just how destructive anger can be, even righteous anger, when it is vented at full force. For this reason, Isaiah reminds us in verses 7-14 that God's anger is tempered with His love and mercy. We cannot hope to come near God in terms of holiness, righteousness, or justice, and when our anger breaks out, it is often destructive because it is not tempered with love.

We are warned in James 1:19-20:

> *"So then, my beloved brethren, let every man be swift to hear, slow to speak, slow to wrath; for the wrath of man does not produce the righteousness of God."* —James 1:19-20

In regards to living in times of oppression, withdrawing into silence or bursting out with destructive anger are two responses to feeling powerless when facing an enemy.

Silence plays out in a desire to hunker down into defensive positions, hide behind barriers and walls, and withdraw into places where the enemy cannot get to us. But isolation is destructive because it breaks the fellowship we need to strengthen us.

As watchmen, we can let an oppressor silence us when we should speak the truth to a fallen world because of our fear of persecution. Confrontation is something most of us would rather avoid, and when we do speak out, it can be with explosive and destructive anger.

We can resort to destructive anger when we try to take the power back from our oppressors by force. A desire for vengeance can fuel anger and cause us to seek our own justice when we lash out in word or action instead of leaning on God's power.

We see the effects of silence and isolation as well as the destructiveness of hate and anger at work in the world right now. It is a reaction to oppression, but it is also the tool of oppressors. It is very easy for those who are oppressed to become oppressors themselves, because they seek power over their lives and the lives of others. If we are going to survive the oppression, we cannot stumble in responding to the oppressor with angry words or actions which will only fuel the hate and anger, nor can we let them drive us into silence. We have to find a healthy balance.

Questions for Reflection:

Stumbling block: Remaining silent

- How do you see yourself as a watchman?
- Have you remained silent in times when you shouldn't have? Why?
- Is there something you need to speak up about now?

- Watchmen are called to speak the truth of what they see and know. Why is speaking the truth necessary when removing stumbling blocks from another person's path?

- Have there been times when you should have spoken the truth, but didn't? Why?

Stumbling block: Destructive anger

- Is God's destructive anger something we are meant to model in our relationships with one another and the world? Why or why not?

- How can anger prevent us from communicating God's love and mercy to people?

- Is there anger in your life that you are holding onto? Why?

- Does acting or speaking in anger resolve things or restore peace?

- Does your anger take the form of remaining silent?

- When you have spoken the truth, have you done so without using destructive or angry words?

- Has anger prevented you from communicating God's mercy to the "Canaanites" around you?

All oppressions begin with a person walking away from God and God's ways. All oppressions end with a return to God and God's ways, but that return is not just about battling a physical oppressor in your life. If getting free of the physical opponent is all you are focused on, then you have missed the point. The point is to refine you, to teach you how to fight a spiritual fight, and to drive you back to God when you have gotten off the path.

Are you feeling fearful and seeking comfort right now? Are you in despair over the circumstances in which you find yourself? Are you feeling powerless—like you want to withdraw into silence or break out in anger?

If you are already feeling this way, you need to reassess your vision of God's power, His love, and in what kingdom you are placing your identity and hope.

The return must begin with repairing a mindset that has lost its vision of God and the kingdom. When we stumble over these, they can lead us deeper into oppression or increase the weight of oppression.

It might be that your oppression stems from one or more of these stumbling blocks, in which case the oppression will not be lifted until you have dealt with the issues you are facing.

These stumbling blocks are also ways that we oppress and afflict one another. Do you shame people? Do you react with destructive words or silence? If you do, then that is your Canaanite side at work, and you are the oppressor. You need to stop these behaviors and repair the brokenness you have caused before the Lord has to step in and contend with you personally to stop the damage you are doing to others.

It might be that your oppression is not caused by any fault of your own, but by sin in another person's life that is impacting you. It may be that God has sent you into oppression for the express purpose of having that experience so that you can help others in the same oppression, as He did "Me" in Isaiah 51.

These are the issues we must come to terms with when facing oppression or coming out of it. We will apply these in the Judges narrative to come, as we look at how Israel stumbled in times of oppression, and take a lesson from that.

JUDGES, PART 2: THE JUDGES

Judges 3:8–16:31

LESSON 4

Oppression #1: Othniel

READ

Judges 3:7-11

BUILD THE PICTURE

Oppression #1, Judges 3:7-11

1. **How does this oppression come about for Israel?**

   It began with everyone in Israel doing what was right in their own eyes, throwing off God as King, and pursuing their lusts through Baal and Ashtoreth worship.

2. **What do we know about the oppressor?**

   His name is Cushan-Rishathaim, king of Mesopotamia, and he oppresses Israel for eight years.

   Cushan means "blackness or darkness."
   Rishathaim (plural of *risha* or wickedness) means "exceeding wickedness."

3. **Where is he from?**

   Problem #1: He is called king of Mesopotamia. Mesopotamia is a grand sweep of ancient lands that today includes parts of Turkey, Syria, Iran, Iraq, and Kuwait. At the time of this narrative, this area was not yet organized into a cohesive kingdom of any kind. So, calling Cushan Rishathaim "king of Mesopotamia" seems a misnomer. For the purposes of our picture, we will consider him a king who reigns over an extensive but as yet unidentified kingdom.

   (Note: When building the Old Testament pictures, don't force the imagery. If it is vague in the text, leave it vague in the picture.)

   Problem #2: Archaeological records have not found any evidence of a king by this name from anywhere in Mesopotamia.

When this happens in Biblical study, it is the practice of scholars to look outside the immediate area to see what is happening in other countries that might provide clues as to the identities of people in the text. In this case, Egyptian records were found indicating a Syrian king usurped the Egyptian throne for a period of time that roughly aligns with this oppression in Israel's history.[1] The records note that the usurper brought with him an army of those "who had once been slaves in Egypt," that is, Israel.

Syria is part of northern Mesopotamia, so that fits roughly with the description of Cushan Rishathaim being a king of Mesopotamia. How could a Syrian king muster an Israelite army? He had already occupied and brought Israel under subjection. For this reason, it is *speculated* that Cushan Rishathaim might be this Syrian king who oppressed Israel and is an early version of a king of the north battling a king of the south that we find later in Israel's history.

That being said, for the purpose of defining this particular picture of Cushan Rishathaim, we will stick with only what the text literally gives us and not include this speculation.

Return of Othniel

4. The pattern: What was Israel's response to the oppressor and what was God's response to Israel?

Israel cried out to God, and God responded by raising up a judge/deliverer for Israel. *(Note: this will become a pattern with some variations that we will study throughout the narrative.)*

5. What do we know of Othniel? (Recall from Judges 1:11-15.)

Othniel, prince of Judah, cleared the way and conquered Debir so that the children of Israel could claim their inheritance. As a reward he was given Caleb's daughter as the bride, and received a dowry of a field plus the upper and lower springs of water as part of the blessing.

We discussed how Othniel is the picture of Christ in His first coming,

---

[1] A. Malamat, "Cushan Rishathaim and the Decline of the Near East around 1200 B. C.," *Journal of Near Eastern Studies*, Vol. 13, No. 4 (The University of Chicago Press, Oct., 1954), pp. 231-242, https://www.jstor.org/stable/542244, Accessed: 03-05-2020 02:40 UTC

when he cleared the way to the Holy of Holies (the *debir*) so that we could obtain salvation and claim a place in His Kingdom.

This first picture of Othniel was associated with Joshua's work to take the Land.

6. **Roughly how much time has passed since Othniel conquered the Land with Joshua?**

   After Joshua died, another generation rose, and almost immediately, it seems, fell into idolatry and this oppression. They were oppressed for eight years before Othniel rose up to deliver them. So it had been, at the very least, eight years, but really much longer.

7. **How are Othniel's roles different this time?**

   In his first appearance, he was only there to take the Land and establish the inheritance in conjunction with Joshua's work. This time he comes as judge and deliverer.

PICTURE SUMMARY

Israel is occupied by a foreign king whose identity (as yet) remains unknown and reigns over an extensive kingdom that is (as yet) undefined. The picture of his reign is one characterized by darkness and exceeding wickedness. Having completed the first work, Othniel reappears in the narrative as judge and deliverer of his people in a time of great spiritual darkness and exceeding wickedness. He goes to war with the oppressor, vanquishes him, and expels him from the Land.

APPLY THE PICTURE

PROFILE OF THIS OPPRESSION

If we were to boil this picture down into its elements, we see a people being occupied and oppressed by a ruler or regime whose reign is characterized by darkness, corruption, and exceeding wickedness.

8. **How do we see this play out in our world today?**

   This model is ubiquitous through our world, even in our own country. It will reach its fullest expression in the End Times when an as yet unidentified "king" will assume reign over "Mesopotamia," an as yet, undefined world kingdom. Then the world will be given over to darkness and exceeding wickedness.

9. **This is a follow-on picture of Othniel. In his first appearance, he was a type of Christ in His first coming. What picture do we have of him this time?**

   This time He is Christ in His second coming as deliverer and judge.

> ## Questions for Reflection:
>
> In general, all oppressions will begin with being occupied.
>
> - With what are you occupied? Has something taken up your emotional, mental, and physical energies, or taken your thought life captive to the point of being obsessive or oppressive?
>
> - How can you become "conscripted" with tasks in a way that becomes oppressive?

BUILD THE PICTURE

King of the North vs. King of the South Scenario

The main picture of this first oppression is meant to pair with Othniel as a picture of Christ. But before we leave the discussion of this oppression, I would like to briefly explore the alternate scenario of Cushan Rishathaim being a type of king of the north who occupies Israel as he battles with the king of the south in Egypt. This is a model of oppression in Israel's later history that can have an application for us, but it will not be one highlighted in the Judges' narrative. So let's discuss it.

APPLY THE PICTURE

PROFILE OF THIS OPPRESSION

This oppression can come about when you get stuck in the middle of a fight between two people. This is not your fight; they bring the fight to you. It begins with two people doing what seems right in their own eyes (but not God's eyes). They get into a power struggle over something—an earthly kingdom or material thing—and they involve you in their dispute.

One or the other may show up on your doorstep seeking support. They will demand your comfort, your loyalty, your emotional support, maybe your physical support, etc., and they will begin to occupy you. They will occupy your thoughts, your time, your energy, and even your resources. They may even occupy you physically—they may end up living with you for a period of time. Over time, their occupation becomes draining and oppressive for you, and you begin to resent them.

Questions for Reflection:

Have you ever been caught in a fight between two people or warring factions? Who hasn't? This can play out on a national, community, or family level. At some point, you may ask yourself, "How did I get into this mess?" Good question.

- How *did* you come to be involved? Looking back, was it avoidable? (It might not have been.)

Oppressed people can bring us into their oppression when they seek us for comfort or support. (Remember the first stumbling block—seeking comfort in transient things? They may be using you for this.) If the situation was unavoidable for you, then you may end up like "Me" in Isaiah 50 who God sends alongside an oppressed person to help them over their stumbling blocks—but that means going through the ordeal with them to a greater or lesser extent. It can be a difficult enough task dealing with their stumblings, but the experience can be compounded by your own personal struggle in reaction to them.

- How do you keep yourself from stumbling over feelings of anxiety, self-pity, powerlessness, etc., as you enter into this person's oppression with them? How do you keep from being sucked into the "dark side" with them?
- In response to God's command to remove the stumbling blocks, how do you help them get refocused on a relationship with God and dealing with issues like fear, despair, self-pity, shame, guilt, anger, silence, etc.?

My thoughts: I am not a counselor by any stretch, but as we saw in the Isaiah passages, all these stumbling blocks revolved around a darkened

Three Kinds of Rest: Survey of Usage

	Rest		
	Shabath "Ceasing"	**Nuach** "Sitting Down"	**Shaqat** "Quietness"
Mentioned in the **Books of the Law** (Gen.–Deut.)	**26 times** Ceasing from work: Sabbath day (Gen. 2:2), Sabbath year, Jubilee You shall make leaven cease in your homes for the Feast of Unleavened Bread (Exo. 12:15) "While the earth remains, seedtime and harvest, cold and heat, winter and summer, and day and night shall not cease [shabath]." (Gen. 8:2)	**18 times** Noah's ark rested on Mount Ararat (Gen. 8:4) The ark of the covenant rested during the wilderness wanderings (Num. 10:36) Rest promised when Israel enters the land under Joshua (Deut. 12:10)	**0 times**
Mentioned in the **Book of Joshua**	**2 times** "Then the manna ceased [shabath] on the day after they had eaten the produce of the land..." (Josh. 5:12) *This rest does not describe Joshua's work.*	**6 times** "The LORD gave them rest all around, according to all that He had sworn to their fathers..." (Josh. 21:44) *This is the rest associated with Joshua's work.*	**2 times** "And the land rested from war" (Josh. 11:23, 14:15)
Mentioned in the **Book of Judges**	**0 times** *This is not the kind of rest associated with the judges.*	**0 times** *This is not the kind of rest associated with the judges.*	**6 times** And the land had rest for 40 or 80 years (Jdg. 3:11, 30; 5:31, 8:28)

> *view of God's power, God's love, and the heavenly kingdom we are supposed to be pursuing (as opposed to an earthly kingdom or material gain). It may be that they need these pictures built up in their understanding before they can begin to deal with their issues. So talk to them about God's power, God's love, and that view of a more glorious kingdom.*

Kinds of Rest

"So the land had rest for forty years..." —Judges 3:11a

The word "rest" crops up repeatedly in the Scripture. God rested on the Sabbath. Noah's ark rested on Mount Ararat. When God brought Israel into the land, He gave them rest all around, according to all that He had sworn to their fathers. Joshua and the judges gave the land rest. These are all kinds of rest, but in the Hebrew they are different kinds of rest. If we are going to interpret the picture correctly, we need to know which form of rest we are dealing with.

The analogy: Anyone dealing with children has at some point issued the three-fold command: Stop what you are doing, sit down, and be quiet. The command will be met with varying amounts of resistance, and it may quickly resolve into a multi-stage engagement.

You may succeed in getting the child to sit down, but that does not mean they have ceased doing anything. They will simply continue doing it while sitting down.

You may get the child to sit down, but that does not mean they are quiet. Achieving quietness while sitting down is a greater level of effort. So we understand that just because we achieve the "sitting down" expression of "rest" does not mean we have achieved the other two.

The concept of rest in the Scripture is divided along similar lines. There is the ceasing, the sitting down, and the quietness, each described by a different Hebrew word. They are: *shabath, nuach,* and *shaqat,* respectively.

a) **Shabath is "the ceasing."** This is the word from which we get Sabbath, when God ceased from work, and it is found in the commands for keeping the Sabbath day, festival Sabbaths, Sabbath years, and Jubilees. But it is not limited to the Sabbath.

Genesis 8:2 says: *"While the earth remains, seedtime and harvest, cold and heat, winter and summer, and day and night shall not cease [shabath]."* A great ceasing will happen at the end of time when the earth will cease its work.

In Exodus 12:15, there is a command to make leaven "cease" or *shabath* from your homes for the Feast of Unleavened Bread. In the book of Joshua, this kind of rest is only mentioned in regards to the manna ceasing or *shabath*-ing when Israel entered the Land, but it does not describe Joshua's work.

Shabath rest is never mentioned in the book of Judges.

b) **Nuach is "the sitting down."** This is the word from which we get names such as Noach (Noah) and Manoach (Manoah, Samson's father). *Nuach* gives us the picture of a positional "sitting down" rest. Noah's ark rested (*nuach*-ed) on Mount Ararat. In Israel's wilderness wanderings, the ark of the covenant would go before them and wherever it rested (*nuach*-ed), that is where Israel camped.

According to Deuteronomy 5:14, your servants should be allowed a "sitting down" on the Sabbath. Note that the "sitting down" is a separate act from the "ceasing" of work. If they had been the same, the additional command would not have been needed.

In Deuteronomy 12:10, God promises Israel will have a *nuach* rest in the Land under Joshua, and this promise is fulfilled (Joshua 21:44). The *nuach* rest is associated with Joshua's work in giving Israel a <u>positional</u> "sitting down" in the Land.

Nuach rest is never mentioned in the book of Judges, and is not associated with the work of the judges.

Side note: There is a noun that spins off of the verb *nuach*, which we should note. *Manoach* means a place of rest, and is found in Genesis 8:9 where it says that Noah's dove found no rest *(manoach)* for the sole of her feet. Similarly, in Deuteronomy 28:56, Israel finds no rest for the sole of her feet when she is cast out among the nations for her disobedience. It is also used in the narrative of Ruth 3:1 where Naomi says, *"My daughter, shall I not see rest for you?"* where marriage is being sought as a resting place (and so Ruth lays herself down at Boaz's feet). The only allusion to this rest in the book of Judges is in the name of Samson's father, Manoah (or *Manoach* in the Hebrew), which is very significant, but we will discuss that when we get to Samson's narrative.

c) **Shaqat is "the quietness."** This kind of rest is never mentioned in the books of the Law. It first shows up in the book of Joshua when he gives the Land rest from war (Joshua 11:23, 14:15), and again in the Judges' narrative when the judges give the Land rest for 40- and 80-year spans of time (Judges 3:11, 3:30, 5:31, 8:28). It also describes the people of Laish who were a "quiet" people—a people at rest—and, therefore, easy prey for the Danites to conquer.

Shaqat **is the rest associated with the work of the judges.**

10. Which rest is associated with God's work?

The *shabath*, or ceasing. This is the rest that was established in the beginning and will be reestablished at the end.

11. Which rest is associated mostly with Joshua's work?

Joshua gave Israel the *nuach* rest—the positional "sitting down" place in the Land of their inheritance. In this, Joshua is a picture of Jesus. Jesus gave us salvation—the *nuach* rest, the positional place in the kingdom. With His death on the cross, Jesus established our inheritance in His kingdom and conquered the Enemy who had the power to push us out of that inheritance.

Just because Jesus put this enemy to rest for us on one level does not mean we have rest across the board. We still have work to do and an enemy to overcome. We live among Canaanites. We live with a carnal "Canaanite" side within us. We battle these enemies throughout life, and we fail miserably at times, for which we must repent and return to the Lord. When we repent, the Savior reminds us of our place in His kingdom, and He sends the Holy Spirit to do His refining work in us, just like the judges did with Israel.

12. Which rest is associated mostly with the judges' work?

The *shaqat*, or quietness. The judges did not have to continually re-establish Israel's inheritance in the kingdom. They were not tasked with giving the *nuach* rest. Joshua accomplished that, and it was a permanent condition. The judges only intervened to bring Israel back when they repented after failings and to give them times of *shaqat* or quietness in the midst of oppression and battle.

Thus the book of Judges' picture focuses on the repentance aspect of our experience—our daily battle with the Canaanites that remain in and around us, our failings, and the *shaqat* rest we experience as we walk this path. The judges model the Holy Spirit who prompts us to return to God when we fail, helps us in the battle, and gives us times of rest between failings.

13. How is the *nuach* rest different from the *shaqat* rest?

Nuach is permanent and completed. *Shaqat* is temporary and on-going.

14. Which kinds of rest do we experience in our Christian walk?

We experience the *nuach* rest at the point of salvation. We experience the *shaqat* rest along the journey. But we have not yet experienced the *shabath* rest as it says in Hebrews 4:8-9:

> *"For if Joshua had given them rest, then He would not afterward have spoken of another day. There remains therefore a rest for the people of God. For he who has entered His rest has himself also ceased from his works as God did from His."* — Hebrews 4:8-9

Note how Joshua's rest is different from the rest that remains, which is described as God ceasing from His work. The writer of Hebrews separates the two different experiences of rest. We have yet to enter into the *shabath* level of rest, and the *shabath* level will not happen until all of creation—both man and land—cease their work, per Genesis 8:2. The *shabath* rest is paired with the experience of the new heaven and new earth described in Revelation 21.

Questions for Reflection:

- What are the dangers of extended periods of rest?

- Forty- and eighty-year spans of time mark generational shifts. What are some dangers inherent in generational turnovers?

LESSON 5

Oppression #2: Ehud and Shamgar

READ
Judges 3:12-31

BUILD THE PICTURE

Oppression #2, Judges 3:12-14

1. **What do we know about the oppressor?**

   He is Eglon, King of Moab. He gathered Ammon and Amalek, and together they marched against Israel. They pushed across the Jordan and retook the "City of Palms," also known as Jericho from Deuteronomy 34:3. Eglon established himself as king and put the children of Israel under tribute for 18 years.

   Eglon means calf-like, from the root *egel* meaning "calf," and he is very fat. (Enter into the picture, one fatted calf. And what is a fatted calf good for? Slaughter.)

2. **Why did God choose Moab for this oppression? What was Moab's history with Israel?**

   At one time, Moab was family (Lot was Abraham's nephew); but over generations, Moab became an antagonist.

   In the book of Numbers, Israel bypassed Moab without bothering them, but then Moab launched a campaign against Israel from behind—first, when Balak hired Balaam to curse Israel (Numbers 22), and then when Moab engaged Midian to help draw Israel into Baal worship (Numbers 25). Phinehas dealt with the Midianites, but not with Moab (Numbers 31). Moab faded back into the landscape for a while and made no move against Israel in Joshua's day. When Moab comes after Israel here in the days of the judges, Israel had been at rest for forty years and had fallen back into her old evil ways.

Moab is an enemy from the past. Israel did not see them as an enemy at first, but they turned out to be one.

Moab is also a reminder of a past failing. Moab is the one who previously led Israel into harlotry and idolatry. God prevented Israel from being taken captive by Moab then and cleansed them of that past sin, but now Israel has fallen back into the same idolatrous lifestyle. And Moab returned to take them captive.

Note: When God sends specific oppressors to Israel, the external oppressor is often a reflection of or comment on Israel's internal condition. The country had already drifted into idolatry and wickedness and were oppressing and afflicting one another. So God sent them into the hands of an oppressor to make them experience what life becomes when sin and oppression reach their fullest extent.

3. **Why would this enemy take Jericho? What was Jericho's significance to Israel?**

   Jericho was the ruins of the first battle Israel fought when they entered the Land—a reminder of God's power, the battle He fought and won for them, and a place that Joshua laid waste. The ruins remained as a testament to the Lord's might and kingship.

   Forty years of rest passed, and with it, Israel became another generation removed from those events. Jericho was a battle that a previous generation had to fight, but this generation no longer guarded. Not only had Eglon invaded Israel, he had begun to rebuild on Jericho's ruins. Note: he lived in a dwelling with an "upper room"—not an insignificant structure.

4. **The pattern: What was Israel's response to the oppressor? What was God's response to Israel?**

   The children of Israel were oppressed; they cried out to the LORD; the LORD raised up a deliverer. This is the same as last time. (Next time will be different.)

Ehud, Judges 3:15-30

5. **What do we know of Ehud?**

   He was the son of Gera, from the tribe of Benjamin. He was the man appointed to take the tribute to Eglon. He was left-handed and had made himself a sword.

   Ehud means "I will be praised"
   Gera means "a grain" (as in, the smallest measure)

   In other words ... *"By the smallest measure, I will be praised."*

6. **Why mention that he was left-handed?**

   In the Hebrew, it doesn't actually say that he was left-handed. It says his right hand was *itter* which means "closed" or "shut"—it closed in on itself and was impeded. He was handicapped and left-handed by necessity. Therefore, he made himself a dagger that could be wielded with the left hand and carried it on his right thigh. Ehud appeared weak but had a hidden strength.

   Side note: This is a defect that afflicts a number of men of Benjamin. Judges 20:16 notes that Benjamin marshaled seven hundred fighting men who had closed right hands and yet could sling a stone with skill in combat. They were at a disadvantage in hand-to-hand combat, but from a distance they were deadly. This is the only time this condition is mentioned in Scripture.

7. **What is Ehud's role(s) ?**

   He is a representative of Israel. The children of Israel were under tribute to Eglon who reigned in Jericho (Benjamin's land). They sent their tribute to Ehud in Benjamin, and Ehud then carried it to Jericho and presented it to Eglon. As representative of Israel, Ehud was forced to abase himself before Eglon.

   God raises Ehud up as a deliverer (*moshia*). His role of deliverer is more pronounced than his role as judge. The text doesn't specifically state that Ehud was a judge, although he is considered one. There is that element of restraint present in the land that is one of the earmarks of the judges, and he gave the land rest as the judges would.

8. **Why did Ehud stop when he came to Gilgal? What was Gilgal's significance to Israel?**

   Gilgal was the place where Joshua set up the memorial stones taken from the Jordan River during their crossing into the Land to remind Israel of their deliverance from Egypt (Joshua 4:18-20). It was also the place where Israel renewed her covenant with God by circumcision and celebrating the Passover (Joshua 5).

   Joshua 5:9 says:

   > "Then the LORD said to Joshua, 'This day I have rolled away [galal] the reproach of Egypt from you.' Therefore the name of the place is called Gilgal to this day."

   Gilgal means "wheel" in the sense of whirling or rolling away. It comes from the root word *galgal* meaning "wheel, whirl, or whirlwind."

   Similarly, the word *galal* used in the verse. It means "to roll away" and is often in reference to rolling back a stone that blocks a well or a cave. When we think of a stone being rolled back, of what do we think? The stone rolled away from Christ's tomb. Did Christ roll away our reproach before God along with that stone when He arose out of that grave? Yes, He did. The rolling away of reproach is part of the picture of the deliverer, isn't it? Hold that thought.

9. **What stood at Gilgal in Ehud's day?**

   In Ehud's day, stone images or quarried stones—stone idols shaped by the hands of men for cultic purposes—stood in place of the memorial. Ehud stopped at Gilgal and remembered what he was meant to remember.

   - He remembered God in His power Who delivered Israel from bondage. Was Eglon any stronger than Egypt?
   - He remembered God's love as He bound Himself in covenant to His people.
   - He remembered Joshua's work and the permanent inheritance that Israel was meant to have in the Land.

   Ehud remembered and turned back to Eglon, saying: *"I have a secret message for you."*

10. **When King Eglon looked at Ehud with his crippled arm, what kind of assumption do you think the king made about Ehud having a secret message for him?**

    A handicapped man was certainly no threat. Being unable to work, he may have resorted to making his living as an informer.

11. **What was the message he delivered to the king?**

    A sword in the belly. The text belabors the picture of Ehud's attack, the goriness of Eglon's death, and the excessive delay of Eglon's servants that allowed for Ehud's escape. It is an epic moment.

12. **Ehud escaped to Seirah (aka *Seirath*). What is the picture behind the word *Seirah* and its root words?**

    Seirah means "shaggy" or "rough" in the sense of being rough-haired or bristly like a goat (also like a head of barley), but if you stop with just this definition, you will miss the picture. This is a case where you have to dig deeper.

    The root verb, *sa'ar*, means "to bristle with horror over a coming violence and to sweep or whirl away as if taken by storm." It carries intense negative emotion paired with an experience of violence, much like when your hair stands on end from seeing a tornado coming at you.

13. **How does *sa'ar* describe the battle that ensued between Israel and King Eglon?**

    At Seirah, Ehud blew the trumpet and whipped Israel into a whirlwind of action. Israel stormed violently out of the hills against the Moabite invaders, overrunning Jericho and seizing the fords of the Jordan. Israel killed 10,000 Moabite men of valor, just as the LORD said they would in Leviticus 26:6-8:

    > "I will give peace in the land, and you shall lie down, and none will make you afraid; I will rid the land of evil beasts, and the sword will not go through your land. You will chase your enemies, and they shall fall by the sword before you. Five of you shall chase a hundred, and <u>a hundred of you shall put ten thousand to flight; your enemies shall fall by the sword before you</u>." — Leviticus 26:6-8 (emphasis added)

    Eglon attacked Israel with the combined forces of the Ammonites and Amalekites and brought Israel into oppression. God retaliated by sending one handicapped man, Ehud, son of Gera, to take down Eglon. *"By the smallest measure, I will be praised."*

14. How many years of quietness does Israel have after Ehud?

Eighty years.

PICTURE SUMMARY

Israel had been at rest for forty years (since Othniel) and had reverted to idolatry—the same idolatry that joined them with Moab before.

Now Moab came back into their life like a vengeance and established a position of power and authority over the unguarded ruins of Jericho. The memorials of God's power and covenant with His people were taken over by the enemy and replaced with idols and tributes to other gods who made Israel pay and pay and pay.

Then the deliverer returned from Gilgal to kill the "fatted calf" who had fattened himself on God's people. He whipped Israel into a whirlwind of action. They stormed violently out of Seirah to slay their oppressors.

APPLY THE PICTURE

PROFILE OF THIS OPPRESSION

Imagine we (like Israel) have begun to slip back into an old way of life that we once battled to put behind us. We assumed our earlier victory over that issue was permanent, so we don't guard ourselves in that area as we should. Suddenly, an enemy from "back in the day" shows up in our life as a reminder of that old failing which is also our current failing. We become swamped with guilt of past failings and succumb to fear, shame, and humiliation, as we allow the enemy to take God's place in our life.

Guilt was one of the major stumbling blocks we studied in Lesson 3. It is an oppression that takes us from behind. Issues that we have battled in the past—like old ruins—become weak spots where the enemy can attack us and bring us into oppression.

There may be a physical person in our life who uses guilt and shame to control us. People who wield guilt may not be people we consider our enemies, but they are. They can use guilt to bind us to them through obligation, and they can assume a place and a power over us that they have no right to have—unless we give it to them. And once they have achieved that foothold, they make us pay and pay and pay.

Questions for Reflection:

- Is there someone in your life who holds past failings over your head and makes you pay and pay and pay, so to speak?

- Do you do this to others?

- How do we model Ehud in overcoming the stumbling blocks of this oppression?

  My thoughts: Ehud remained in bondage until the day he remembered God's power, God's love and promises, and the picture of the kingdom as it was meant to be. When he remembered those things, he overcame the fear, the guilt, the shame, and the sense of powerlessness. After that, the enemy had no power over him.

- Ehud is a savior figure. How does our Savior, Jesus, help us rally and overcome this oppression?

  The Savior came out of Gilgal—out from behind the stone that had been rolled away, taking with it our reproach. He defeated the enemy with a decisive blow, and now challenges us to remember the things we should remember—that our guilt and shame have been removed.

- How do we deal with the person who uses guilt to control us? What is an appropriate response?

BUILD THE PICTURE

Shamgar, Judges 3:31

1. **What do we know about Shamgar, son of Anath?**

   Very little except that he also was a deliverer, and that he killed six hundred Philistines with an ox goad.

   Shamgar means "sword."
   Anath means "answer."

   In other words, by way of *answer*, God sends the *sword*—except the sword wields an ox goad.

2. **What is an ox goad and what is its purpose in general?**

   An ox goad is basically a stick with a sharp, reinforced point used to prod sulky animals into action. It is a common tool.

3. **What is the Hebrew word for ox goad, what does it mean, and what does it add to the picture?**

   In Scripture, there are two words in the Hebrew and one in the Greek for the word "goad." I want to combine all of them into the picture of the goad.

   The Hebrew word used in this particular passage is *malmad*, from the root verb *lamad*, which means "to teach or discipline." A *malmad*, therefore, is the incentive to learn. A pricking of discipline and conviction keeps us on the right path. The goad also spurs us to act—to apply our learning but also to contend for the faith.

   The other Hebrew word is *dorbon* (pronounced door-bone). It describes the words of the wise in Ecclesiastes 12:11:

   > *"The words of the wise are like goads, and the words of scholars are like well-driven nails, given by one Shepherd."* —Ecclesiastes 12:11

   The comparable Greek word is *kentron,* an iron goad that delivers a sting like that of bees or scorpions. Thus, to kick against the goad (Acts 26:14) is to offer perilous or ruinous resistance.

   When we pull all these pictures together, we see that while the ox goad has a literal purpose in prodding oxen to move, it also has this figurative picture of teaching through discipline, and the man who resists the lesson does so to his own ruin. Shamgar's ox goad taught the Philistines a lesson in this case, but it gives us a lesson as well.

4. **The text says Shamgar "_also_ delivered Israel." Since Shamgar follows Ehud's narrative, this implies a comparison between Shamgar and Ehud. Compare Shamgar to Ehud.**

- Ehud's narrative contained much detail; Shamgar's narrative, none.

- Ehud was physically handicapped but fashioned himself a strong weapon beforehand. Shamgar was not mentioned as being handicapped but was armed with a weak weapon—a common tool that he had at hand.

- Ehud fled to the mountain and marshaled an army. Shamgar stood where he was (wherever that was) and fought alone.

- How many men did Ehud and Shamgar each kill? The text only mentions Ehud killing one enemy personally, while Shamgar kills six hundred.

- Ehud delivered Israel. Shamgar also delivered Israel. Was Shamgar any less effective than Ehud in achieving the overall goal? No.

PICTURE SUMMARY

Shamgar models for us this basic message: Stand where you are, do what you can with what you have, and it will be enough.

APPLY THE PICTURE

We may look at ourselves and think we are ill-equipped to deal with the enemy because we don't have sufficient knowledge, speaking abilities, or "weapons." Shamgar's ox goad teaches us otherwise. We don't need seminary or college degrees. We don't need a command of Hebrew or Greek. We don't need to be great debaters or know all the prevailing world beliefs and arguments. We don't need an army of support. A lack of all those things should not stop us from being bold in the face of the enemy as Shamgar was. We, as common people equipped with common tools and faith, can be just as effective when we realize our strength is not in ourselves but in God.

In Matthew 10:16-20, Jesus warned His disciples that persecutions were coming, but He gave them this reassurance:

> *"But when they deliver you up, do not worry about how or what you should speak. For it will be given to you in that hour what you should speak; for it is not you who speak, but the Spirit of your Father who speaks in you."* —Matthew 10:19-20

5. **Does that mean we shouldn't strengthen or equip ourselves as Ehud did in areas where we know we have a weakness?**

   Was Jesus saying that we don't have to prepare ourselves to face this enemy? Can we neglect the learning aspect of Bible study and the equipping of ourselves, thinking that we will just open our mouth and perfect, inspired words will pour out of us and slay our enemy? No! I think we as believers can become lazy when we think that all we have to do is love and trust God but make no effort to improve our understanding or work out our faith. How you react when events burst on you suddenly will reflect the training of your mind and heart. If you feel you are weak in an area (like Ehud), sharpen your sword.

   Study the word! Equip yourself, and in the day when you are called to speak, that knowledge and understanding will give you strength. The Word of God is an ox goad, but it is a weak tool only when wielded by those who lack conviction and faith.

Questions for Reflection:

- **Read 2 Corinthians 10:3-5.** We fight a spiritual enemy. What is our main weapon in the battle?

- Does the Word of God feel like a sword or an ox goad to you?

  My thoughts: Sometimes the Word of God can feel like an ox goad—when you wield it, it pricks the enemy just enough to get them angry, and then they turn on you and attack you. If you wield it without conviction, then it will remain a weak weapon.

- Based on your faith in God, His power, and your knowledge of His Word, how equipped do you feel to take on the Philistines in life?

LESSON 6

Oppression #3: Deborah and Barak

READ
Judges 4–5

BUILD THE PICTURE

Oppression #3, Judges 4:1-3

1. When did this oppression begin?

It began after Ehud died. Eighty years then passed and another generation came on the scene—one which had not known the mighty works of the LORD first hand, nor did they know how to war.

We should note that Shamgar fell somewhere in between Ehud and Deborah. He is a contemporary of Ehud, but also mentioned in the Song of Deborah. He was included in the Judges' narrative for the sake of comparison and example without being a time marker of years gone by.

2. What do we know about the oppressor?

Jabin, King of Canaan, reigned in Hazor (Naphtali's territory) for twenty years. He was paired with a commander named Sisera, who lived in Harosheth HaGoyim and commanded nine hundred chariots of iron. Together they had control over an extensive area of the Jezreel Valley.

Jabin is different from the first two oppressors we studied in Othniel's and Ehud's accounts in that he is a Canaanite. The first two had been invaders from outside the Land, but Jabin is from within the Land. He is also paired with this commander, whereas the others have no counterparts. The Jabin–Sisera duo will be balanced by the Deborah–Barak partnership.

3. **How do the meanings of the people and place names add to the narrative picture?**

   Jabin: Jabin means "he whom God considers." That seems like an odd definition for a name, and yet it lends itself to consideration. Do you ever wonder if God sees the oppressor that is making your life a misery? Does God even see your plight, and if He does, why doesn't He do something about it?

   When you have been in oppression for a long time, you can become convinced that God has forgotten you and doesn't see the affliction you are in. We saw Israel voice the same concern in Isaiah 49:14 when we studied that second stumbling block of despair and self-pity. Thinking that God doesn't see or consider your plight is a stumbling block. God sees the oppressor. He sees and considers him.

   Hazor: The proper name Hazor comes from the common word *hasor* meaning "castle" from the root word *haser*, meaning "court or enclosure"—a fortified city. Hazor was something of a royal city in northern Palestine in the territory allotted to Naphtali. The root verb, *hasar*, means to blow the trumpet, as a king would. So, Jabin sits in his castle blowing his trumpet over Israel.

   Sisera: Sisera means "battle array"—appropriate for an army general who commands nine hundred chariots of iron.

   Harosheth HaGoyim means "woodland of the Gentiles" or "the cuttings of the Gentiles," but I want to dig deeper into the name Harosheth.

   Harosheth: the proper name stems from a common word, *harish*, describing a flat or plowed area of land like the Jezreel Valley where Sisera deploys his chariots. Digging deeper into the root word etymology, we find the common word *harosheth* means "carving or skillful working." This word is used in Exodus 31:5 to describe the cutting of stones and carving of wood by a skilled craftsman for use in the Tabernacle:

   > *"In cutting [harosheth] jewels for setting, in carving [harosheth] wood, and to work in all manner of workmanship."* —Exodus 31:5

   Keep digging. The root verb for *haroset* is *harash*. *Harash* has two separate usages in the Scripture.

   > **Definition 1:** *Harash* means "to cut in, plow, or carve" in the sense of using a tool to cut or dig at something—such as a plow

to cut the soil (1 Kings 19:19) or an engraving tool to cut wood or stone. Figuratively, *harash* describes a whip that furrows a man's back (Psalms 129:3) or plowing in a sense of digging out or devising something, only the tool you are using is a person instead of an object. The word has about it a sense of plotting or devising things in secret (1 Samuel 23:9)—the crafting of something below the surface. It implies a treachery has happened.

Definition 2: *Harash* means to remain silent, be dumb, speechless, or deaf. In the Scripture, it is often translated as holding one's peace, often in context with a crime being committed or covered up. In Genesis 34:5, Jacob knew about Dinah's rape but he *harash*-ed over the matter—he held his peace. A person knows what is going on but turns a blind eye to it or keeps silent at times when he ought to speak up.

The full picture of *harash*: *Harash*-ing happens when an oppressor uses a tool to carve out a place—to overcome and subdue a people. Sisera is Jabin's tool for carving out an empire within Israel. Sisera's tools are iron chariots. Everyone knows what is going on, but no one says anything. They don't speak up against the oppressor or the oppression, but withdraw into silence and hold their peace.

Israel's oppressor carved out an empire in the Jezreel Valley, and Israel didn't fight back. Twenty years passed before Israel broke her silence.

Deborah and Barak, Judges 4:4-9

4. **The pattern: How did God's response to Israel's cry differ from previous oppressions?**

    In the past two oppressions, the children of Israel cried out, and God immediately raised up a deliverer in response. This time, the children of Israel cried out to the LORD, and the LORD sent word by a prophetess who was also a judge. The judge became an intermediary between God and His people.

5. **What do we know about Deborah, the wife of Lapidoth?**

    Deborah was a prophetess and a judge, but she was not intended to be a deliverer of Israel. She was located, literally, between Ramah and Bethel, very near Shiloh. In Jewish culture, a woman would not consult privately with men in a house, so she sat outdoors under the palm tree of Deborah, and the people came to her there for judgment.

But consider the meanings of the names Ramah and Bethel relative to each other.

Bethel means "house of God" and is located on the Shiloh side of where Deborah sat.

Ramah is the proper name that springs from the common word *ramah*, meaning "a hill or lofty height." In other places in Scripture, *ramah* is universally associated with idol worship—the high hills upon which Israel set up altars and asherah poles for illicit worship (cf. Ezekiel 16:24-25, 29, 31).

Figuratively, Deborah sat between the house of God and a high place used for idol worship, which is appropriate since she judged and was intermediary between God and an idolatrous people. The palm tree adds a little more to the picture. Palms are unique from multi-branched trees in that they have a single, upright heart. The palm tree of Deborah evokes a sense of Deborah having an upright heart.

She was called Deborah, and she was the "wife of Lapidoth." Let's consider the picture that comes out of the names Deborah and Lapidoth.

Deborah: Deborah means "bee." Obviously, she is not a literal bee, but she is bee-like in a sense. We have a general understanding of bees, but God has some particular uses for bees in Scripture, mentioned in four passages. Let's examine these contexts briefly and pull together the overall picture of bee uses.

> *"And the Amorites who dwelt in that mountain came out against you and chased you as bees do, and drove you back from Seir to Hormah."* —Deuteronomy 1:44

When Israel went charging into the Land without God, the Amorites chased Israel out of a place where they should not be, like bees do. God used bees to chase people out of places. (Is Deborah chasing someone out of a place they shouldn't be? Yes, in a couple of ways, as we will see.)

> *"After some time, when he [Samson] returned to get her, he turned aside to see the carcass of the lion. And behold, a swarm of bees and honey were in the carcass of the lion."* —Judges 14:8

These are the bees that Samson finds in the lion's carcass doing what bees do—they swarm over a place as a united body and take it over. They are a hive of industry, and yet it is a unified effort, and they move with orderly motion.

> *"All nations surrounded me, but in the name of the LORD I will destroy them ... They surrounded me like bees; They were quenched like a fire of thorns; for in the name of the LORD I will destroy them."*
> —Psalm 118:10, 12

In Psalm 118, the speaker appears to be one who is either of a kingly or military persona and speaks of nations that have swarmed around him like bees and encompassed him; but he defeats them by the LORD's help. (Read verses 10-12 to get the full context.)

> *"And it shall come to pass in that day that the LORD will whistle for the fly that is in the farthest part of the rivers of Egypt, and for the bee that is in the land of Assyria."* —Isaiah 7:18

Isaiah 7:18 comes out of the Immanuel Prophecy, where the LORD tells King Ahaz that He is sending the Assyrian king to take Israel out of the Land. The bee is figurative of the Assyrians who will swarm over the land of Israel and occupy it in a time of the LORD's judgment of Israel.

Dig deeper: Remember, these nouns often have actions at their root. The noun *deborah* comes from the root verb *dabar* which means "to speak." Now, how do we get a noun that means "bee" from a verb that means "speak"? What does a bee have to do with speaking? Whenever you get a sudden segue from one word to another that seems completely disconnected, you will find a connection when you put the pictures together.

The full picture of the bee: God uses bees to drive people out of places. They swarm over a place and take it over as a unified body moving in orderly motion. They can be figurative of the nations who swarm over Israel and occupy it in a time of judgment, but are defeated by a king or military leader. (Jabin is like a bee in this sense, but then God sends Deborah and Barak to drive him out.)

How does the bee speak? With a sting.

How does a bee-like prophetess and judge speak? With a sting.

How does God use Deborah? He uses her to drive people out of places where they shouldn't be.

Lapidoth: Deborah is also called *eschet Lapidoth* or the wife of Lapidoth. The usual word for "wife" is the Hebrew word, *ishash*, which can be translated as either woman or wife. Lapidoth is understood to be her husband, but the wording is not definitive.

Lapidoth means torches, flames, or that which gives light. Thus, the phrase *eschet Lapidoth* can be rendered woman of flames, wife of flames, woman of light, or wife of a man whose name means flames or torches. Lapidoth may reflect the husband and wife's vocation. Jewish tradition holds that Deborah was a maker of wicks for the Tabernacle lampstand.[1]

6. **What do we know of Barak?**

    Compared to Deborah, little description is made of Barak. We know he is the son of Abinoam and lives in Kedesh of Naphtali. But there is more to the picture of him when we consider the meaning of these names.

    Barak: Barak (or more correctly rendered, *baraq*) means "lightning" or "lightning flash," as in light glittering off a wielded sword. Where the common word is used in Scripture, this "lightning" or "glittering sword" is expressly reserved for the LORD's use.

    > *"If I whet My glittering sword [baraq], and My hand takes hold on judgment, I will render vengeance to My enemies, and repay those who hate Me."* —Deuteronomy 32:41

    His father is Abinoam. **Abinoam** means "My father [*abi*] is pleasantness [*noam*]." Following the meaning of *noam*, we find a description of all that is delightful, pleasant, kind, beautiful, and well-favored. It is the description of what life is like for a people walking with God and experiencing His blessing. Such was the place in which Barak was brought up—a place that his father's generation, or perhaps his grandfather's generation, had prepared for him. Prior to the oppression, Israel had experienced eighty years of relative peace and prosperity. This was the life, or the view of life, that Barak inherited; but he is now under oppression.

---

1 Kadari, Tamar. "Deborah 2: Midrash and Aggadah." Jewish Women: A Comprehensive Historical Encyclopedia. 20 March 2009. Jewish Women's Archive. (Viewed on February 10, 2021) <https://jwa.org/encyclopedia/article/deborah-2-midrash-and-aggadah>.

Barak lives in Kedesh beside Hazor. **Kedesh** means "holy place or sanctuary." It is an interesting addition to the imagery of his father's name. In the shadow of Hazor's oppressive presence, Barak has clung to his "sanctuary." It is his safe place, a place of pleasantness created by his father's generation. It is perhaps something like what Christians describe as the "holy huddle," insulated from the secular world. Instead of battling the oppressor, God's "glittering sword" chose to remain sheathed and at rest.

7. **What was Deborah's message to Barak?**

    "... Has not the LORD God of Israel commanded, 'Go and deploy troops at Mount Tabor; take with you ten thousand men of the sons of Naphtali and of the sons of Zebulun;" —Judges 4:6b

    "Has not God commanded . . ." This is stated in the present perfect tense, meaning God told you at some point in the past, but you haven't done it yet, so He is continuing to tell you . . . go! Hello, Barak, glittering sword, what are you waiting for? God told you in Deuteronomy 32:41 how He would use you. Don't you trust God to keep His promises?

8. **Why did Barak want Deborah to come with him?**

    Keep in mind, Barak was of the generation that had been raised in the 80-year span of quietness and rest in the land. He had never seen war and didn't know how to fight. He had heard the stories of God's power but never experienced it first-hand. He was being asked to step out in front of a seasoned general armed with nine hundred chariots, when all he had was an army of volunteers who, like himself, didn't know the first thing about warfare. He had no confidence in himself, let alone God.

    He had not grasped the fact that God has already assured the victory for him. God said He would deploy Sisera and deliver him into Barak's hands. Barak had only to step out in faith.

    Instead Barak set up conditions that had to be met before he would do his part. He would not move unless he had a counselor to guide him.

9. **What was the consequence for Barak's lack of faith?**

    Deborah told him there would be no glory for him in the journey. The final victory would go to a woman.

PICTURE SUMMARY

Jabin sat in his castle, reigning over the richness of the Jezreel Valley, blowing his trumpet, and oppressing the people. Meanwhile, Barak, God's glittering sword, remained sheathed in his pleasant sanctuary—his safe space where there was beauty and pleasantness and grace and favor.

Barak ignored the reality around him. He held his peace as the *harash*-ing was going on around him. He ignored God's command to do something about it because he didn't want to deal with the bully in his own backyard. So, God sent Deborah after him.

Deborah was a judge and a prophetess. She was a bee who spoke with a sting. She spoke God's words to His people to drive them to action and repentance, but she had a particularly stinging rebuke for a leader who had not dealt with the marauding bees who had swarmed over the Land and taken up residence. She was the bee and the woman of flames sent to chase Barak out of his comfort zone and light a fire under him, so to speak.

Barak went, but not willingly. He became defensive and created conditions that Deborah had to meet before he would do his part. While Deborah agreed to go with him, there was a loss of reward for his lack of faith.

APPLY THE PICTURE

PROFILE OF THIS OPPRESSION

Jabin is a Canaanite, so he can represent an antagonist outside of yourself who you are battling, or he can represent a war with the Canaanite side within you.

The profile of an external "Canaanite" antagonist: There is an antagonist you have allowed to remain in your life who assumes an authority over you that is not rightly theirs. The antagonist gains power over you to the point where they have the ability to impact your freedom, well-being, and livelihood, and they retain power because you perceive them as being stronger—backed by authority, physical strength, wealth, influence, or even public opinion.

Everyone sees and knows about the bully in the backyard, but no one (including you) stands up to them. Everyone holds their peace and lets the bully have his way until the oppression is unbearable.

The profile of an internal "Canaanite" antagonist: Your carnal side can gain authority over you—not by force but because you give it authority. It can gain power over you and affect your freedom, well-being, and livelihood. Whatever form this aggressor takes—perhaps cravings for power, status, wealth, physical addictions, or even the need for validation and public support—it brings you into a form of bondage to it.

> ## Questions for Reflection:
>
> **External antagonist:** Do you have a Jabin in your life?
>
> - Is there someone in your life who you have had to finds ways around, either to avoid or cope with them?
>
> - Do you find yourself seeking sanctuary or "safe spaces"—a place where they can't find you or areas of your life where they are not allowed entry? If so, what does your sanctuary look like?
>
> - Does trying to find a way around the problem or ignoring the problem bring peace or more oppression?
>
> - When God convicts us of a need to deal with an oppression that has taken over our lives, how do we respond to the person He sends to light a fire under us?
>
>   *My thoughts: We can get into a battle of wills with the person telling us to deal with our problem, and forget that God is the one who issued the command. One of the ways we avoid having to act is to make conditions that someone else has to meet before we do our part.*
>
> - What support do you feel you need to deal with this antagonist? Is a perceived lack of support or guidance keeping you from dealing with the problem?
>
> - What do you lose in your journey when you follow Barak's example?
>
>   *My thoughts: The whole point of going through trials is to give us the experiential relationship with God—to get a sense of His power, love, and faithfulness to us. It is meant to be a glorious one-on-one encounter, but it becomes diluted when we throw people into the role that should be God's.*
>
>   *That doesn't mean that we don't need help at times in battling oppression. God sent Barak in with ten thousand foot soldiers. But if*

> *all we have is faith and an ox goad, that should not stop us. When we become dependent on transient, often shortsighted, human counselors for comfort, guidance, and reassurance to the point that we cannot act without them, then we lose the glory of the journey.*
>
> **Internal antagonist:** Have you given reign of your body to your "Canaanite" side?
>
> - What are you struggling with in terms of a spiritual walk?
> - Is there something that you are pursuing that is having a negative effect on your life and the lives of those around you?
> - What is the source of its power?
> - What do you feel you need in order to deal with this internal antagonist?

BUILD THE PICTURE

The Battle, Judges 4:10-24

10. What are the battle details? (These are going to change when we read the Song of Deborah, so take note):

- **What tribes did Barak call?** Zebulun and Naphtali.
- **How many men went up to Mount Tabor with him?** 10,000.
- **What was the outcome?** The LORD went out before Barak and routed Sisera's army with the edge of the sword before Barak, just as the LORD promised. Sisera's army fled, and Barak and his army pursued them all the way to Harosheth HaGoyim (appropriately, the *harash*-ings or digging out of the Gentiles). Sisera escaped on foot to the tent of Jael.

Remember: King Jabin had *harash*-ed Israel—he had carved out his empire using Sisera and tools of iron. God contended with the Canaanite king by sending Barak, His own glittering sword, to dig Sisera out of the Jezreel Valley. God *harash*-ed back by plowing right through Sisera's army as easily as a plow cuts the earth, and Barak and his army were left to clean up. At Deborah's command, they swarmed over the Jezreel Valley and drove the enemy out (in a bee-like fashion).

11. Did Barak argue with Deborah this time when she told him to go?

No, he didn't, unlike last time. This time he immediately moved forward. As easy as it is to come down on Barak for his balking, we have to remember this man is named among the greats in the hall of faith in the book of Hebrews (Hebrews 11:32). How is it that he is counted as a man of great faith when his effort falls short of glory, according to Deborah's prophecy?

One of the integral themes running through the book of Judges is the contrast between what man sees as right in his own eyes and what is right in God's eyes. We judge Barak by the facts laid before us in this narrative, and the balance tips in judgment against him being a man of faith. But what is faith in God's eyes? Is a little step of faith after much balking still a step of faith? It would seem that God recognizes and rewards even small steps of faith. Isn't that encouraging to consider?

I admit, in building this study, I have had my own Barak moment. As I delved into the deep issues that come out of these lessons, I immediately felt swamped with insecurity over my lack of personal experience in many of these areas. I have not had to wrestle with a lot of the thorny questions I have been posing so far (and to come), and to me, that is a bad thing, because how could I presume to teach something without that knowledge? I did not wish to pose as some great expert or a counselor, which I am not, and I was afraid that I would come off insensitive or harsh or flat-out wrong in my analysis. The first thought in my head was that I needed a counselor to walk with me through this—someone with experience or at least a higher level of learning than myself who could tell me when I was being shortsighted. I tracked down as many "experts" as I could—various members of counseling staff, pastors, their wives, missionaries in the field—to see if they could give me a broader view of the application of these things than I understood myself, and while I received a modicum of advice, which I appreciated greatly, it never felt like it was enough. And I balked and fretted over it a good long while until God finally impressed on me the message that all I needed to do was stand where I was and do what I could with what I had, and it would be enough. And I had to laugh at myself. Duh. So, this is me learning my lesson along with you, and taking a little encouragement from Barak in knowing God will count this as a step of faith, however small. And I beg your forbearance with me in these lessons as I work through these scenarios. Enough. Back to the lesson.

12. What do we know about the Kenites?

As you will remember from the first lesson, the Kenites are a clan of the Midianites who separated themselves from the Midianite nation and went to live in the Judean desert in Othniel's day. Heber's family had further split from the Kenite clan and moved north to camp at Zaanaim beside Kedesh.

Let's look at the meanings of the names Heber, Kenite, Jael, and Zaanaim, and see how they add to the picture in the narrative.

Heber: Heber means "comrade," one who comes alongside you, with whom you have affinity and fellowship. The proper name springs from the common word *heber,* meaning "association, company, or band" (keep in mind, there are good and bad associations). The root verb means "to unite or join with."

Kenite or Qayni: *Qayni* (plural noun) means "smiths" as in blacksmiths—makers of weapons and wielders of hammers. It would appear that these semi-nomadic people were itinerant craftsmen of metalworks.

Qayin (singular noun) means "smith," but also "spear," in the sense of fixity, like a tool used to pin something to the wall or ground. So, they were makers of weapons that were used to pin things in place. We should note there is a variant meaning for this word. It is also the word from which we get the name Cain, the son of Adam, and we have some blending of imagery when we put the two contexts side by side. Cain was a man who struck down his brother, and then became a wanderer whose progeny were dwellers in tents, workers of metal, and musicians. (Cain's lineage ended at the Flood, so the Kenites are not of his line. Only the imagery is shared.)

Qayin is derived from the root verb *quwn,* which means "to strike a musical note (such as a hammer on metal) in accompaniment to a funeral lament."

Jael: Jael means "mountain goat," in the sense of one who ascends or rises up in terms of excellence or being profitable the way a mountain goat ascends the mountain heights. Interestingly, the root verb *ya'al* means "to gain, profit, or benefit." This is a picture of a person who rises up to be profitable, beneficial, or otherwise valuable to another person. This most certainly describes Jael in aiding Barak.

When you look at the verses where *ya'al* is used, you find an interesting study of "gain" and the means by which you attain or lose it. In light of our earlier discussion of pursuing gain by Ashtoreth ways, I will give you some examples of people or things that are a profitable or unprofitable in terms of *ya'al* by God's definition:

"Treasures of wickedness profit [ya'al] *nothing, but righteousness delivers from death."* —Proverbs 10:2

"They were all ashamed of a people who could not benefit [ya'al] *them, or be help or benefit, but a shame and also a reproach."* —Isaiah 30:5

"Those who make an image, all of them are useless, and their precious things shall not profit [ya'al]; *they are their own witnesses; they neither see nor know, that they may be ashamed. Who would form a god or mold an image that profits* [ya'al] *him nothing?"* —Isaiah 44:9-10

"Thus says the LORD, your Redeemer, The Holy One of Israel: 'I am the LORD your God, Who teaches you to profit [ya'al], *Who leads you by the way you should go.'"* —Isaiah 48:17

"The priests did not say, 'Where is the LORD?' And those who handle the law did not know Me; the rulers also transgressed against Me; the prophets prophesied by Baal, and walked after things that do not profit [ya'al] *. . . Has a nation changed its gods, which are not gods? But My people have changed their Glory for what does not profit* [ya'al]." —Jeremiah 2:8, 11

"O LORD, my strength and my fortress, my refuge in the day of affliction, the Gentiles shall come to You from the ends of the earth and say, 'Surely our fathers have inherited lies, worthlessness and unprofitable [ya'al] *things.'"* —Jeremiah 16:19

Jael most certainly knew where her profit lay, and rose up to do her part in securing that gain.

Zaanaim: The place name, Zaanaim, means "removings" or a place of "taking down," as in a tent being put up, only to be taken down again. It has the feel of a way-station where travelers might stay the night and then move on. The Kenites pitched their tent here in this temporary place for the very purpose of taking down a tent, so to speak, except the tent was a man over whom a covering has been thrown. In his taking down, a kingdom was taken down with him.

13. Why does Sisera seek refuge at the Kenite camp instead of Hazor with King Jabin, and why does Jael's tent seem a good choice?

In the space of a day, a veteran general with a tremendous army miraculously lost the entirety of his fighting men and nine hundred iron chariots to what, in his estimation, was nothing more than a handful of untrained volunteers under Barak. Deep in enemy territory, alone, on foot, and without resources, the military man made some decisions as to where to go and how to save his own life. The coast was the nearest escape route, except it was controlled by Israel, so his only other option, really, was to head north toward Hazor and King Jabin.

If you were a general who had just lost your entire army and control of the kingdom, would it be wise to return to your king, seeking protection? Of course not. The king would have you killed if only to vent his fury with you. Perhaps for this reason, Sisera turned aside and sought refuge in the camp of Heber the Kenite at Zaanaim near Kedesh. Heber was an itinerant blacksmith without any kingdom of his own, who resided as a guest in Israel's land and was a neutral party, as the text notes.

The choices we make when events break suddenly on us reflect our values, heart, and the training of our minds. If our core values are wrong, if we cling to the wrong kingdom in this life and pursue the wrong kind of gain, then the choices we make will be wrong, even if they seem right in our own eyes.

Sisera and Jael make an interesting comparison in the choices they made when events broke on them suddenly.

Sisera was a trained military man who assessed his situation according to military strategies, operational risk, and earthly reward. His whole identity, purpose, and values were based on the army he commanded and the kingdom he had carved out for King Jabin. He came to this crisis in his life with his mind trained down a particular path, which drove the decisions he made in dealing with that crisis.

Judges 4:17 specifically points out that Sisera fled to the tent of Jael, wife of Heber the Kenite, and not to Heber himself. That seemed a curious point to me, and when I gave this study in a classroom setting, I asked my students: why choose Jael's tent rather than Heber's? Why would Jael's tent have seemed a strategic solution to Sisera's problem, and why was it, in fact, the wrong choice? One of my students, Mr. Peter Johnson, offered a very good answer, which I include here:

> This decision by Sisera may have seemed like a safe move to him for a number of reasons. First, Jael's tent was in the camp of Heber, her husband, and peace existed between Heber and King Jabin. Secondly, Sisera would view a woman as an unlikely threat. Thirdly, if he hid in a woman's tent, no one would enter her tent looking for him while she was occupying the entrance and denying that he was present. Middle eastern custom at the time would not allow for anyone uninvited to enter her tent while she was occupying it.
>
> In the culture of that time, the host's obligation to an *invited* guest who entered the host's tent was to protect the guest, even above the protection of the host's own family. However, such an obligation was conferred *only* as the result of an invitation extended by the dominant male in the camp. Jael, as a consequence of this situation, had no responsibility to protect Sisera.[2]

So, if Sisera had entered Heber's tent and appealed to him for help, Heber, as head of the clan, would have been bound by the Middle Eastern rules of hospitality to protect Sisera, even with his own life, whereas Jael was under no such obligation. The very fact that she invited Sisera in should have raised a warning flag, since it was a scandalous act for any man to enter a married woman's tent without the consent and presence of her husband. It was for this same reason that Deborah sat outside beneath the palm to judge rather than grant audiences to men behind closed doors. But then Sisera is not basing his choices on these considerations. To a weary and desperate military man, Jael is not a physical threat, and that is foremost in his

---

[2] For more information about the middle eastern customs of hospitality, I recommend the article "Travelers and Strangers: Hospitality in the Biblical World" by Dennis Bratcher, published online on The Voice, Biblical and Theological Resources for Growing Christians; Christian Resource Institute; http://www.crivoice.org/travelers.html.

mind. She is neutral, unarmed, hospitable toward him, and her tent would be an unlikely place for anyone to look for him.

Neutral parties are only neutral until you force them into a position of having to make a choice. As her actions attest, Jael's heart was already decided in favor of Israel and Israel's God, regardless of the peaceful relations her clan had with King Jabin. She is a good model for us as believers in this, that she lived at peace with the world around her, yet maintained her beliefs and convictions and acted on them accordingly when the situation demanded it.

How does a woman react to the sight of a desperate and dangerous military commander still in battle array, standing outside her tent? Speaking from a woman's viewpoint, I would have shut the tent against him and hid. But then Jael was the wife of the camp's leader, and perhaps a response seemed obligatory. She offered him hospitality as the wife of the camp leader, and it was a strategic act to get him to drop his defenses. She offered him milk instead of water and a "covering" as he rested—literally a blanket or rug, but figuratively protection. And then she picked up a tent peg and hammer and nailed him to the ground.

Why choose a tent peg and hammer as a weapon? She was the wife of an itinerant blacksmith and lived in a tent. Tent pegs were readily available, as was a hammer.

Like Shamgar, she did what she could with what she had at hand, and it was enough. Jael's choice was based on a correct understanding of which kingdom was more profitable to her and what she stood to gain by taking down Sisera.

PICTURE SUMMARY

Unknown to Barak, he had a comrade, Heber, whose family had come alongside him. They were transient people in his life, but they ended up here in the fight at just the right place and time to help Barak defeat a final enemy. These Kenites were the "smiths" whom God brought into this battle to strike a particular blow against Israel's enemy.

Jael rose up to wield the hammer and was given the honor of striking that musical note that became the death song over Israel's enemies. Indeed, she was exalted in song—the Song of Deborah.

APPLY THE PICTURE

Jael presents us with a model of an intercessor who works behind the scenes on behalf of a struggling believer. An intercessor by scriptural definition is one who stands in the gap and fights or pleads for justice and mercy (Isaiah 59:15-16, Ezekiel 22:29-30).

Christ is the chief intercessor for us in His role as our high priest, and the remembrance of our justification through His death on the cross can become our strength in battling enemies:

> *"Therefore I will divide Him a portion with the great, And He shall divide the spoil with the strong, Because He poured out His soul unto death, And He was numbered with the transgressors, And He bore the sin of many, And made intercession for the transgressors."* —Isaiah 53:12

> *"But He, because He continues forever, has an unchangeable priesthood. Therefore He is also able to save to the uttermost those who come to God through Him, since He always lives to make intercession for them."* —Hebrews 7:24-25

> *"What then shall we say to these things? If God is for us, who can be against us? He who did not spare His own Son, but delivered Him up for us all, how shall He not with Him also freely give us all things? Who shall bring a charge against God's elect? It is God who justifies. Who is he who condemns? It is Christ who died, and furthermore is also risen, who is even at the right hand of God, who also makes intercession for us. Who shall separate us from the love of Christ? Shall tribulation, or distress, or persecution, or famine, or nakedness, or peril, or sword? . . . Yet in all these things we are more than conquerors through Him who loved us."* —Romans 8:31-35, 37

The Holy Spirit is also an intercessor.

> *"Likewise the Spirit also helps in our weaknesses. For we do not know what we should pray for as we ought, but the Spirit Himself makes intercession for us with groanings which cannot be uttered. Now He who searches the hearts knows what the mind of the Spirit is, because He makes intercession for the saints according to the will of God."* —Romans 8:26-27

While we do not fight the battle physically as Jael did, we, too, are called to be intercessors in how we help one another in times of spiritual battle, specifically through prayer. Very often, the people for whom we pray are unaware of our work on their behalf, or they discover it sometime after the battle is over. There are many verses in the New Testament directing us to intercede for one another in prayer, but here are a few:

> *"Therefore I exhort first of all that supplications, prayers, intercessions, and giving of thanks be made for all men, for kings and all who are in authority, that we may lead a quiet and peaceable life in all godliness and reverence."* —1 Timothy 2:1-2

> *"For I know that this will turn out for my deliverance through your prayer and the supply of the Spirit of Jesus Christ,"* —Philippians 1:19

> *"For this reason we also, since the day we heard it, do not cease to pray for you, and to ask that you may be filled with the knowledge of His will in all wisdom and spiritual understanding;"* —Colossians 1:9

> *"Now I beg you, brethren, through the Lord Jesus Christ, and through the love of the Spirit, that you strive together with me in prayers to God for me, that I may be delivered from those in Judea who do not believe, and that my service for Jerusalem may be acceptable to the saints, that I may come to you with joy by the will of God, and may be refreshed together with you."* —Romans 15:30-32

Questions for Reflection:

In Lesson 3, we talked about the seven stumbling blocks in oppression from Isaiah. One had to do with having the right values and perspective of the kingdom we are pursuing. Sisera illustrates the "Canaanite" for us.

- Sisera was a man whose whole identity and purpose was wrapped up in gaining and protecting an earthly kingdom. What is the danger of sourcing your identity, comfort, and hope in earthly kingdoms, leaders, and material things?

- To what extent have you anchored your own identity to a country or leaders, or focused your effort on securing material gain or an earthly kingdom? If you were to lose these things today, where or to whom would you turn?

- What happens when that identity collapses?

> If you aren't struggling, that doesn't mean you shouldn't be in the battle.
>
> - How are Deborah and Jael models for us in dealing with believers like Barak?
>
> - What weapons or tools do we need to be effective in helping a person deal with oppression?

The Song of Deborah, Judges 5

General observations about the song:

- **It is written in archaic Hebrew.** Even Jewish scholars have had difficulty in translating it, which is why there is a great deal of variation in translations.

- **The song differs from the narrative.** It follows the general flow of the narrative with "then" statements: "Then" the people were under siege (v8), "then" Deborah and Barak arose (v11), "then" the battle begins (v13), "then" the retreat (v22). But it has some additional information not included in the narrative and a different focus.

- **It is written in the first person.** You are meant to identify with the speaker as if you are saying these words.

- **It is poetic literature,** which means the text will incorporate **figurative language** such as metaphors, similes, hyperbole, personification, and symbolism.

- **The song is structured around three sets of comparisons.**

    o **Part 1 (5:2-11a)** compares God's kingship and power in contrast to powerless Israel who serve other gods

    o **Part 2 (5:11b-23)** compares battle details: Israel's warriors to the Canaanite kings

    o **Part 3 (5:24-31)** compares two women: Jael and Sisera's mother

We will walk through the text in parts.

BUILD THE PICTURE

Part 1: Powerful God, Powerless Israel, Judges 5:2–11

Part one sets up a contrast between God's power and Israel's powerlessness without Him. It begins and ends with the praise of God and is framed by a repeated structure of theme and command:

Opening theme (verse 2): *"When leaders lead in Israel, when the people willingly offer themselves, Bless the LORD!"*

Command (verse 3): *"<u>Hear</u>, O kings! Give ear, O princes! I, even I, will sing to the LORD; I will sing praise to the LORD God of Israel . . ."* (emphasis added)

Closing theme (verse 9): *"My heart is with the rulers of Israel who offered themselves willingly with the people. Bless the LORD!"*

Command (verse 10-11a): *"<u>Speak</u>, you who ride on white donkeys, who sit in judges' attire, and who walk along the road. Far from the noise of the archers,³ among the watering places, there they shall recount the righteous acts of the LORD, the righteous acts for His villagers in Israel . . ."* (emphasis added)

Between these two bookends, we find a picture of God in verses 4-5 contrasted with Israel in verses 6-8.

14. Compare and contrast the pictures of God and Israel.

Picture of God: This description is reminiscent of the Isaiah 40 passage we studied previously. God strides into battle with all of creation at His command, and creation melts and gushes forth in the outpouring of power and grandeur.

Picture of Israel: Where God is powerful, Israel is powerless. The highways were deserted, and the people walked by winding roads. Village life ceased as the people withdrew into the fortified cities, only to have the enemy follow them to the gate and battle them there. This

---

3 Far from the noise of the archers (*hatsim*): The *hatsim* (those who divide) is a vague term. In the context of battle, it may refer to archers who march in divisions. In the context of watering places, it may refer to shepherds dividing flocks at those places. Either way, the *hatsim* are very noisy, and yet here, the praise of God is louder. According to the Jewish Study Bible (JPS, 1985), the phrasing might be summarized: The praise of God's righteous acts will be so loud that the noise of the *hatsim* will sound like a distant echo.

is the exact picture of the consequences described in Leviticus 26 that God promised to send upon Israel for their disobedience and idolatry.

The Hebrew word for highway is *orach,* meaning "path or open road." In a literal sense, the roads were unsafe to travel openly, perhaps because of wild beasts or bestial, lawless men. Thus, the people used byways—crooked or winding paths that skirted these hazards.

But *orach* is also figurative of a path or way of life. A way of life—God's way of life—ceased, and the people chose a different way of life. They chose paths of coping and avoidance in an effort to live in their oppressive conditions. As the people gathered in fortified cities for protection, community life fractured and fell apart, bringing isolation. The gates became the battleground. However far Israel withdrew, the enemy still pursued them. The text notes that not a spear or shield was seen among forty thousand. Forty thousand denotes warfare on a national level (not just one city).

This is the figurative path Israel has taken: Keeping in mind the stumbling blocks we studied, Israel's unfaithfulness and pursuit of Baals and Asherahs led to oppression, then fear, then despair, shame, and powerlessness, and ended in silent withdrawal. They hunkered down into defensive, fortified positions and hid behind walls. Withdrawal led to isolation and a loss of a sense of community.

That was the course down which their byway led them. Why did all this happen? Because they chose new gods.

Their condition continued until the days of Deborah. The text says Deborah arose like a mother to Israel. In the Old Testament Hebraic culture, the title "mother" does not necessarily denote a blood relation. A mother can be one who has the upbringing of a person and teaches them the Law and holy living. As a judge and prophetess, Deborah fulfilled these roles and is given the honorary title of mother.

15. **Why are Shamgar and Jael mentioned by name together?**

    They are positioned in the text between the descriptions of God and idolatrous Israel and are a contrast to Israel in that they remained true to God. In spite of the oppression in which they lived, they stepped forward to fight with common tools and uncommon valor, whereas the rest of Israel is pictured as withdrawing and battling from behind fortified gates without weapons.

> ## Questions for Reflection:
>
> Forsaking the highway for the byway leads us down a path strewn with stumbling blocks: Idolatry ... oppression ... fear ... despair and powerlessness ... destructive anger or silence.
>
> - Do you, personally, feel yourself on this path somewhere with some personal oppressor you are dealing with?
> - If so, where have you stumbled? (If you are feeling fear, despair, shame, destructive anger or silent withdrawal into isolation, then you have stumbled over one of the stumbling stones.)
> - When you look at our country, where are we on this path as a nation?
> - Regardless of the direction the country goes, do you personally have to stay on this path?
> - Israel took the path of withdrawal into silence for twenty years. Why isn't silence and withdrawal a good solution?
> - Does withdrawing into "safe spaces" or fortifications fulfill our mandate to go out into the world?

Part 2: Israel versus the Canaanite Kings, Judges 5:12-23

OVERVIEW

The narrative segues from the grand overview in Part 1 to a focus on the battle in Part 2. The text follows the narrative flow with "then" statements in verses 11, 13, 19b, and 22:

> "... Then the people of the LORD shall go down to the gates." (11b)
> "Then" marks the calling of Deborah and Barak.
>
> "Then the survivors came down ..." (13)
> "Then" marks the calling of Israel and details who participated or not.
>
> "... Then the kings of Canaan fought ..." (19b)
> "Then" marks the battle.
>
> "Then the horses' hooves pounded ..." (22)
> "Then" marks the retreat.

Judges 5:13 and 23 create bookends within the battle sequence by a repetition of phrases:

> "... *The LORD* came down for me *against the mighty*." *(13b)*

> "Because they did not come to the help of the LORD, to the help of *the LORD against the mighty*." *(23b)*

These bookends establish the LORD as the deliverer. Though the rest were participants, the battle belonged to the LORD. He was the one who called Barak to gather Israel, and He was the one who called Sisera to battle through an undisclosed means. He was the one who deployed Sisera's army and delivered it to Barak. There is no single human deliverer named in this narrative. The LORD alone stands as the deliverer of His people.

While there is a general mention of the battle in Part 2, the focus is more on the participants than on relating the battle details. Verses 13-18 establish who of Israel did and did not participate. Deborah's words give an assessment of each tribes' participation. Verses 19-23 give us a view of the Canaanite kings in battle with earthly and heavenly forces. The section ends with the Angel of the LORD rendering judgment against a certain faction in much the same way that He delivered judgment at Bochim.

THE ASSESSMENT OF ISRAEL'S WARRIORS

16. Who are the survivors (*sariyd*, remnant) in verse 13?

If we are following the flow of the narrative, then the remnant are those who came through the oppression and called upon the LORD to be saved.

As I read that, I get a sense that the LORD used the oppression as the testing ground for His people to see which among them would return to Him. Only a remnant survived, and it was this remnant that He now exerts Himself to deliver.

17. Who participated? (verse14-15a)

- **Ephraim** "whose roots are in Amalek." It is unclear whether Amalek was meant as a proper name or a common phrase meaning "dweller of the valley."
- **Benjamin.**
- **Machir** (that is, West Manasseh as opposed to Gilead or East Manasseh).

- **Issachar.**
- **Naphtali.**
- **Zebulun**, "those who bear the recruiter's staff." (NKJV) Again, this phrase is a difficult translation. The Hebrew phrase is *b'shevet sofer,* or the "stick" of "counting or accounting." It can be translated either as those who bear the staff of command and marshal a number of people, such as a muster-officer, or those who are called to give an account, such as a scribe (this last phrasing lends itself to the KJV translation). The context of the passage is the accounting of those who participated in battle and those who did not, so either translation fits within the greater context.

Zebulun and **Naphtali** are further honored with a second mention in verse 18. These details differ from the narrative in Chapter 4 where only Zebulun and Naphtali are mentioned as being called by Barak. It would appear that a multitude more participated.

18. Who did not participate and why not?
- **Reuben** had great resolves of heart.
- **Gilead (Gad/East Manasseh)** stayed on the other side of the Jordan and did not cross over to help their brethren.

    These tribes east of the Jordan had been commissioned by Moses and Joshua to help their brothers claim their inheritance, but once that obligation was finished, it would seem that these tribes returned to their side of the Jordan and stayed there. The tribes west of the Jordan were left to deal with their own ongoing problems.

    The tribe of Reuben is given special attention. Geographically, Reuben was the farthest from the fight. The text notes that they had *"great resolves of heart"* and yet not enough resolve to get involved, apparently. They commiserated, empathized, agreed that the oppression was just awful, but didn't lift a finger to help. Judges 5:16 asks:

    > *"Why did you sit among the sheepfolds, to hear the pipings [sherukah] for the flocks? The divisions of Reuben have great searchings of heart."*— Judges 5:16

    Sherukah means to whistle in a sense of calling with a whistle or pipe, as a shepherd to his flock. It can also mean to whistle at someone with hissing and derision.

Reuben's call to battle does not come from Barak. Barak only called Zebulun and Naphtali according to Judges 4:10. So, who called the rest? The LORD, the Great Shepherd. The tribe of Reuben ignored the call of the Great Shepherd whistling for His sheep because they were too busy tending their own flocks to come. They knew they should go to help, they had great resolves of heart, but in the end, the call from home was louder and stayed them.

The LORD warns that the pipings, the *sherukah*, will turn to hisses of derision and scorn for those who forsake the Shepherd when called:

> *"Because My people have forgotten Me, they have burned incense to worthless idols. And they have caused themselves to stumble in their ways, from the ancient paths, to walk in pathways and not on a highway, to make their land desolate and a perpetual hissing [sherukah]; Everyone who passes by it will be astonished and shake his head."* —Jeremiah 18:15-16

- **Dan** remained on his ships (Hebrew: *oniya*)—merchant ships, as implied by the term's usage in other Scripture verses. Dan had business to attend and could not come.

- **Asher** had the most vague of reasons. It simply says they remained by the seashore. The battle was right on their home front, and yet they remained on the seaside, which perhaps indicates something of where their loyalties lay. The sea is symbolic of the Gentile nations, and Asher remained on the sea's side.

The same could be said of Dan, who put off entering battle for the gain to be made by seafaring pursuits.

THE BATTLE WITH THE CANAANITE KINGS (Judges 5:19-22)

19. Where was the battle? Was this an earthly or heavenly battle?

". . . then the kings of Canaan fought in Taanach, by the waters of Megiddo . . ." Physically, the war is fought in the Jezreel Valley. Taanach and Megiddo are major cities in the valley, and Kishon is a literal river. The battle is fought between Israel and the Canaanite kings in a physical sense, but the battle really is the LORD's.

"They fought from the heavens; The stars from their courses fought against Sisera." The imagery evokes the picture of a heavenly, spiritual

battle as much as a physical one. Israel is personified as stars, a metaphor taken from Deuteronomy 1:10 and 10:22 *("the LORD your God has made you as the stars of heaven in multitude")*.

"The torrent of Kishon swept them away, that ancient torrent..." This imagery ties back to the opening picture of the LORD striding into battle with the forces of creation at His command: *"... the heavens poured, the mountains gushed..."* (Judges 5:4-5).

We get a sense that this is both an earthly and heavenly or should we say, spiritual battle. Unlike the previous oppressions, there was no human deliverer named in this narrative. Barak, Deborah, and Jael all had a part in overcoming this oppressor, but only God shines as the true deliverer.

20. **The Hebrew word for "courses" in verse 20 is *mecillah*. How is that Hebrew word translated in other Scripture verses and what is the implication of that picture when added to this narrative?**

    Literally, the *mecillah* is a highway, a raised road, or a public road. (This is a different highway than the *orach*. When you look up the word *orach,* you get a different set of verses with a different picture from what the *mecillah* describes. It is important to identify which highway is being described to get the right picture).

    In 2 Chronicles 9:11, it is literally the grand, terraced staircase leading to the Temple and king's palace.

    Figuratively, it is used here in Judges 5:20 to describe the path of a star in heaven or a grand causeway in which the battle rages (that is, the Jezreel Valley).

    In keeping with the picture of the grand staircase leading to the Temple, the highway is the way of the upright who depart from evil (Proverbs 16:17) and the way of return to God (Isaiah 40:3, 62:10).

    > *"... Prepare the way of the LORD; make straight in the desert a highway* [mecillah] *for our God.'"* —Isaiah 40:3

    > *"... Prepare the way for the people; Build up, Build up the highway* [mecillah]*! Take out the stones..."* —Isaiah 62:10

    The *mecillah* takes us back to those Isaiah passages about the stumbling stones that we studied in Lesson 3. This picture of the *mecillah* recalls the commands to prepare the way and remove the stumbling stones and reinforces the theme of helping one another in the battle here in the Song of Deborah.

Part 2 ends with a judgment and curse against those who did not help, delivered by the Angel of the LORD.

> *"'Curse Meroz,' said the Angel of the LORD, 'Curse its inhabitants bitterly, because they did not come to the help of the LORD, to the help of the LORD against the mighty.'"* —Judges 5:23

21. Who was Meroz?

Meroz is an unidentified people—perhaps Israel, the nations, or both. The name means "refuge," yet in practice they offered no help.

For whatever reason, they did not join the battle. It is not that they didn't help their brethren. It says that they did not come to the help of the LORD, and judgment was rendered on them by the Angel of the LORD. (This is an echo of the judgment of Bochim.)

APPLY THE PICTURE

The Song of Deborah emphasizes the theme of helping one another in battling oppression. We fight a spiritual battle that works itself out in our physical world. All are called to help those battling in the *mecillah*, and Deborah and the Angel of the LORD rebuke those who don't help.

How do we respond to the Shepherd's call when commanded to help those battling in the *mecillah*?

22. How can we fall into Reuben's model?

Reuben heard the call and had great resolves of heart, but didn't lift a finger to help. We might speculate why. Maybe the battle seemed too far away to be of help. Maybe the obligations at home in tending their flock took precedence. Maybe it was sheer laziness and not wanting to leave the comfort of home. Whatever the reason, the piping of the flocks kept Reuben at home.

James 2:14-17 makes the analogy between helping people and faith without works:

> *"What does it profit, my brethren, if someone says he has faith but does not have works? Can faith save him? If a brother or sister is naked and destitute of daily food, and one of you says to them, "Depart in peace, be warmed and filled," but you do not give them the things which are needed for the body, what does it profit? Thus also faith by itself, if it does not have works, is dead."* — James 2:14-17

What good is your faith if it is nothing more than wishing people well in their battle? Maybe we rationalize that we have our own battles to fight and so choose not to extend ourselves and risk getting embroiled in someone else's troubles.

Granted, we cannot meet all needs for all people, and sometimes the best we can offer is to pray for them. But if there is a particular need that the Lord has impressed on us, and if we do not respond to His call, then we have become a Reubenite.

23. How can we fall into Dan's model?

Dan is a variation of Reuben in that his merchant business kept him too busy to help. Granted, we must work to support our families, even to provide for the needs of those in battle, but when the call comes from the Lord, these reasons can become an excuse for not responding.

But there are other considerations. In our current culture, work demands are on the rise. They can obligate us to work seven days a week, often with overtime, or create such chaotic work schedules that it becomes difficult even to maintain fellowship with other believers. Gainful employment can become a master over us, demanding all of our energies and leaving no breathing room for godly pursuits. Just finding time to take care of our own family flock is an effort. This, too, can keep us from heeding God's call to battle.

Apart from needful employment, the pursuit of earthly riches can derail us from being effective co-laborers. This aspect speaks to the stumbling block of wrong values and the pursuit of the wrong kingdom. God called Dan to the battle for the spiritual kingdom, but Dan preferred the earthly kingdom. What is earthly wealth when a person needs help in returning to a spiritual relationship with God?

24. How can we fall into Asher's model?

Asher also preferred to stay by the sea's side, to a point that their loyalties could be questioned. There didn't seem to be any impediment keeping them from joining the fight. It wasn't like they lived any distance away, as Reuben and Dan did. The battle was right in their backyard, and yet they wanted no part of it.

What man can remain unmoved when the fighting is right outside his door? The spiritual war rages around us, and yet we often fail to heed the call when it comes, for reasons only we know.

25. How does Meroz describe us? Read Matthew 25:31-46.

Matthew 25:31-46 describes a judgment day when Christ will return and gather the nations before Him to separate the sheep from the goats. In the passage, the nations are undefined, just like Meroz, and the separation is made based on who offered help, just like Meroz. There are those on the one hand who responded to the needs of those who are hungry, thirsty, naked, and in need of physical help and fellowship. On the other hand, there are those who do not respond to the same needs.

Barak raised the call to battle, but it really wasn't Barak to whom the tribes were rallying. It was the Angel of the LORD. We would like to think that if Christ Himself needed help then we would respond without a second thought, whereas if someone like Barak called for help, we might prioritize. But Matthew 25:45 makes it clear that it is the Lord Himself that we failed to respond to when we ignored the call to help. When the sheep and the goats ask the Lord when they failed to minister to Him in His need, He responds:

> *"Assuredly, I say to you, inasmuch as you did not do it to one of the least of these, you did not do it to Me.' And these will go away into everlasting punishment, but the righteous into eternal life."*
> *—Matthew 25:45-46*

Everlasting punishment is the curse on Meroz.

There is a cost associated with not heeding the Good Shepherd's call when He summons us to the highway to remove the stumbling blocks for those struggling to return to Him. The stumbling blocks may be as simple as a physical need, or as consuming as helping a person work out of an addiction. But if we receive such a call, there will be no mercy for us if we do not show mercy.

> ## Questions for Reflection:
>
> - If the Lord has placed someone on your heart who needs help, have you reached out to them yet? If not, why not?
> - How do you know if the Lord is calling you?

Part 3: Jael versus Sisera's Mother, Judges 5:24-31

Directly following the curse in verse 23, we find a blessing (*barachu*). Jael is honored, and her killing of Sisera is retold in elaborate detail. Sisera's fall was epic and made further ignoble by having died at the hand of a woman—a disgraceful death for Sisera and also a blow to Barak's honor.

In the second half of this section, Jael is starkly contrasted to Sisera's mother.

26. Compare Jael and Sisera's mother. What do we know about each?

Jael, wife of Heber the Kenite	Sisera's mother (unnamed)
Gentile (for Israel)	Gentile (against Israel)
A woman in a tent: transient, without permanence	A woman in a lordly house: solid, established, of nobility in her world
She waited alone to hear the outcome of the battle	She waited with her noble women to hear the outcome of the battle
She acted with wisdom	They are described as wise, yet were clearly without understanding
Her focus is on doing what is right in the Lord's eyes	Their minds were focused on the spoil—embroidered garments, girls

Jael was just a traveler passing through. She was without substance or permanence, wealth or finery, and yet she possessed wisdom and vision beyond that of the world's wisest noblewomen. She seemed out of place, and yet we see that God brought her to this place in her life for a very specific purpose. Like Shamgar, she shines as a heroic example of a simple woman who stood where she was and did what she could with what she had at hand, and it was enough. After this narrative, she is never heard from again, and yet her legacy lives on in song.

Conclusion

Jabin wasn't overthrown overnight, but without Sisera, the kingdom was lost, as it said in Chapter 4:

> *"And the hand of the children of Israel grew stronger and stronger against Jabin king of Canaan, until they had destroyed Jabin king of Canaan."* —Judges 4:24

By contrast, the Song of Deborah ends, not with battle details, but with a victory cry and description of God's people at rest.

> *"Thus let all Your enemies perish, O LORD! But let those who love Him be like the sun When it comes out in full strength." So the land had rest for forty years."* —Judges 5:31

Translation Exercise

Before we leave the Song of Deborah, I want to give you a taste of the translation difficulties scholars faced in trying to make sense of the archaic Hebrew. We are going to examine two words in the opening phrase of Judges 5:2:

> *"When <u>leaders lead</u> in Israel, when the people willingly offer themselves, Bless the LORD!"* — Judges 5:2 (NKJV)

This is transliterated from the Hebrew:

> *B'<u>proa paraot</u>* b'Yisrael, be'it-na-dev am, barchu Jehovah.

Proa is a form of the verb, *para*, which has multiple usages in Scripture. It can mean:

1. To lead, act as leader
2. To let go, let loose, ignore, let alone, untended
3. To be let loose, be loosened of restraint (for vengeance)

Paraot is one of two ways that the noun *pra* is rendered in a plural form. The other rendering is *peraot.* Remember, the original Hebrew did not include vowels. The "a" in *pra* is the Hebrew letter *ayin* and is not considered a vowel as we consider it in English. Other vowels have to be added to make these words pronounceable.

Adding an "a" at the beginning renders it *paraot.*
Adding an "e" at the beginning renders it *peraot.*
These words have very different meanings.

Paraot means "leaders." This fits the context of the battle narrative. Paired with the verb, we get translations such as leaders leading or leaders being turned loose on an enemy for vengeance.

Peraot means "locks of hair." This word is a specific reference to taking a Nazirite vow in which the locks of hair are left untrimmed (let loose or left untended). This word fits the verse's context of people offering themselves, presumably the leaders as well at the people. Paired with the verb, we get translations such as locks of hair leading (perhaps a reference to a leader being a Nazirite) or locks of hair being let go or untended (untrimmed).

Most Christian translations lean toward the use of *paraot*, or leader, so we get translations like the following:

"When leaders lead in Israel, . . ." (NKJV)

"That the leaders took the lead in Israel . . ." (ESV, RSV)

"When the princes in Israel take the lead . . ." (NIV)

The King James Version sidesteps the translation difficulty by not mentioning leaders at all:

"Praise ye the LORD <u>for the avenging of Israel</u>, when the people willingly offered themselves."

Jewish translations, however, choose *peraot*, or locks of hair, in their translation:

"When the locks go untrimmed in Israel . . ." (Jewish Study Bible, JPS, 1985)

"When men let grow their hair in Israel . . ." (JPS, 1917)

The use of *peraot* over *paraot* has the curious effect of shifting the focus away from the battle narrative to a focus on the people's relationship with God, which I think is fitting. The Song of Deborah in Chapter 5 differs from the narrative account in Chapter 4 in how it highlights and emphasizes the participants and their relationships, first to God and then one another, rather than offering yet another recounting of the battle's details.

That being said, there is a prophetic picture of a deliverer yet to come that is veiled in the opening and closing verses of the Song of Deborah. This picture only appears when *all* the meanings of *para*, *paraot*, and *peraot* in verse 2 are pulled together in their fullness along with the closing verse.

Here is the amplified version of Judges 5:2, 31:

"When [God raises up a leader who is under a Nazirite vow and without restraint and turns him loose on His enemies for vengeance], *when the people willing offer themselves, bless the LORD! . . . Thus let all Your enemies perish, O LORD! But let those who love Him be as the sun when it comes out in full strength."*
— Judges 5:2, 31

We should note that the Hebrew word for "sun" is *shemesh*, and one who is like the sun is *Shimshon*, or Samson. Samson was a Nazirite who lived his life with little restraint, and yet the LORD raised him up as a leader in

Israel and turned him loose with a vengeance against the Philistines. In addition to being physically strong, his strength was like the sun when it came out at full strength in exposing the treacheries of the Philistines and Israel alike.

Deborah's words give us this prophetic view of a deliverer yet to come, but the picture is veiled by archaic, ambiguous words and because our reading of these verses is in context of the narrative of Deborah and Barak. We are not looking for a picture of Samson in this place.

As it is with the prophetic picture of Samson here, so it is with the prophetic pictures of the Messiah in the Old Testament. To see them, you must consider the words outside of the context of the near events. We will return to this picture when we reach the narrative of Samson.

LESSON 7

Oppression #4: Gideon

READ

Judges 6-8

BUILD THE PICTURE

Oppression #4, Judges 6:1–10

What do we know about this oppression?

1. **Who were the Midianites, Amalekites, and people of the East, where did they come from, and what was their history with Israel?**

    There was no defined king or leader in this oppression, but rather an onslaught of invaders. The Midianites were the ringleaders of the group, but they brought with them the Amalekites and "people of the East."

    According to Genesis 25:1-6, the Midianites were descendants of Abraham and Keturah who Abraham sent to "the east," away from Isaac's inheritance. Amalek was the grandson of Esau, and his people settled in southern Canaan (Genesis 36:12). So, the "people of the East" in this case denotes the desert tribes ranging south-southeast of Israel.

    The Midianites were the people with whom Moses stayed after he fled Egypt. Moses married Zipporah, a Midianite woman, and even invited her family (the Kenite clan) to come with them to the Land. In contrast to the Kenites, the rest of the Midianites were treacherous in their dealings with Israel. During Israel's wilderness journey, Balak king of Moab told the elders of Midian that Israel was so numerous that they would "*. . . lick up everything around us, as an ox licks up the grass of the field . . .*" (Numbers 22:4), and Midian conspired with Moab to take Israel captive and exploit them. (Not surprising, Midian here does to Israel as they once falsely accused Israel of doing to them.)

Midian helped Moab lead Israel into idolatry, and ended up in a battle with Phinehas. Phinehas wiped out five princes of Midian who were vassals of King Sihon of the Amorites living in what became the territory of Reuben (Numbers 31, Joshua 13:21).

2. **How did they oppress Israel?**

   The invading hordes came up from the southern deserts and crossed Israel's borders in caravans with the intent of taking Israel's produce and destroying whatever was left. They entered Israel from the east, traveling up along the trade route called the King's Highway which runs from the gulf of Aqaba (Midianite land) through Edom, Moab, and onto the Plains of Moab which is Reuben's and Gad's territory. From there they crossed the Jordan into Israel's rich interior. The text says that they fanned out and destroyed the land as far as Gaza in Judah and the Jezreel Valley where Gideon is located.

   These invaders were different from the other oppressors we have studied so far in that they had no intent to remain in the land and rule it. They would wait for the harvests, then raid, destroy, and leave. They did this year after year for seven years. For this reason they were described as locusts.

3. **How did Israel cope with the physical oppression?**

   Israel went underground, literally. Instead of living openly, they withdrew into hiding. In the days of Deborah, village life ceased as the people sought the protection of the cities. Now, not even the cities were safe. The people were driven into the mountain strongholds.

   Dens, caves, and mountain strongholds are all natural fortifications and hiding places, often with underground water sources. But they are also dark and deserted places, dwellings for base creatures, and used as places to bury the dead. For Israel to seek refuge in such places is a reflection of their having returned to a base, wilderness-like lifestyle.

   This was not the first time Israel opted to withdraw into silence, but it was the first time they had been driven underground.

4. **The pattern: When the people cried out, what was God's response?**

   The Lord sent a message by a prophet. This is similar to last time with Deborah, except that this prophet differs from Deborah in some significant ways.

5. **Compare the prophet with Deborah:**

   Deborah was identified by name. This prophet was not.

   Deborah was a prophetess and a judge. This prophet was just a prophet.

   Deborah's message was for Barak specifically, to call him to help deliver Israel. There was a sense of hope and imminent salvation for Israel in Deborah's words. This prophet's message was for all of Israel and was merely a rebuke. Don't you remember Egypt? Don't you remember who I am? Don't you remember what I told you? What did you expect when you started down this path?

   Notice the Exodus theme. When the people began to do what was right in their own eyes, they slipped back into that wilderness lifestyle. God brought on them the locust plague of Midianites, their enemies from that journey, who then oppressed them in this cyclical pattern which robbed them of fruitfulness and purpose. They might as well have been walking in circles in the wilderness. The resounding message was "Don't you remember Egypt?" The Exodus theme will continue through the narrative of Gideon.

THE PICTURE OF THIS OPPRESSION

Israel had been in the Land some two hundred years and had forty years of relative peace and security. Caravans of migrant nomads from the southeastern deserts amassed on its borders and came streaming into the land in waves to take what they could, and then left. This happened over and over, year after year after year.

These migrants weren't concerned with ruling Israel or becoming lawful, contributing citizens. They were only there to take what they could. Agriculture was the hardest hit. The nomads took the crops, devastated the land, and left Israel impoverished.

APPLY THE PICTURE

There are enemies, physical and spiritual, in this world that can drive God's people underground so that they no longer practice their faith openly. It is one of the enemy's tactics to weaken resistance by systematically removing vital resources from a person's life—the right to meet and worship, the access to basic needs such as food, housing, medicine, and employment. Life for believers in these circumstances is oppressive, and yet God is with them even in the wilderness.

On the other hand, there is an oppression that a society can inflict on itself, and its roots can trace back over several generations. Remember, Israel had had forty years of rest, and another generation had risen. Over those forty years of ease, God's people became immersed in a godless society that began to erode God's truth, His vision, and His presence in their lives. Over time they came to accept and assimilate worldly beliefs and values, and succumb to the world's oppression. But that is the effect of living with the Canaanites, not the Midianites. The Canaanites are the unidentified, ever-present influence that affect Israel's response to this crisis. Like Israel, we, too, have Canaanites around us who can influence our response to national or community crises.

THE PROFILE OF THIS OPPRESSION

A people invade a land for the purpose of exploiting the benefits meant for its citizens. They have no wish to be citizens or contribute to the welfare of the land. They come to take as much as they can, and when the resources are exhausted, they leave. They devastate entire communities, and the results affect the entire nation.

Here in the United States, this profile has worked out in two very controversial ways in our history. These issues continue to be very explosive topics, and there are believers on both sides of the fence, so to speak. The point is not to argue one position over another, but to illustrate and acknowledge why we have such varied opinions on how to deal with these national issues and what factors are influencing our decisions. In answering the questions, feel free to express opinions you have heard that may not necessarily be your own.

Model #1: Migrant caravans come up in waves out of the southern Mexican desert seeking to cross the American border.

- What motivates these people to enter the country?

- What do you think they would do if the U.S. suddenly had no more resources to offer?

- Many of us live beside or work with undocumented immigrants already in the country. How do they influence our response (for or against)?

- We live among a wide variety of nationalities who do not embrace our belief in God, our worldview, or even our national identity. How do they influence our response (for or against) when we are faced with migrant caravans coming across our border?

- Even after years of being constantly raided, Israel made no effort to secure its borders against the raiders, and we can see the condition of Israel as a result. Is this a model we should follow or not?

Model #2: In 2020, rioters swept in waves through America's communities.[1] They looted and burned community businesses and homes and then left the communities devastated. Small businesses closed. Grocery stores closed. People were left homeless. Police protection and medical services became almost non-existent. Communities were left without food, protection, shelter, and jobs, and crime became rampant in the streets.

- Why were rioters allowed to sweep through communities with impunity?

- How did rioting become an acceptable act in our society?

BUILD THE PICTURE

Gideon and the Angel of the LORD, Judges 6:11–24

Note the distinct break in the narrative between Judges 6:10 and 11. It is almost as if the LORD left Israel to stew in their condition while He began to work with Gideon.

6. Who was Gideon?

Gideon was the son of Joash the Abiezerite.

---

[1] This model is based on the first-hand report of a missionary church ministering in inner city Chicago in 2020.

The name **Gideon** means "hewer" or "one who cuts down or chops off." **Joash** means "given by the Lord." **Abiezer** means "father of help."

In other words... *"the hewer, given by the Lord, father of help."*

Not a bad name for the man whom God used to cut down an enemy who had been mowing down Israel for years.

7. **Where was Gideon from?**

   Gideon came from Ophrah in the territory of West Manasseh, somewhere between Shechem and the Jezreel Valley.

   The name **Ophrah** derives from the common word *opher,* meaning "young stag," which is only used in the Song of Solomon as a description of the Beloved who pursues the Shulamite girl (a picture of God married to His people).

   The name **Manasseh** is also a curious addition to the picture. Joseph gave this name to his son, saying, *"for God has made me forget all my toil and all my father's house"* (Genesis 41:51).

   Together, a subtle picture is painted in the mixing of these names. The first is a picture of the ideal relationship between God and His people, depicted in the setting of a lush and fruitful land. The other is an echo of Egypt and a man being separated from his toil and his father's house as Joseph was for the purpose of saving his people.

   Israel's relationship to God is anything but ideal, and the land is anything but lush now that the Midianites have eaten every leaf in sight. But that is the picture God wants it to be. Out of this place, God calls Gideon from his toil in the field (threshing grain in a winepress) to be deliverer of his people and return Israel to their relationship with God and the Land to its lush fruitfulness.

8. **What time of year was it, and why was that significant?**

   Gideon was threshing wheat in a winepress. If there was any kind of a wheat harvest happening, that indicates a time of year roughly around May to June. The winepress was not needed until the grape harvest in August-October, so Gideon was harvesting in a place where the enemy wouldn't suspect.

   The wheat harvest officially began on the Feast of Weeks, aka Pentecost. Interestingly, Pentecost is also the feast that marks the giving of the Holy Spirit to God's people in New Testament times. We noted in Lesson 2 that the judges were likened to the Holy Spirit in their purpose. Gideon was the second judge upon whom the Holy Spirit came, given by God, the great Father of Help, and he began his work in the days of harvest.

Gideon was raised up as both judge and deliverer (*moshia*), so there will be a picture of Christ as well in his narrative, as we will see.

9. **Who initiated the conversation between Gideon and the Angel?**

The Angel of the LORD initiated it. God always initiates the relationship and the calling of His people. The main thrust of this conversation was to establish who God was in Gideon's life.

10. **Based on his response in verse 13, what was Gideon's relationship with the LORD like?**

> *"O my lord, if the LORD is with us, why then has all this happened to us? And where are all His miracles which our fathers told us about, saying, 'Did not the LORD bring us up from Egypt?' But now the LORD has forsaken us and delivered us into the hands of the Midianites."*
> —Judges 9:13

Gideon was a product of his generation. He had heard the stories all his life but had never personally witnessed God's power in action. He was victimized, cynical, despairing, and removed from a personal relationship with the Lord.

The lack of experiential knowledge of God is one of the consequences of doing what is right in your own eyes. God keeps to the path He has established. When you walk the path with Him, you will see Him in action and see how He works out things. When you leave His path, you lose the experience that comes by walking with the Lord.

11. **How had Gideon stumbled in his thinking?**

He failed to grasp God's power and sovereignty, and despaired of God's love. His words are an echo of Isaiah 49:14, *"But Zion said, 'The LORD has forsaken me, and my Lord has forgotten me.'"* He was suffering from feelings of powerlessness. The Angel of the LORD's words about being a *"mighty man of valor"* must have seemed like a cruel joke, seeing as Gideon was hiding in a winepress just to thresh a pathetically small amount of wheat.

12. Gideon thought God had abandoned Israel. Where was the LORD actually?

Standing right beside Gideon.

13. When did Gideon realize he was speaking with the LORD?

> "Then the LORD turned to him . . ." —Judges 6:14a

There is a literal turning point in conversation. The turning implies that maybe the Angel of the LORD hadn't been looking at Gideon directly before, but then He did. The Angel of the LORD brought Himself face-to-face with Gideon and said:

> ". . .Go in this might of yours, and you shall save Israel from the hand of the Midianites."

The rioters are in the streets. The caravans are getting ready to stream across the border. Go, do something about it.

> ". . . Have I not sent you?"

Who was the "I" to Gideon? Who was the Angel of the LORD identifying Himself with? The LORD.

> "So he said to Him, 'O my Lord, how can I save Israel? . . .'"

Notice how Gideon changes the title from "lord" to "Lord" when he responds. The switch from lowercase "l" to uppercase "L" in the English indicates a change in the Hebrew words. Gideon used the word *Adonai* here instead of *adoni*. *Adoni* is a title of respect used toward men in general, but *Adonai* is an emphatic form of the word used only for God. Gideon was beginning to suspect he was speaking to the LORD or, at least, an emissary of the LORD.

14. What reasons did Gideon give for not doing what the Angel of the LORD was telling him to do?

Gideon said, I am one man. I am weak. My father's clan is the least in the tribe and I have little support, even in my father's house. Such self-deprecating language is common in Middle Eastern conversations, but it is nevertheless a way of saying, as politely as possible, that what is being asked is impossible.

15. How does the Angel of the LORD counter Gideon's objections?

The Angel of the LORD tells Gideon: *"Surely I will be with you, and you shall defeat the Midianites as one* [echad] *man."*

We should note the Hebrew word used here for "one" because there are two words in Hebrew that are translated as "one."

Yachid means "one" in the singular sense—one and one alone. *Echad* means "one" in the corporate sense—as being one of a group, or first, with the understanding that there is a second, third, etc.

Echad is used in Genesis 2:24 where man and wife become one flesh. They are two individuals, and yet they are one (*echad*). *Echad* also describes the first Day (Genesis 1:5). Day and night combine into one day, and that day is *echad*, the first of a group of days comprised of both a day and night. Deuteronomy 6:4 declares that the LORD is *echad*—He is one, and yet He has a corporate oneness in the expression of His being.

The Angel told Gideon *"I will be with you"* and that Gideon would defeat the Midianites as *"one [echad] man."* Gideon was not as alone as he thought he was, nor was God asking him to tackle this national problem on his own. Even so, if it was just you and the Angel of the LORD against the locust hordes, would you feel confident of victory? Maybe, if you were sure the Angel really was the LORD . . .

16. What proof did Gideon request that the Angel really was the LORD Himself?

Gideon asked for a sign. He sought an experiential validation of the growing conviction that maybe he was speaking with the LORD. And the LORD granted Gideon the sign. Gideon brought an offering and the LORD accepted it.

Angels don't accept worship in this manner. Only the LORD accepts offerings, and then only when they are made on approved altars and done according to His direction. Gideon offered the broth-soaked bread and meat on the rock as directed, and the Angel of the LORD set them on fire. When they were consumed, the Angel of the LORD departed. So, Gideon's conviction was confirmed. Verse 22 says that he perceived that he had been talking to the Angel of the LORD, and was horrified. But God reassured him with the statement, *"Peace be with you; do not fear, you shall not die."*

17. What did Gideon do when he realized it really was the LORD?

After nearly having a heart attack, Gideon stepped into the relationship with God instead of fleeing from it. He built an altar which he named "YHWH Shalom" or "God-is-peace." Was Gideon's life at peace? Not by a long stretch. But in his spiritual relationship with God, he found a moment of peace.

APPLY THE PICTURE

If God is with us, then why is all this happening to us? Where are all His miracles? Why has He not kept His promises?

When our lives become embroiled in oppressive circumstances—whether from our own choices in life or another person's choices that have sucked us into oppression—we can be tempted to ask the same questions Gideon asked. And we, too, can come to the false conclusion that God has forsaken us. But those are the words of a person who does not see God sitting right next to them in the middle of their oppression.

The Angel of the LORD's model for encouragement

Encouragement is a vital first step in helping someone prepare to battle an oppression in their life. The Angel of the LORD makes a series of statements to Gideon that are a good model for us to follow in giving encouragement. Consider the basic psychology behind these statements.

"The LORD is with you, you mighty man of valor!"
> Reassure your Gideon that God is with them. Reestablish how God sees them. They might respond with cynicism as Gideon did, but then they are seeing themselves from their own eyes and not God's eyes.

"Go in this might of yours, and you shall save Israel from the hand of the Midianites. Have I not sent you?"
> Reestablish the commission and God's expectation of them.

"Surely I will be with you, and you shall defeat the Midianites as one man."
> Isolation is a stumbling block in dealing with oppression. It can make a person feel powerless, fearful, and despairing, and rob them of sound thinking. Address the feelings of isolation. Establish that the enemy can be defeated, and with God's help, they have the strength to overcome the enemy.

> ## Questions for Reflection:
>
> Frustration may come from wrong expectations of God. We may not be seeing either the situation from His perspective or what He is trying to accomplish. If you are feeling frustrated with God, consider:
>
> - What is your expectation of life as a child of God?
> - When you fall into oppression, what do you expect God to do?
> - What does God expect you to do?

BUILD THE PICTURE

Gideon Destroys Baal in His Father's House, Judges 6:25–32

God established who He was in Gideon's understanding, then commanded him to reestablish God in his father's house. God gave Gideon the challenge: "Will you obey My voice?" (an echo of the prophet's rebuke of Israel in verse 10).

God gave Gideon some very strong commands in Judges 6:25-26:

> "... tear down [haras] the altar of Baal that your father has ..."
> **Haras:** to throw down, tear down a thing, or overthrow a people

> "... and cut down [karath] the wooden image that is beside it."
> **Karath:** to cut down, cut off as a garment, cut covenant with

> "and build an altar to the LORD your God on top of this rock [ma'oz] ..."
> **Ma'oz:** a stronghold, place of strength, a place from which you draw strength

Idol worship had established a rock—a stronghold—in Joash's house. God tells Gideon to make a public statement of faith by overthrowing the stronghold, cutting covenant with Baal, and erecting an altar and a worship of God in its place.

Gideon took ten men of his own household and did the deed by night because he was afraid having a battle with: 1) his father, and 2) the men of the city.

18. What is the reaction from the men of the city?

They came out in the morning and found the deed done. An investigation ensued. When they discovered that it was Gideon, they demanded that Joash hand him over to be killed.

19. How did the men of the city gain authority over Gideon's father and his house?

They shouldn't have had any authority, and yet they were bold enough to demand that Joash turn over his son to be put to death. Joash must have given them that authority, or at least, he did not challenge them when they assumed the authority.

At the beginning of Judges 6, it said that the children of Israel had gone underground, and yet there were some like Joash still living out in the open. They contended not just with the foreign invaders, but with these Canaanites who demanded the right to rule over them.

Where the battle was at the city gates in Deborah and Barak's day, the battle was now brought to the very door of Israelite homes.

While men like Joash bowed to the Canaanite ways, it only took a flash point for peaceful relations to burst into a fiery confrontation. When this happened, Israel ended up fighting a battle in multiple arenas. You can't fight a war abroad and on the home front at the same time. God initiated this confrontation by using Gideon as the flash point to settle the battle on the home front before tackling the greater threat.

20. What is Joash's reaction?

Oddly, Joash wasn't the first to react. He didn't seem overly affected by the loss of his household idols, nor did he say anything until the men of the city came for Gideon. He seemed more affected by the demand that his son be put to death than the supposed crime against Baal. He did not defend Baal. He actually challenged Baal's godship by demanding he plead for himself. But Joash never once affirmed his loyalty toward God either.

21. Why did Joash give Gideon the name Jerubbaal?

Joash clearly had no intention of handing over his own son to be put to death. So, he made a show of defending his son to the men of the city in a way that allowed him to sidestep the fight by pushing his son out front. Instead of showing his loyalty to God and making this a fight between God and Baal, Joash made it a power play between Gideon and Baal. Instead of glorifying God, Joash glorified his son in the eyes of the Canaanites and gave him a new name—Jerubbaal. Jerubbaal means "Let Baal plead."

What Joash did was to make an idol of his son. He lifted Gideon up to be a contender on par with the Canaanite gods. Gideon might as well have been a Canaanite god in his father's eyes. Joash was idolatrous at heart. His loyalties switched from Baal to his son, but for the wrong reason.

Gideon was the man that God saw face to face. He was the struggling believer, newly reestablished in his faith and uncertain of what he was doing. He was feeling his way through this new mission the Lord had given him and was weak even in his own assessment of himself.

Jerubbaal was the idolized hero in people's eyes. Jerubbaal was the man who dared take down Baal, the untouchable, the great man of God who stood up to the Canaanites, and the epic hero who took on the Midianite oppressor and prevailed.

From this point on, the author will use these names interchangeably, but with a purpose. Whenever the focus and glory is on God, Gideon will be called Gideon in the narrative. But whenever Gideon is exalted as the idolized hero in the eyes of the people, the author will refer to him by the name Jerubbaal.

APPLY THE PICTURE

In an effort to live at peace with the world around us, we may bow to some of the secular world's demands, but at what point do we as Christians draw the line? When they try to dictate how we live our faith in our own houses or deal with sin in our family? When they demand we give them our children?

- In what ways has the secular world demanded a right to our children?
- In what other ways does the secular world seek entry into our homes, and how do we battle it?
- What happens when extended family comes to live in our house with us and brings their Canaanite ways with them? How do we deal with

the Canaanite influence within our own homes? What if they are our grown children who are returning? What if they are our elderly parents who need our care? What if they are step-children, or other step-relations?

Questions for Reflection:

- What battles of faith are you facing right now?

- In what arenas have you had to battle (within yourself, your family, your community)?

- Both Gideon and his father were apprehensive over standing up to the men of the city. Has fear kept you from stepping up to a confrontation with ungodly people where your faith was concerned?

- Fear is a stumbling block. What combats fear?

BUILD THE PICTURE

Gideon Prepares for War, Judges 6:33–7:8

On the heels of the confrontation with the men of the city, the Midianites, Amalekites, and people of the East made a thrust into Israel and set up camp in the Jezreel Valley.

In response, the Spirit came upon Gideon, and he gathered Israel to him. His family (the Abiezerite) gathered to him. He sent messengers to Manasseh, Zebulun, Asher, and Naphtali. The text does not mention any call to Ephraim or Issachar (which seems odd since the battle is playing out in Issachar's land).

THE SIGN OF THE FLEECE (Judges 6:36-40)

22. How long did it take for the sign of the fleece to play out?

Gideon gathered everyone together, and they waited three days (two nights) for Gideon to get on with the fight. Why? Because Gideon was waiting for a sign from God. Note: This was Gideon, not Jerubbaal—the humble man who was feeling his way through the crisis.

On the first night, Gideon put a fleece on the threshing floor and said to God:

> "if there is dew on the fleece only, and it is dry on all the ground, then I shall know that You will save Israel by my hand, as You have said." —Judges 6:37

Note: Gideon acknowledged that it would be the LORD saving Israel, not himself. The next morning, he wrung a bowlful of water out of the fleece, but the ground was dry. So, that was God's confirmation.

On the second night, Gideon put a fleece on the threshing floor and asked God for the opposite:

> "Do not be angry with me, but let me speak just once more: Let me test, I pray, just once more with the fleece; let it now be dry only on the fleece, but on all the ground let there be dew." —Judges 6:39

And God confirmed it.

Can you imagine the pressure on Gideon as a leader through all this? The enemy had swarmed over the land, the battle was rapidly setting up, but Gideon has not yet launched into action. Waiting for God's answer was a test of faith for Gideon. His delay was also a sign of a good leader. There is tremendous pressure on leaders to act immediately under such conditions, especially from followers who are walking by what is right in their own eyes. Regardless of how they are feeling inside, an outward expression of calmness and deliberate, authoritative actions on the part of leadership in times of crisis does much toward steadying the people and encouraging them.

Questions for Reflection:

- How long do you wait to decide on a course of action when dealing with a crisis or threat?

- Have you ever requested some kind of confirmation from God before making a particular decision? If so, what was the confirmation, and how long did you wait for it?

THE CALLING OF ISRAEL (Judges 7:1-8)

23. Why did the narrative lead with the name Jerubbaal instead of Gideon in verse 1?

This is a clue as to who is getting the glory. Jerubbaal was the hero who the people followed out to the battle field and rallied behind. But it was the man and not God who they wanted to see in action.

24. What was God's assessment of the people?

The people were there to glorify themselves. God intended to send most of them home *"lest Israel claim glory for itself against Me, saying, 'My own hand has saved me.'"* God needed Gideon to weed out those who were really there to fight from the looky-loos and glory-seekers. So He set up a testing ground for Israel.

THE FEAR TEST

25. Where did the battle set up?

Israel set up camp beside the Well of Harod or Eyn Harod. **Eyn Charod** means "eye of trembling and fear." (Wells are likened to eyes in that they weep water.)

The Midianites, Amalekites, and people of the East set up camp across the valley from Israel at the base of the **Hill of Moreh**.

Moreh means "teacher." Its root word, *yara*, means "to cast out, shoot out, throw, or pour out," which can have different applications depending on who is doing the casting and what is being cast.

- An archer can *yara* arrows.
- God can *yara* rain on the earth (imagine Him flicking his fingers and casting out water droplets).
- A teacher can *yara* when he shoots out a finger in making a point or showing a student something.

With *yara*-ing, there is a cause and effect—something is sent out, followed by an expected result or response.

God instructed Gideon to bring Israel to Eyn Harod, the "eye of trembling and fear," where he told the people to cast their eye on the enemy sprawled in the valley below them at the foot of the "teacher." There Gideon demanded from them a self-assessment. If any of them were fearful, let them go home.

Judges 7:12 tells us:

> *"Now the Midianites and Amalekites, all the people of the East, were lying in the valley as numerous as locusts; and their camels were without number, as the sand by the seashore in multitude."*
> — Judges 7:12

From where Israel stood at Eyn Harod, the enemy looked unconquerable. But then they were looking at the enemy from their own eyes, not God's, and were estimating the enemy's power against their own abilities, not God's. The Well of Harod was the breaking moment for those who had neither vision or heart to fight, and twenty-two thousand out of the original thirty-two thousand volunteers immediately turned and went home. Only ten thousand passed the fear test at Eyn Harod.

THE WATER TEST

There are two kinds of people in this scenario: Those who squatted and carried the water to their mouth with their hand (keeping their head up and lapping out of their hand), and those who kneeled and put their face in the water to suck the water up.

26. What made lapping superior to kneeling?

There is the tactical consideration: In combat, the man who remains upright is less vulnerable and responds quicker to an enemy threat than a man who gets down on both knees and puts his face in the water. A kneeling man is easily overcome.

The physical body language also bears witness of the inner heart for which God is looking. When God brought Israel out of Egypt, the first thing he had Moses do was lift their heads (In Numbers 1:1, the phrase "take a census" is actually "lift the head" in the original Hebrew). The man with a lifted head is a free man. He sees farther in terms of distance but also in terms of goals. The man with a bowed head is still a slave, if only subconsciously.

God was looking for free men who would remain upright in battle. Of the ten thousand volunteers who survived the fear test, only three hundred passed the water test.

APPLY THE PICTURE

27. Why exempt a person because of fear?

According to the Law, fear is a reason to be exempted from battle:

> "The officers shall speak further to the people, and say, 'What man is there who is fearful and fainthearted? Let him go and return to his house, lest the heart of his brethren faint like his heart.'"
> —Deuteronomy 20:8

According to 2 Timothy 1:7, fear stands opposed to three things:

> "For God has not given us a spirit of fear, but of power and of love and of a sound mind." —2 Timothy 1:7

Fear is contagious. Fear is a stumbling block.

Fear makes a person feel powerless, and the natural reactions of fight or flight will kick in but without the control needed for an army to accomplish its objective. God's army needs to identify with His power and act with control according to His direction.

It is out of His love for them that God sends this deliverer to save the people. If the people are still afraid, even with this tangible savior standing beside them, they will not be effective in dealing with the oppressor. (Feelings of unworthiness can also influence a person's willingness to fight.)

A fearful person does not exercise sound judgment because fear and panic drive decision-making. A fearful person will do what is right in his own eyes and seek his own personal good at the expense of the greater mission.

BUILD THE PICTURE

Gideon Goes to War, Judges 7:9–25

THE VISION OF THE BARLEY LOAF

28. Why didn't fear disqualify Gideon?

Gideon had a daunting enemy before him and all these desperate people behind him waiting for guidance and expecting him to be fearless and bold. He was, after all, Jerubbaal the great hero in most of their eyes. But Gideon knew he was not the hero. He knew he was groping his way through this, but God had set him to this task, so he was going to do it.

To be afraid and yet remain obedient is a rare quality in a leader. Gideon had already passed the qualifying tests in God's eyes. God knew the position Gideon was in, and in His great compassion, God granted him the luxury of a face-saving moment to deal with his fear away from public eyes. He gave Gideon the command, "Arise, go down . . ." but added the little "if" clause—not as a judgment against Gideon, but as an added incentive. He sent him down to the camp with just a servant and just to listen.

29. Why did God send Purah with Gideon? What was Purah's significance as part of the bigger picture?

Purah, Gideon's servant, is a minor character in the narrative as Gideon's moral support and back-up in this precursory expedition. But the meaning of his name alone adds tremendous detail to the bigger picture of what God was preparing to do to the Midianites.

The proper name, Purah, is derived from the common word *porah*, meaning "leafy bough" in the sense of an exalted, high, spreading branch of a tree full of lush leaves. That is the literal use of the word, but the word is never used in its literal sense in Scripture. This word is only ever used in a figurative sense of great nations that God is getting ready to cut down, specifically in context with Israel, Midian, Assyria, and Egypt (Isaiah 10:33, Ezekiel 17:6, 31:5-6, 8, 12-13).

God sends Purah as an encouragement to Gideon, but for us, reading this account at a later date, it is a clue to the bigger picture. Remember: Hebrew words are keywords. They connect passages, and their contexts help clarify and expand the bigger picture.

The name Purah is the first introduction of the *porah* imagery into the Scripture. This battle with the Midianites will be a benchmark for similar "cutting downs" and is recalled as a particular example in a future engagement with Assyria, as it says in Isaiah 10:26, 33:

> "And the LORD of hosts will stir up a scourge for him like the slaughter of Midian at the rock of Oreb; . . . Behold, the Lord, the LORD of hosts, will lop off the bough [porah] with terror; those of

> high stature will be hewn down, and the haughty will be humbled."
> — Isaiah 10:26, 33

Dig deeper. The root verb for *porah* is *pa'ar*. *Pa'ar* means to glorify, beautify, adorn (as leaves adorn a lofty tree branch). Depending on who is getting the glory, it can also mean to embellish or be boastful (self-glorification).

In verse 14, to whom did the Midianite guard give glory for the take-down when he saw the vision of the barley loaf? Gideon—but the guard did not neglect to mention that it was God who delivered Midian into Gideon's hands. And Gideon responded by giving glory to God, as well.

Note: the tree motif will carry through into the narrative of Gideon's son, Abimelech, in Judges 9.

30. How did the barley loaf imagery in the vision add to the picture?

Barley in the Hebrew is *sehora*, from the root *sa'ar*, meaning "to bristle with horror over a coming violence and to sweep or whirl away as if taken by storm." It carries intense negative emotion paired with an experience of violence. (It is the same root word that we discovered when we looked into the name Seirah in Ehud's account.)

A bristling horror was going to sweep into the Midianite camp, yet it would be like an imagined horror—a bad dream—because no physical combatant would enter the camp. Gideon and his men would stay outside.

Barley and barley fields often figured in acts of judgment (Exodus 9:31, Numbers 5:15, 2 Samuel 21:8), and barley was used for offerings made by fire and as repayment of debts. The Midianites had come to consume the wheat and barley of the Land, but now the barley, as an agent of judgment, would destroy them.

In the guard's dream, this bristling horror knocked over a tent. Think about the sounds made by a tent falling over. There is an initial clacking as the structure collapses, followed by the usual scramble of human occupants to set it right, and a moment of relative chaos. The *sound* that the barley loaf makes is as much a part of the picture as the sight of the barley loaf.

(See if you can find a sound clip of a tent falling over and listen to it. I found one at https://www.audiosparx.com/sa/summary/play.cfm/crumb.1/crumc.0/sound_iid.163483. The sound is very much like pitchers breaking!)

THE BATTLE (Judges 7:16-25)

31. With what did Gideon arm his men?

A trumpet and a pitcher with a torch inside. That is all.

32. What was Gideon's strategy?

- Divide into three companies and surround the Midianite camp.
- Wait until the dark of the night and changing of the guard.
- Hit the enemy with the sounds:
    - The sound of the trumpet
    - The sound of pitchers breaking
    - The battle cry of "for the LORD and for Gideon!"
- Let the torches (*lappidoth*) shine out.
- Stand and listen.

Gideon and his men engaged the Midianites at the middle watch—around ten o'clock at night when the night was very dark and it was hardest to see. The darkness made sounds unnaturally loud and torches exceedingly bright, which would be all the more terrifying to a superstitious people like the Midianites. It was also the time of the changing of the guard, when the guards would be drowsy, distracted, and least attentive to an attack.

33. The attack relied heavily on the use of sound—what was being heard as opposed to what was seen with the eyes. What sounds did the enemy hear and what did Gideon's men hear?

The sound of a pitcher breaking can easily mimic the clack of a tent falling over, the clatter of weapons, and the tramp of feet. Add to that the sound of trumpets and a battle cry, and you have all the sounds of an approaching army. These were the sounds the Midianites heard.

Gideon's men heard the enemy's cry of fear, the clash of swords, and running feet.

APPLY THE PICTURE

34. This battle was won more by hearing than seeing. What lesson do we take from that?

The book of Judges emphasizes the people's failing when they walk by what they see with their eyes. What they needed was to see a little less and listen a little more.

Being obedient to God is more a matter of listening than seeing, and there is an element of blindness in how this war is waged. All Gideon's men were asked to do was to stand where they were with what they had in hand, follow their leader, and let God do the rest. God used short-sighted men and common, weak things to accomplish His purpose to His glory.

35. What is the purpose of breaking the pitchers?

Read 2 Corinthians 4:5-10. Paul describes us as empty pitchers with torches inside, except the torch is God's light inside us. Sometimes, our earthen vessels must endure breaking as part of the battle.

The purpose of our breaking is to let God's power and glory be revealed to a darkened world. Our breaking becomes a witness to the darkened world: that we believe in a spiritual kingdom and spiritual reward richer than the physical kingdom and physical gain.

In this battle, we may have to endure the breaking of our bodies—the taking down of our physical tent, even to death. Though we lose a physical kingdom, we gain a spiritual kingdom and reward if we endure.

To willingly allow ourselves to be broken is the test of our understanding of God's power and lordship over our lives, but also to see if we have grasped the greater vision and values of the kingdom. The moment of breaking can be the point at which we stumble out of fear, anger, or the desire to cling to the transient things of this world that have only the appearance of power and strength.

BUILD THE PICTURE

36. Once God routed the Midianites, how did the battle play out—what path of retreat did the Midianites take, and who else from Israel got into the fight? (Judges 7:24-25)

The LORD routed the Midianites and they retreated from Beth Shittah (or Beth Acacia) to Zerereah all the way to Abel Meholah by Tabbath.

The men of Naphtali, Asher, and Manasseh pursued them with Gideon and the three hundred, but it doesn't seem that they continued with Gideon and his men when they cross the Jordan. It is not clear whether the Midianite army split at the ford with half heading south and the rest crossing the Jordan, or if there were simply more Midianites camped along the lower Jordan. Either way, Gideon needed help to secure the Jordan boundary, which is why he called Ephraim.

37. What did the men of Ephraim accomplish?

They secured the fords at Beth Barah and upward, and captured two Midianite princes, Oreb (the raven) and Zeeb (the wolf). They killed Oreb on the rock of Oreb and Zeeb in the winepress of Zeeb, then took the heads to Gideon.

Both the raven and the wolf are unclean animals. In a sense, this is a symbolic putting away of uncleanness from Israel.

Gideon Confronts the Men of Ephraim, Judges 8:1-9

The men of Ephraim took issue with Gideon for waiting until the eleventh hour to call for their help in the battle.

38. What was at the heart of Ephraim's grievance?

They wanted a greater part of the glory for themselves. They were greedy and arrogant.

39. How did Gideon respond to their grievance?

He gave them a placating answer. He reminded them that even though they were called in the eleventh hour, they were still given an equal, if not richer, share of the reward. In fact, they finished their work and achieved the goal before Gideon and his men did. Gideon and the three hundred must press on for their reward.

The Ephraimites swept onto the scene in the eleventh hour, did their part almost effortlessly, and claimed the reward. Gideon and the three hundred are still in the battle and must press on with great effort before they accomplish their mission and claim the reward. Do you think Gideon and his men deserved a greater reward for having fought the more strenuous battle?

APPLY THE PICTURE

40. Compare Gideon's calling of the Ephraimites to Jesus' parable about the workers of the eleventh hour (Matthew 20:1-16).

There is a task that needs accomplishing in God's vineyard, i.e. Israel. **In Judges,** it is the battle with the Midianites who are destroying the Land. Gideon and his three hundred are pursuing two princes of Midian, which is the same task that the Ephraimites have been given. **In the parable,** all the workers are contracted for a denarius regardless of time worked. It is about achieving a goal, not the money.

Workers are called at different times. **In Judges,** Gideon called the three hundred and they began the battle. Later, Asher, Naphtali, and the rest of Manasseh joined. Finally, Ephraim was called at the last. **In the parable,** the landowner sought workers at the third, sixth, ninth, and eleventh hours. Gideon's men were the workers of the first hour who end up working the full day (they endured testing, took up the chase, and still had more battle in the offing). The Ephraimites were workers of the eleventh hour who only worked for an hour (they were only part of the chase).

Here is the twist. In the parable, the workers of the *first* hour were the ones who complained. **In the Judges account,** it was the workers of the *eleventh* hour (the Ephraimites) who complained.

But they both complain for the same basic reason. They were not focused on the kingdom but on their own personal reward, as if the kingdom was determined by merit.

Having worked the whole "day," Gideon's men would have had every right to complain about the Ephraimites doing so little and yet reaping the honor of dispatching two kings. Gideon's men were still in the battle while Ephraim's work was done. We could imagine them appealing to Gideon, saying, *"These last men have worked only one hour, and you made them equal to us who have borne the burden and the heat of the day"* (Matthew 20:12).

But Gideon's men did not say that. The reason they were selected in the first place was because they were not glory seekers like so many in Israel (Judges 7:2). They cared only that the goal had been accomplished, personal glory aside.

Instead, it was the Ephraimites, who only worked for one "hour," who complained over only having a part in the chase and not the battle (as if Gideon's men had fought the battle. In reality, Gideon's men just stood around while God fought the battle). The Ephraimites' complaint was clearly based on the assumption that Gideon and his men would get more glory for having battled longer. They are glory- and status-seekers at heart.

Gideon smoothed their puffed-up feathers by pointing out that even though they were only in on the chase, they still took what was the greater honor (at that time) in killing the two generals.

> *"... What have I done now in comparison with you? Is not the gleaning of the grapes of Ephraim better than the vintage of Abiezer?"* —Judges 8:2

Is not the gleaning—that which is taken last—better than the first? Isn't it a greater honor to have taken down two princes rather than a host of foot soldiers?

Gideon did not mention that there was more of the battle to be fought and more princes to be pursued, nor did he invite the men of Ephraim to join the three hundred. Instead, he let the Ephraimites walk away with a false pride in their accomplishment.

In the end, Gideon and his men accomplished the same goal as the Ephraimites. Both parties pursued two sets of princes and took their prizes, though one worked longer than the other to accomplish it. Like the workers in the parable, each got the same "wage" for their effort. But the goal was achieved in such a way that the glory-seeking Ephraimites were rebuked. It is almost like God saying to them, *"Friend, I am doing you no wrong. Did you not agree with me for a denarius? Take what is yours and go your way. I wish to give to this last man the same as to you."* —Matthew 20:13-14

This episode with the Ephraimites and the parable both paint a portrait of people who do their work in the kingdom out of wrong values and wrong goals. There are those who want more honor because they have battled longer, and there are those who want more battle just for personal glory. The whole point is how you weigh reward—by your own scales or God's scales. In Gideon's case, it pleased the Lord to give the workers who finished last the same glory as those who finished first.

The parable ends with a grim reminder that many are called, but few are chosen.

41. **Recap: How many were called and how many chosen?**

    Thirty-two thousand were called; three hundred were chosen.

42. **Why were so many cut?**

    They would have taken glory for themselves instead of giving it to God, or they would have failed to accomplish the mission out of fear and a lack of faith in God.

43. **Gideon called Ephraim to battle untested. Would the men of Ephraim have made the original cut?**

    I think it is doubtful. We should note that Gideon waited for the Lord to test the people and took His direction over who to cut or not cut. When Gideon called for untested Ephraim, he does it for expedience, but without asking the Lord, and it has some consequences.

Questions for Reflection:

In the midst of battling the external oppressors, a leader can find himself battling a second front—this time with his own people. Brothers who should be helping and supporting the effort add to the conflict and oppression when they decide to pursue what is right in their own eyes and let their Canaanite side rule them.

- As a leader, how do you respond when your co-laborers in ministry get angry with you because they covet a more prestigious role in the ministry than you are giving them? Do you give them the soft answer like Gideon did?

> When necessity arises and immediate help is needed to spearhead a ministry objective, filling the slot with untested volunteers may get the job done, but may also bring leadership some grief.
>
> - How is Gideon's experience with the men of Ephraim a warning?

BUILD THE PICTURE

Israel chased the Midianites from **Beth Shittah** (house of wood) toward **Zerereah** (oppression/fortress) as far as **Abel Meholah** (meadow of dancing) by **Tabbath** (celebration).

The battles in the "house of wood" and the "fortress of oppression" had been won as far as the outside enemy was concerned. Then Gideon and the three hundred crossed the Jordan and came to Succoth and Penuel. Succoth will be another picture of a house of wood and Penuel will be another picture of an oppressive fortress. These should have been places where Gideon and his weary men were greeted with celebration, rest, food, and comfort, but they were not. Instead, Gideon found himself fighting another version of these battles, this time with his own countrymen.

THE MEN OF SUCCOTH AND PENUEL

44. Why Succoth? What does "Succoth" mean to Israel?

> **About Succoth:** This was the original site where Jacob put up booths for his cattle and built a house for himself.
>
> **Succoth** (or Sukkot, pronounced sue-coat) is the plural of *sukkah* or "booth," a temporary makeshift shelter made from whatever brush or branches are at hand and often used for animal shelters. A *sukkah* can also refer to a thicket or overgrowth of branches that creates a shelter.
>
> **Succoth embodies a very particular Bible picture** that began with Jacob in his big tent with his flock resting in *sukkot* around him. That picture became part of the Exodus experience—as Israel wandered in the wilderness, they painted this picture of God in His big tent surrounded by His flock camped in *sukkot* around Him. In the wilderness, the *sukkot* were unadorned houses of wood.

When Israel came into the Land, that picture then carried into the **Feast of Tabernacles** (aka Sukkot), where God's children gathered together yearly to camp in *sukkot* around His tent after the harvest. Sukkot was a time of rest and rejoicing in God's provision and protection. The *sukkah* tents were decorated with the fruits and greenery of the harvest—except in Gideon's day, the Midianites had taken all the harvest, fruit, and leaves. The picture of Succoth as a place of celebration and rejoicing, rest, provision, and protection was gone. A fruitless, leafless, hopeless existence was what life had become under Midianite oppression, and Succoth had reverted to the character of "houses of wood" in a wilderness.

45. Under whose protection and provision had the men of Succoth sought "shade"?

Instead of seeking shade under God's protection and provision, the men of Succoth have taken shelter under the great Midianite tree that God was sending Gideon to cut down. The *porah*—exalted leafy branches—were the Midianite princes, Zebah and Zalmunnah.

> **Zebah** means "deprived of protection," as a sacrificial animal for which there is no longer a chance of reprieve.

> **Zalmunnah** also means "deprived of protection," in the sense of being without shade.

These are the princes upon whom the men of Succoth were placing their hopes and allegiance.

46. Why Penuel? What is significant about Penuel?

About Penuel: The name **Penuel** means "facing God." Penuel was the place where Jacob once came face-to-face with God, wrestled with Him, and prevailed, although he came away broken. It was a place where blessing was bestowed on those who cling to God in the midst of their struggle with Him, and in spite of being broken at His hand.

But this generation didn't have an experiential knowledge of God nor did they recognize the savior that God had sent. They made decisions by what was right in their own eyes, and they were no longer clinging to God as Jacob had.

The word "tower" is *migdal* in the Hebrew, which comes from the root *gadal*, meaning "to become great or important, promote, make powerful, praise, magnify." The men of Penuel had built a symbol of power and glorification of themselves over the site that should have been a humbling reminder to cling to God for provision and protection. From their tower, they looked down at Gideon, their savior, and spoke loftily—deprecatingly—to him.

47. What did Gideon promise he would do when he returned?

To Succoth: *"I will tear their flesh with the thorns of the wilderness and with briers!"*
To Penuel: *"When I come back in peace, I will tear down this tower!"*

APPLY THE PICTURE

48. Read Matthew 25:31-46. How did the men of Succoth model this parable for us?

We studied Matthew 25:31-46 in the Song of Deborah, when Israel was assessed for helping or not helping when called to battle. The same applies here. When the savior (Gideon) made his first appearance at Succoth and Penuel, his men received no help when he asked for it. When he returns a second time, he will come in judgment, and the lack of help will be remembered. The men of Succoth and Penuel were examples of those in the parable who didn't help when called, and judgment is determined against them.

Questions for Reflection:

- Where do you seek shade in life?
- Are the people who oppress you also the ones on whom you depend for shelter and needful things?
- Can the fear of losing what little you have keep you in oppression?
- When a fellow believer has looked down on you loftily or spoken to you loftily, what kind of response did it provoke in you?
- Have your words ever provoked that reaction in others?
- Does a self-righteous stance create more conflict or bring peace?
- Does it add to oppression in a believer's struggle or relieve it?
- Does it help or hinder the Savior's mission?

The Final Battle, Judges 8:10-17

The Midianites went to ground at Karkor on Israel's eastern border. They started with an army of one hundred and twenty thousand but were now reduced to fifteen thousand—still more than Gideon's three hundred. Gideon's men were still outnumbered fifty to one.

49. What do the names Nobah, Jogbehah, and Karkor mean and how do they add to the picture?

Nobah means "barking."
Jogebehah means "lofty" or "haughty."
Karkor means "foundation" in the sense of being "dug in, secure, or entrenched."

Gideon and the three hundred passed by Succoth and Penuel without receiving any help. Then they skirted around Nobah and Jogbehah by following a nomad trail and caught Midian where they felt secure. To win the battle, Gideon and the three hundred had to rout the Midianites at their "foundation."

50. How did the "barkers" and "lofty" add to the Midianites' feeling of (false) security? Why would Gideon skirt these places?

The "barkers" and the "lofty" are watchmen of sorts—at least they should be. The "barkers" raise the alarm when the enemy is near. The "lofty" have the advantage of seeing from a higher plane and can see more clearly and, therefore, more strategically. At least, that is what they will argue.

51. In Isaiah 56:10-12, why do the watchmen, the "barkers," cease barking?

"His watchmen are blind, They are all ignorant; They are all dumb dogs, They cannot bark; sleeping, lying down, loving to slumber. Yes, they are greedy dogs which never have enough. And they are shepherds who cannot understand; They all look to their own way, every one for his own gain, from his own territory. 'Come,' one says, 'I will bring wine, And we will fill ourselves with intoxicating drink; Tomorrow will be as today, And much more abundant.'" —Isaiah 56:10-12

Watchdogs aren't always on watch. They can be sleeping. They can be distracted and grow lazy with too much feasting. They aren't overly discerning—they will bark at the enemy, but also the neighbors, other dogs, squirrels, doorbells—whatever comes into their territory, whether it is an enemy to you or not. Sometimes they bark just to hear their own voice.

APPLY THE PICTURE

In this section, a number of stumbling blocks are put in Gideon's way as he pursued the enemy. The men of Ephraim, Succoth, and Penuel are all his kinsmen, and yet they increase his struggle with their self-serving complaints, discouragement, and self-righteousness. Nobah and Jogbehah are also Israelite holdings, yet Gideon skirts these places without seeking help from them. The reason for this is not stated, but one might speculate from their names that the "barkers" and the "lofty" would have distracted Gideon's men from their mission and wasted precious energy.

52. What forms do the barkers and the lofty take in our world today?

As believers in this age, we do not see hand-to-hand combat so much as we fight a war of words and ideologies. Our world is full of barkers. They are on social media, TV, news stations, blogs, etc. Not a day goes by when someone doesn't raise a howl over something regarding social injustice or conspiracy (real or imagined). They are noise makers that demand our attention, and we can get sidetracked into fighting a battle with the barkers rather than pursuing the real enemy, which is why the enemy likes to put them up as a front that we have to overcome.

If we can get past the barkers, we must then contend with the lofty—the experts, the scientists, the psychologists, the strategic marketers, and all those who purport to have the higher or broader view of things. They are people who will present us with facts and evidence that are often skewed to make a persuasive argument that suits a particular agenda. Ultimately, they rely on their own understanding and view the situation by what is right in their eyes, not God's eyes. The enemy hides behind these as well.

It is good to follow Gideon's example in skirting these combatants.

BUILD THE PICTURE

Gideon and the three hundred caught the enemy where they felt secure, routed them at their foundation, captured Zebah and Zalmunna, and marched them back to Succoth.

53. How did Gideon deal with the men of Succoth when he returned?

He "taught" the men of Succoth—scourged them with whips made of thorns and briers.

Succoth, with its associated picture of the Feast of Tabernacles, was meant to be a picture of Messiah's kingdom to come, but the men of Succoth had corrupted the picture by denying the savior his rightful place and establishing foreign kings over them. The shadeless, thorny branches that they had used to build their houses of wood became the tools of judgment for teaching them who the rightful king was.

Imagine Christ returning some day to confront those of His people who had corrupted the kingdom picture and given themselves over to the Antichrist. What will be their punishment?

54. Why did Gideon kill the men of Penuel when he said he would only tear down the tower?

Self-righteous people usually fight having their towers torn down instead of humbling themselves as they should.

Question for Reflection:

We are not called to go around tearing down people's towers of self-righteousness, but when our own tower needs tearing down, God often uses circumstances, fellow believers, and even unbelievers as catalysts to confront and convict us.

- Do we fight them, and if so, to what end?

    My thoughts: The fight may not end in a physical death as it did with Gideon and the men of Penuel, but we can fight each other to the death of the relationship.

Gideon's Legacy, Judges 8:18-35

55. How did Zebah and Zalmunnah describe Gideon?

They described him as the son of a king.

56. Why didn't Gideon kill them himself? Why give the task to his son, Jether?

Though he was not king, Gideon's action was very kingly. He treated Zebah and Zalmunnah contemptuously as a superior toward an inferior by ordering them to be killed in this manner. It is one thing for a king to be killed on the battlefield against seasoned warriors or even by another king as equals, but it is a slap in the face for a king to be killed by a young boy in front of everyone.

The name, **Jether,** means the "remainder, remnant, excellence, or abundance." It describes a man's legacy—what remains of his excellence and abundance that is often embodied in his children and passed on to the next generation. Jether was Gideon's son—the son who was expected to step into his father's shoes and take up the fight in the next generation. Remember: One of the reasons for these oppressions was to teach the next generation how to war.

57. Was Jether's youth a reason not to engage the enemy, or was it a failing on his part?

I suppose it can be argued both ways, but my view tends toward a failing for a few reasons. To be standing in Succoth with his father and the three hundred meant that Jether must have followed his father in battle, so he couldn't be so very young as to lack the physical strength. In terms of his faith, he was no younger than his father, really.

Gideon had not seen the Lord in battle, but stepped out in faith and was victorious. He was a good model this for his son, yet Jether refused to follow his example. While we might make an allowance for youth, I think it is a failing on Jether's part. This will be the last we see of the young man.

58. How did the son's refusal to step up reflect on the father in the face of his enemies?

The father had already fought and won the battle. It is to the father's glory that the son should take up the sword and finish the fight. It would have been humiliating for Gideon. Because of his son's failure, Gideon's own reputation were on the line. He was obligated to take glory for himself against his enemies personally.

59. How did Gideon respond to the men of Israel pressing the kingship on him?

He gave glory to God by refusing the kingship for himself and his sons and declared that God was King. Even so, he made himself a golden ephod out of the enemies' golden earrings. (This was reminiscent of Aaron making the golden calf out of golden earrings in the wilderness journey. It was a moment of stumbling.)

60. Over the course of the narrative, Gideon built two altars and an ephod. The ephod became a stumbling block for him and his house where the altars did not. Why?

Because the ephod was a tribute to Gideon and not to God. I think his desire to make a legacy for himself with the golden ephod was a reaction to the humiliation he felt when his son—who should have been his legacy—failed to step up and deal with the enemy. Gideon sought a tangible means of tribute to himself to replace the son who disappointed him. Humiliation is one of the stumbling blocks that are part of the dynamics of oppression.

61. Why did the text switch between the names Jerubbaal and Gideon in verses 29-35?

What happens when the hero (Jerubbaal) returns home and becomes just a regular man (Gideon) again? Heroes like Jerubbaal don't remain heroes in people's eyes for long. As soon as he dies, he and his family are forgotten.

Questions for Reflection:

- Why might parents feel shame and humiliation when their children fail to follow in their footsteps in the faith and take up the battles?

- How do they overcome these feelings without stumbling?

- How must Christ feel when we fail to take up the commission He has given us, after the battle He waged to assure us victory?

APPLY THE PICTURE

God's Three-Step Process for Dealing with Oppression

Step 1: Address the person

When God deals with oppression, He focuses on the individual first and foremost. He addressed Gideon's faith and brought him into a right relationship and understanding of Himself, encouraged him, strengthened him, and invested in him the understanding of His power and love.

For us, righting our relationship with God is the first step to dealing with our oppression and begins with considering our own situation. Are we on the path that we should be or have we slipped into doing what is right in our own eyes? Is there sin we need to deal with? We need to set things right in our own life before we presume to tackle the bigger issue.

Step 2: Address the house

Being a witness for God in an ungodly world begins on the home front. Having righted Gideon's relationship with Himself, God then sent him to confront the idolatry in his father's house. It is important to note that God's objective was not for Gideon to bring his father's house into submission to God's ways and right that spiritual relationship. That is an unrealistic expectation, for Gideon and for us. We can see from Joash's response that while Gideon may have destroyed the idols in his father's house, nothing Gideon did really changed his father's heart toward God. Gideon's stand may have inspired the grand upwelling of support from family and nation, but it fell far short of returning the people to God and had the negative effect of making him an idol in people's eyes.

Rallying support for Gideon was not God's goal in sending Gideon to deal with the idolatry in his father's house. God's goal was to test Gideon's conviction in doing what God was asking of him, even when he knew he had no support from family or friends. Was God's power enough to sustain him? Would he obey God's voice?

Ideally, a leader should bring his house into a right understanding and relationship with each other and with God before tackling the greater battle, but achieving the heart change and return to God is not always possible with family. It is important to understand that God doesn't make us responsible for that, as if we had that kind of power. If we approach this step with that unrealistic expectation, a lack of success can derail us from pressing on to deal with the oppression in our lives. What God wants to see from us as individuals is that we are convicted enough to stand up and fight for Him and for His ways, and that we have grasped the understanding of His power working in us and through us.

For us, this step may involve reconciling and righting the relationships we have with our family, or it may mean establishing boundaries they cannot cross with us. It may mean standing up to outsiders and saying "as for me and my house, we will serve the Lord!" But this effort is more for our benefit than others. Nothing may change within the family sphere, but we will know in our hearts where we stand with the LORD. We must pass this test of our relationship with Him before going on to the greater issue.

Step 3: Address the congregation/community/nation

Gideon's actions had the effect of gathering the people to him to throw off the Midianite oppression. Even so, many who joined the "movement" came with wrong expectations and motivations, and God made it a point to whittle down those numbers where the world would embrace them. When a person enters a spiritual battle, his house and his people should be with him so that he isn't fighting the battle on a second front; but it is better to go into that fight with God alone, or just a few godly individuals, than with many glory-seekers.

62. Why does the process need to follow this order?

Why is it necessary for a person to deal with their own sin before they start hacking away the altars and Asherah poles in other people's lives? What happens when a leader whose own life and family are out of control tries to deal with sin in the greater congregation? They are ineffectual and come across as self-righteous hypocrites, according to Matthew 7:3. It is important to understand that when a person fails to conquer his or her internal Canaanite side and bring it into submission, then the battle is lost on *all* fronts.

This model is also used for selecting leadership in the church. Paul instructs Titus to choose elders whose characters are exemplary and above reproach but who also have an orderly, God-fearing family life.

> *"if a man is blameless, the husband of one wife, having faithful children not accused of dissipation or insubordination. For a bishop*

must be blameless, as a steward of God, not self-willed, not quick-tempered, not given to wine, not violent, not greedy for money, but hospitable, a lover of what is good, sober-minded, just, holy, self-controlled," —Titus 1:6-8

63. **More and more, our society is embracing the idea of group "movements" to effect social reform in a top-down approach—making systemic changes at the national level first that then drive change at the individual level. This stands in contrast to God's bottom-up method of effecting change through singular individuals.**

    - Is the top-down approach as effective as the bottom-up approach? Why or why not?

    - What are some dangers inherent in group "movements"?

    - Do groups "empower" individuals as they purport? If so, how? If not, why not?

SECURING BORDERS

One key aspect in all of these oppressions is the need to secure and maintain borders and boundaries where the Enemy is not allowed to cross. Gideon had to re-establish and secure the boundaries of his nation, his own home, and even his own person when people tried to lift him up above his station.

We are not Israel. We are not battling a physical enemy for a physical kingdom in this age. However, there are boundaries that we must maintain for us to live as believers.

64. **What kinds of boundaries do we have to establish and maintain?**

Questions for Reflection:

"If God is with us, then why is all this happening to me? Where are His miracles? Why has He not kept His promises?"

If you are asking these questions, then you are at the same place where Gideon began. Gideon went from a man convinced God had forsaken him to a man who overcame a daunting enemy with courage. He told his men *"Look at me and do likewise..."* Let's look at what Gideon models for us in dealing with oppression.

When Christ turns to us and says, "Okay, let's deal with your oppression. Get yourself in order, get your house in order, then we'll tackle the rest of the world," what does that entail?

Getting yourself in order . . .

- What if that means acknowledging that you got yourself into oppression because you were doing what was right in your own eyes? Are you prepared to admit that and take the steps needed to repent and resolve those issues?

- Are you ready to submit to Christ's kingship over you, embrace His values, and fight the battle on His terms?

Getting your house in order . . .

- What if that means confronting family members with sin?

- Are you ready to reestablish boundaries in your own house?

- Are you ready to face a possible fight with outsiders over the right to live your faith, even within your own home?

Battling the enemy . . .

- How did Gideon battle?

- Based on Gideon's experience, what should you be prepared for? Prepare to:

    o Feel weak against the enemy. God's ways of fighting are not man's ways. God uses weak people and unconventional weapons as strengths in battle.

    o Feel like you are groping your way in the dark. This battle is not won by sight.

    o Listen—to God and leadership—and act on what you hear.

    o Stand where you are, do what you can with what you have.

    o Be broken. You might not win the physical fight, but you will win the spiritual war.

The Sounding of Trumpets: A Prophetic Picture of Christ

Gideon armed his men with trumpets and clay pitchers with torches in them. I touched on the picture of the broken vessel with the light in it but didn't go into the imagery of the trumpets, which is a prophetic picture that I will explain here.

The sounding of trumpets is an important picture in the Scriptures. Israel was commanded to keep this picture alive through the ages by celebrating the Feast of Trumpets (aka Rosh Hashanah) year after year.

> *"In the seventh month, on the first day of the month, you shall have a sabbath-rest, a memorial of blowing of trumpets, a holy convocation."*
> —Leviticus 23:24

On this feast day, Israel is commanded to blow the trumpets as a memorial. A memorial of what? To find that answer you have to consider why trumpets are blown in Scripture.

Gideon's narrative is only one example of trumpets being blown. Gideon himself blows the trumpet twice—once to assemble Israel for war and once at the start of the battle (Judges 6:34, 7:20). Those are two reasons, but there are others.

When you compile *all* the Scriptural reasons for blowing of trumpets, you get a picture of the End Times events portrayed in the book of Revelation.

You also get a picture of Gideon's narrative overall. Even though Gideon blows the trumpet for only two reasons, the other reasons are also illustrated in his narrative in various ways, which means that Gideon's narrative, overall, is a rough depiction of End Times events.

In the following chart, I have outlined the reasons for blowing trumpets drawn from Scripture. Beside each reason, I have matched its parallel in Gideon's narrative, and its projected fulfillment in the End Times. As you can see, Gideon's narrative encompasses much of the End Times picture. It is not in a particular timeline order, but the pieces are there.

Just as the narrative of Gideon's battle focuses heavily on the sounds being heard, the memorial feast focuses on the trumpet (shofar) being sounded in different ways. There are four distinct sound effects created by the shofar blower, and each of them illustrate an element of Gideon's narrative.

The Sounding of Trumpets: A Prophetic Picture of Christ

Reasons for Sounding the Trumpet	Gideon's Narrative	End Times imagery
To mark the beginning of Israel's repentance and return to God (the Feast of Trumpets begins a time of self-examination and testing as Israel prepares for the Day of Atonement). The voices of the prophets are likened to shofar blasts.	Israel cries to the LORD for deliverance, and the LORD sends them a prophet with the message that they should do some soul searching (6:8-10). Also, a time of testing to see who will be chosen to go to battle (7:2-8)	In Jewish thought, the days between the Feast of Trumpets and Day of Atonement are equated with what we call the Tribulation or Days of Awe.
To call Israel to assemble and prepare for war	Gideon blows the trumpet to call Israel to him (6:34-35).	The trumpet of the Rapture (perhaps the calling of the 144,000)
To announce the LORD's arrival on Sinai when He gave Israel the Law.	Gideon coming as judge	Christ coming as judge
To announce the LORD's arrival on the Day of the LORD when He fights for Israel in a time of great darkness (and in the Jezreel Valley)	Gideon and the three hundred sound the trumpets around the Midianite camp at night, and the LORD routes the Midianites (7:16-22)	The Battle of Armageddon
To herald the imminent overthrow of a people.		
To announce the coronation of a king (on the Feast of Trumpets, you announce God as King).	Gideon is offered the kingship over Israel, which he does not take but declares the LORD shall be King (8:22-23).	The celebration and crowning of Christ the Messiah as king.
To herald the coming of the Messiah (Moshia), a Messianic age, and resurrection/restoration.	Gideon is a *moshia* figure and in his days, he brings the nation into a 40-year period of rest (8:21).	The Millennial Kingdom

These are the four sounds:

1) There is a single blast to call the assembly to gather, to battle, and to advance. In that we hear Gideon sounding the trumpet to gather Israel to war.

2) A second set of broken, mournful notes simulates the sound of wailing and repentance, reflected in Israel's cry for relief from their Midianite oppressors.

3) A third set of sharp, staccato notes are meant to simulate the clattering sound of tents coming down, the tramp of feet, and an army breaking camp—or the clatter of pitchers being broken.

4) A final great blast signals the victory and coming of the King, which is Gideon and the three hundred blasting out the trumpets as the LORD sets the enemy's sword against itself and routs them.

Gideon's narrative is magnificent in its depth and breadth of application. It has taken us deep into personal challenges, addressing both physical and spiritual issues on a personal, family, community, and national level. It has presented us with some remarkably relevant social issues to consider, offering a model for encouragement and the steps for dealing with oppression. And if the present time were not enough, it projects a picture of a Messiah to come in a future time of oppression and tribulations.

One Final Scenario

Let's say God raises up another Gideon—a man tagged for a particular ministry purpose and to whom He gives a particular vision. The man embraces the mission, and God blesses him in his ministry to the point where people begin to view him as a great leader and mighty man of faith. He draws great crowds, donors give much money to his ministry, and he does much good for the Kingdom.

As the man grows older, he is expected to pass on his ministry to his son. But the son has neither the vision or mission from God, and isn't willing to step up and assume leadership of the ministry.

When the man dies, he is mourned briefly, and then comes the question over what to do with his ministry, which has now grown to the proportion of a small kingdom. A fight ensues over who will step into his shoes and take over his ministry, sometimes within the family, sometimes by those outside the family.

Why is there a fight? What are they really fighting over? They fight, not because they have been given the mission by God, but because the ministry carries a reputation and honor that they themselves have not had to earn or been able to earn by their own merit.

Enter Abimelech.

LESSON 8

Abimelech

READ

Judges 9

OVERVIEW

A note about the structure of Chapter 9:

Jotham's parable and Abimelech's downfall are narrated in a 3-and-4 literary structure where the first three elements are of like kind while the fourth sets up a climactic contrast.

There is an echo of the narrative in these proverbs:

> *"... There are three things that are never satisfied, Four never say, 'Enough!': The grave, the barren womb, the earth that is not satisfied with water—and the fire never says, 'Enough!'"* —Proverbs 30:15b-16

> *"For three things the earth is perturbed, Yes, for four it cannot bear up: For a servant when he reigns, a fool when he is filled with food, a hateful woman when she is married, and a maidservant who succeeds her mistress."* —Proverbs 30:21-23

The servant who reigns is most definitely an illustration of Abimelech, as is the fire which will characterize him as Jotham's curse plays out.

BUILD THE PICTURE

Abimelech's Coup, Judges 9:1-6

1. **When did this take place?**

   After the death of Gideon and forty years of rest. We should note that this period of rest will be the last time rest was given by a judge. All future judges and deliverers will not bring about an age of rest.

2. **Where did the story play out?**

The narrative played out at Shechem, located roughly in the saddle of land between Mount Gerizim and Mount Ebal. We remember these mountains as the places where the tribes of Israel stood to recite the blessing and cursing when they first entered the Land, as it says in Deuteronomy 27:12-13:

> "These shall stand on Mount Gerizim to bless the people, when you have crossed over the Jordan: Simeon, Levi, Judah, Issachar, Joseph, and Benjamin; and these shall stand on Mount Ebal to curse: Reuben, Gad, Asher, Zebulun, Dan, and Naphtali." —Deuteronomy 27:12-13

Gideon and his house (including Abimelech and Jotham) were from the tribe of Manasseh, which was the house of Joseph, so they would have been the ones to stand on Mount Gerizim to give the blessing.

About Shechem: The word *shechem* means "back or shoulder," the place where a burden is carried. It can also refer a seat of power or a place where a man is beaten for punishment.

Shechem was originally the hometown of Shechem, son of Hamor the Hivite, who was killed by Simeon and Levi for raping their sister, Dinah (Genesis 34). I mention this because the name Hamor will come up later in the narrative.

Shechem was also the place where Joshua reestablished God's covenant with Israel after the inheritance had been divided (Joshua 24). Joshua gathered the people to this place in the shadow of Mounts Gerizim and Ebal and delivered the following charge:

> "And if it seems evil to you to serve the LORD, choose for yourselves this day whom you will serve ... But as for me and my house, we will serve the LORD ... So Joshua made a covenant with the people that day, and made for them a statute and an ordinance in Shechem ... And he took a large stone, and set it up there under the oak that was by the sanctuary of the LORD. And Joshua said to all the people, 'Behold, this stone shall be a witness to us, for it has heard all the words of the LORD which He spoke to us. It shall therefore be a witness to you, lest you deny your God.'" —Joshua 24:15-16, 25-27

In Joshua's day, the people swore to serve God there at the pillar that stood by the oak (or terebinth) tree. Here in Judges 9, they chose a very different king to serve.

3. **What do we know Abimelech?**

   Abimelech was the son of Jerubbaal's (Gideon's) concubine. Notice, he is identified as Jerubbaal's son, not Gideon's son. He was the son of the hero with the reputation, not the humble man of God.

   The name **Abimelech** means "My father is king." *Melech* infers not just kingship, but divine kingship in the Scripture, so the name could be rendered "My father is God the King." This would have been in line with Gideon's statement in Judges 8:23 that the LORD was king over his people. But Abimelech is the son of the hero, not the man of God. Jerubbaal is the idolized deliverer whose reputation was embodied in his golden ephod, a war trophy that became a snare to Gideon and his house. The reputation remained even after his death, and where Gideon had once refused the kingship for himself and his sons, Abimelech sought it.

   Abimelech wanted to be king. He coveted a place and power and glory that were not rightly his. He might not become king of Israel, but he wanted to rule over whatever he could, if only his home town of Shechem.

   Abimelech was a type of rebel who sought to rule a lesser kingdom when the greater kingdom was denied him. He is patterned after Korah (Numbers 16) and Satan in this respect.

   Abimelech was a man with two natures at war in him. He was identified with the father, even with God, but he gave himself over to his Canaanite side.

   In the Judges narrative, it is not specifically stated that Gideon's concubine—Abimelech's Shechemite mother—descended from the Hivites (Canaanites), although Gaal's rant in verses 28-29 implies a distinction between Abimelech's Israelite father and Shechemite mother. For the purpose of this lesson, I will present Abimelech as being of this dual nature—half Israel and half Shechemite.

SEVEN STEPS TO ASCEND A THRONE

Step 1: Identify and appeal to your support base (9:1-2)

> *"Then Abimelech the son of Jerubbaal went to Shechem, to his mother's brothers, and spoke with them and with all the family of the house of his mother's father..." (9:1)*

Abimelech went to his mother's Shechemite side to generate support for his campaign against his father's Israelite side. He reiterated to the Shechemite side of the family, *"I am your own flesh and bone."* In doing this, he gained their support by identifying with them and began to polarize the family and community.

Step 2: Use a skewed argument to create a fight where there is no fight, an enemy where there is no enemy (9:2)

> *"Please speak in the hearing of all the men of Shechem: 'Which is better for you, that all seventy of the sons of Jerubbaal reign over you, or that one reign over you?' Remember that I am your own flesh and bone." (9:2)*

Remember: Gideon said neither he nor his sons would rule Israel. There was only one king—God (Judges 8:23). Gideon's sons were not pursuing kingship, *but Abimelech made people think they were.* Abimelech argued that it would be better to be under the rule of one instead of seventy. That was a true statement, except the people were already under the rule of only one—God. Abimelech wasn't in contention with the seventy. He was in contention with God. Abimelech placed himself in the role of king as replacement for God. The purpose of his words was to draw the people away from an identity and connection with God, and to identify themselves instead as victims and himself as their savior.

Step 3: Let others promote you (9:3)

> *"And his mother's brothers spoke all these words concerning him in the hearing of all the men of Shechem; and their heart was inclined to follow Abimelech, for they said, "He is our brother." (9:3)*

Abimelech's family then spread the word on his behalf and won him support among the men of Shechem. Yes, a man can come to power without ever having to open his own mouth if enough people promote him.

Steps 4 & 5: Generate funding; build an army (9:4a)

> *"So they gave him seventy shekels of silver from the temple of Baal-Berith with which Abimelech hired worthless and reckless men; and they followed him." (9:4)*

Gideon's power base was made up of volunteers hand-picked by God; Abimelech hired his army.

Worthless: The Hebrew word is *req* (pronounced rake) meaning "empty, vain, wicked"—ethically empty men. They were as empty as Gideon's pitchers but without the light inside them.

Reckless: The Hebrew word here is *pachaz*, meaning "to bubble and boil, to be light as froth." They dissipated as quickly as they bubbled up and were of little substance or importance.

Step 6: Slaughter the opposition

> *"Then he went to his father's house at Ophrah and killed his brothers, the seventy sons of Jerubbaal, on one stone..." (9:5a)*

Abimelech ambushed and killed them, execution style, on a rock. The execution was the act of contempt by a superior toward an inferior.

What happened to Jether? He died. Jether shrank from the fight when his father asked him to step up. Do you think his earlier refusal to fight had some consequence in meeting Abimelech's threat? One could speculate.

Step 7: Assume the throne

> *"... they went and made Abimelech king beside the terebinth tree at the pillar that was in Shechem." (9:6b)*

This was the pillar Joshua set up beside the oak when the children of Israel swore to follow the LORD alone and put away the idols from among them. This was where Joshua charged Israel: choose this day whom you will serve! This time the men of Shechem chose Abimelech over God.

THE PICTURE OF THIS OPPRESSION

The oppression begins with Abimelech, a man with a divided identity. He is Israelite in his identity with his father, but Canaanite in his identity with his mother. He covets kingship which has been denied him through his father's Israelite line, and so pursues it through his Canaanite line. He gives himself over to his Canaanite identity and rises to take the throne by lies, treachery, and murder.

APPLY THE PICTURE

THE PROFILE OF THIS OPPRESSION

Embodied within the picture of Abimelech is a man with a divided persona. He is a new man, and yet he has this other carnal "Canaanite" side of him that seeks to dominate him. His Canaanite side (the Enemy) will rise up to take over the new man and eventually consume him by the same steps with which Abimelech took the throne. This is the model of spiritual warfare between the new man and his Canaanite side:

Step 1: The Enemy will appeal to your carnal (Canaanite) side, separate you from your identity with God and Christ, and ask you to identify with your "flesh and bone."

Step 2: The Enemy will present a skewed argument that will play out along the lines of 1 Timothy 6 (throwing off a master in pursuit of gain, serving Baals & Asherah). The Enemy will:

- Create a desire in you for something that appeals to your carnal side (covet).
- Create enmity between you and God where no enmity exists. You will begin to see God or God's appointed leaders as masters who enslave you.
- Create a victim mentality in you and a desire to fight for freedom from the master who is keeping you from achieving the thing you covet (strife).

Step 3: The Enemy will let others promote him (via social networking, news media, advertising, and various communications forms) until the new man is swayed.

Step 4: The Enemy will be well financed by the Baals he serves and will bring his resources to bear in swaying the new man. As the new man begins to turn, the Enemy may suggest (carnal) ways for the new man to resource and finance his new pursuit.

Step 5: The Enemy will be backed by an army of reckless and worthless people—vain, wicked, ethically empty people who bubble, boil, and froth at the mouth. They may take the form of verbal or physical attackers.

Step 6: When the Enemy makes the final push with a show of force, the new man succumbs without a fight.

Step 7: The Enemy assumes the throne in the new man's life and makes him as much a slave as he ever was.

BUILD THE PICTURE

Jotham's Response, Judges 9:7-21

4. What do we know about Jotham?

He was the youngest and only surviving son of Jerubbaal by his wife. Jotham's family had been cut off, and he himself was left a remnant.

Jotham means "God is perfect," with an emphasis on the character of God being complete, morally righteous, having integrity, being sound and wholesome.

Compare his name with Abimelech's name: "My father is king." Abimelech's name, by contrast, emphasizes reputation, nobility, and rulership, but it has been skewed toward a more carnal identity with man and not God.

5. Why does Jotham go to Mount Gerizim?

The name **Gerizim** means "cutting off." Jotham identified with this place in his own condition of being cut off and left a remnant, and he sought justice there. Mount Gerizim was where Jotham's Manassite ancestors once stood to deliver the blessing (Deuteronomy 27:12). The place of blessing was now delivered over to curses and judgment as Jotham demanded a reckoning for the sin done to his family.

From where he stood, it is doubtful that the men of Shechem heard him, so the cry was more to God than with the hope of being heard by men. Victims' cries are like that. God hears them when no one else does.

THE PARABLE OF THE TREES

There is a formulaic 3-and-4 structure in the parable of the trees. Three elements are of like kind, and the fourth is set up as a climactic contrast.

6. What are the three and the fourth?

There are three leafy, fruitful plants compared to a bramble bush, and three refusals compared to one agreement.

7. **The "trees" sought a king (9:8). What were the three who were offered kingship and what did they do?**

   The trees were the olive, the fig, and the grape, and are representative of the best and most noble of Israel. The olive tree produced oil which honors God and man (9:9) and marked the one anointed as king. The fig tree produced sweetness and good fruit (9:11). The grapevine produced wine, the symbol of joy, that cheered God and man (9:13). All three were useful, fruitful, and symbolic of peace and prosperity.

8. **Why did the three trees refuse kingship, and what did their refusal imply about how they value their roles compared to the kingship?**

   They argued that they must cease doing what they were doing to pursue the kingship. They obviously valued their roles as being greater, more useful, or more rewarding than the potential role of king. They didn't want to stop what they were doing to pursue a greater reward.

   Why didn't those who had so much to offer of what is good and holy and fruitful step up? Isn't kingship a better station and reward? There is a bit of a skewed value system here. Remember, the stumbling blocks in oppression include losing sight of the kingdom and clinging to the transient, feel-good pursuits in life.

9. **After the three refusals, the kingship was offered to the bramble. What are the characteristics of the bramble by contrast? (v15)**

   The bramble was unlike the olive in that it had no honor nor gave honor. It produced no fruit, sweetness, or cheer like the fig and the grapevine. It exalted itself as if it were a big leafy tree, offering much shade when in fact it had no shade to offer.

   The agreement was extortionate—if the trees did not crown the bramble, then its fire would burn down the great trees who exalted themselves.

THE INTERPRETATION

10. **What is Jotham's curse?**

    Jotham stepped into his father's shoes as judge and took a stand on Mount Gerizim. He demanded that the people of Shechem consider their actions.

    "If you have acted in truth and sincerity in making Abimelech king, and if you have dealt well with Jerubbaal and his house, and have

> *done to him as he deserves . . . then rejoice in Abimelech, and let him rejoice in you"* —Judges 9:16

Jotham reminded them of the work that Gideon, their deliverer, did for them. He fought for them. He risked his life for them. He delivered them from the hand of the enemy. They should have been eternally grateful to their deliverer for saving them. But instead, the men of Shechem have executed his rightful heirs in favor of the son of his servant.

With great bitterness, Jotham delivered a curse from the mount of blessing. If the people had done right and chosen the right king, then let them rejoice and be blessed. But if they had made the wrong choice and crowned the wrong king, let the fire come out from Abimelech and the men of Shechem and let them consume each other.

By crowning the bramble as king, the people chose for themselves a crown of thorns and brought upon themselves the curse and the judgment.

11. What happened to Jotham?

He fled to the refuge of Beer—the "well"—and dwelt there. Nothing more is heard of him in Scripture.

APPLY THE PICTURE

Even if they had heard Jotham's indictment against them, Abimelech and the men of Shechem would not have repented nor would Abimelech have relinquished the throne, and so they incurred the curse of being burned. We find a similar indictment described in the book of Hebrews.

Read Hebrews 6:4-8

12. How do Abimelech and the men of Shechem model this New Testament pattern for us?

Once wickedness assumes power and there is nothing left to restrain it, it begins to burn as a fire and by its very nature will rage until it has consumed itself, as the prophet, Isaiah, says:

> *"For wickedness burns as the fire; It shall devour the briers and*

thorns, and kindle in the thickets of the forest; They shall mount up like rising smoke. Through the wrath of the LORD of hosts the land is burned up, and the people shall be as fuel for the fire; No man shall spare his brother." —Isaiah 9:18-19

Isaiah's words aptly describe what is going to play out between the men of Shechem and Abimelech.

There can come a point in a believer's life where their Canaanite side—the thorns and briers—can completely overrun their new man. They become so entrenched and hardened to the sin in their life that repentance is not likely to happen. It is at this point that God often allows a devastation to strike their lives. It is often accomplished simply by God lifting His hand from them and letting their Canaanite side rage uncontrolled until it has burnt itself out.

Kingship and Rewards

13. The book of Judges began with a judgment against those who refused to pursue the full inheritance—the reward. What is the reward for us and how does it tie into this idea of kingship?

Our understanding of the inheritance or reward includes earning crowns and being rulers and co-heirs with Christ in the Kingdom. The picture begins in the Old Testament . . .

- Adam and Eve are given dominion in Eden (Genesis 1). This was lost because Adam gave his kingship to the Enemy (Satan). When Adam should have reigned as king over the garden of fruitful trees, he fell under the kingship of the bramble king and was given over to the curse. The kingship was lost, but a promise remained of its restoration in a future Kingdom to come.

- A provision for a future king is made in the Law. *"You shall surely set a king over you whom the LORD your God chooses . . . you may not set a foreigner over you, who is not your brother."*
—Deuteronomy 17:15

- As part of the inheritance of the land by Israel, they were called to rule over the land and subdue it in the books of Joshua and Judges (an echo of Adam and Eve).

    Here in the book of Judges, we have the parable of the trees who sought a king from among their own, but none would step up to take the kingship. Instead they chose the inferior bramble to be king over them, which ends in a curse (again, an echo of Adam and Eve). The book of Judges ends with the statement *"In those days there was no king,"* a critical comment meant to imply that a king would be the only solution to bring Israel out of her condition.

- A future King is pictured and prophesied in the Psalms (2, 8, 110) and reaches its zenith in Isaiah 53:12: *"Therefore I will divide Him a portion with the great, and He shall divide the spoil with the strong, because He poured out His soul unto death..."*

The picture continues in the New Testament with:

- The theology of the book of Hebrews, which details what it means to be partners (*metachoi*) with Christ

- The theology of crowns which presents us with the various crowns believers may gain:
    - The incorruptible crown (1 Corinthians 9:25)
    - The crown of righteousness (2 Timothy 4:8)
    - The crown of rejoicing (1 Thessalonians 2:19)
    - The crown of life (James 1:12, Revelation 2:10)
    - The crown of glory (1 Peter 5:4)

- 2 Timothy 2:11-13, which says: *"This is a faithful saying: For if we died with Him, We shall also live with Him. If we endure, We shall also reign with Him. If we deny Him, He also will deny us. If we are faithless, He remains faithful; He cannot deny Himself."*

- Romans 8:17, which says: *"and if children, then heirs—heirs of God and joint heirs with Christ, if indeed we suffer with Him, that we may also be glorified together."* This then leads into the theology of glorification.

Questions for Reflection:

- Have you ever gone to someone with a serious, legitimate grievance about how they have treated you? What response did you get?

- Has someone ever accused you of dealing wrongly with them? How did you respond?

> - How should you respond when you find out you misjudged the situation?
> - How do you feel about being a ruler in the Kingdom?
> - Is that a reward worth pursuing? Would you fight the Enemy for it?

BUILD THE PICTURE

Abimelech's Downfall, Judges 9:22-57

14. How long did it take God to respond, and how did the curse begin to play out?

God let Abimelech reign unhindered for three years before He initiated the conflict between Shechem and Abimelech.

The curse began to play out on the mountains where Jotham delivered his curse. The men of Shechem set men to ambush Abimelech. Highwaymen infested the mountains, and the highways became unsafe to travel. These men didn't just rob Abimelech. They robbed everyone. They victimized their own people.

The playing out of the curse began with an act of treachery and robbery. Considering that Abimelech took the kingship by acts of treachery, murder, and robbery, this is a bit of eye-for-an-eye justice.

15. What do we know about Gaal?

Gaal was the son of Ebed. The name means "loathing," son of "a slave." He was a foreigner who came to Shechem with his brothers and began to win the regard of the men of Shechem. He was arrogant, a drunkard, and a rebel.

16. What do we know about Zebul, and what was his role in the conflict between Abimelech and the men of Shechem?

Zebul was the ruler of the city, perhaps the head magistrate. His name means "exalted," but by whom? He sent messages that incited and enflamed the men against each other. He was like one of those people who works behind the scenes to stir up dissension.

17. What was Zebul's plan for dealing with Gaal?

Gaal and his brothers were lodged in Shechem along with the men with whom they had been partying. The city gates were shut by night, so Zebul told Abimelech to lie in wait in the fields and ambush Gaal and his supporters when they came out of the gates in the morning.

THE BATTLES

Like the parable of the trees, the battles are narrated in the literary 3-and-4 structure. Here is the breakdown:

Stage 1: Fight against Gaal and his confederates (v34-41)

Stage 2: Fight against the fields/city of Shechem (v42-45)

Stage 3: Fight against the tower of Shechem (v46-49)

Stage 4: Fight against Thebez (v50-55)

The first three are Abimelech's take-down of the men of Shechem. The fourth, by contrast, is Abimelech's own take-down.

STAGE 1: Abimelech fights Gaal and his confederates (9:34-41)

18. What was Abimelech's strategy?

Abimelech's strategy was similar to the strategy Gideon used against the Midianites: Divide his men into four groups, surround the city, and ambush his enemy.

Gaal and his men woke the next morning dull-headed with hangovers only to find themselves in a fight the minute they stepped out of the gate of the city. Zebul stands at Gaal's shoulder, needling him into battle.

Gaal saw one company coming down out of the mountains, and Zebul told him he was seeing things. Gaal saw another company advancing from the middle and a third spring up out of nowhere like magic from the Diviner's Terebinth Tree. When at last Gaal recognized that the threat was real, he went out to fight. The men of Shechem went with him, only to find themselves ambushed and on the run.

19. What was the conclusion of Stage 1?

The battle was a victory for Abimelech. Abimelech fought the battle outside; Zebul drove Gaal and his brothers out of the city and clanged the gate behind them so they couldn't reenter the city.

20. Where did Abimelech go to live after the battle?

Abimelech went to dwell at Arumah, which name means "I shall be exalted." Why didn't he return to Shechem, if he was the king of Shechem? It seems there was a growing distance between Abimelech and the men of Shechem, and Abimelech was now on the outside.

STAGE 2: Abimelech fights against the city of Shechem (9:42-45)

21. What started the next stage of the battle?

It is a little unclear what started things this time. The battle with Gaal was over, right? And yet there was a fire smoldering in Abimelech over this incident with the men of Shechem. He may have dealt with Gaal and his brothers, but why had the men of Shechem joined them so readily? Who else might the men of Shechem embrace as a new king?

Jealousy, suspicion, and fear can easily inflame a man who finds himself challenged and on the outside.

I don't know if those were Abimelech's thoughts, but for some reason, he suddenly began to look on the men of Shechem as an enemy. And so, when word came to him that the people of Shechem were coming out to the fields for the day's work, he staged another ambush.

22. What was Abimelech's strategy?

He divided his company into three parts this time, lay in ambush for the Shechemites to come out of the city, then attacked them. Abimelech and one company took the city while the other two companies took those in the field.

23. What did he do to the city?

He demolished it and sowed it with salt so that the city would be barren and not rebuilt (although it was rebuilt in the days of kings).

STAGE 3: Abimelech fights against the tower of Shechem (v46-49)

24. What started the next stage of the battle?

"It was told to Abimelech . . ." (9:47) Some unnamed party informed Abimelech that there was a contingent of men hiding in the fortified section of the city. Apparently the tower or fortifications of Shechem and the Temple of Baal-Berith were a separate complex from the city.

Again, there was no reason for continuing the battle apart from this grudge that Abimelech held against the men of Shechem. His fire was still burning.

25. What was Abimelech's strategy for dealing with the tower?

Abimelech decided to burn the tower down, so he immediately headed for a nearby wooded hill called Mount Zalmon.

Zalmon means "shady" or "shadowy" in the sense of a shadow casting a likeness of something on the ground. What Abimelech did there was a likeness to the actions of his father, Jerubbaal, but in a very dark way. He and his men began by taking axes and chopping down tree branches, which they then propped up against the tower and lit on fire. Thus, they killed the one thousand men and women who were in the tower. (Think of how large the tower must have been to house a thousand people.)

Abimelech's actions were a shadow picture of Gideon, the hewer, taking down the great *pe'orah*—the exalted branches of Midian—but it is mixed with the imagery of Penuel, where Gideon took down the tower and killed the men who looked down loftily at him and refused to help him and his men.

STAGE 4: Abimelech fights against Thebez (v50-55)

26. What was Abimelech's grievance with Thebez?

He had no grievance. He was just a fire raging out of control.

27. How did this engagement contrast to the other three?

What was the grand resolution? In Thebez, there was a replay of the tower burning scenario, except this time, before Abimelech could set it on fire, an unnamed woman dropped a millstone on his head and mortally wounded him. To keep from being dishonored at the hand of a woman, Abimelech demanded that his armor-bearer—a youth—kill him. And so, he died at the hand of the youth instead of a woman, but it was still a dishonorable death.

28. How the punishment fit the crime: How did God mete out some eye-for-an-eye justice against Abimelech?

Abimelech, the son of a servant, set himself up as rival to God; God set up Gaal, the son of a slave, as Abimelech's rival.

Abimelech scorned his brothers and conspired against them. The men of Shechem scorned Abimelech, their "brother," and conspired against him.

The men of Shechem helped Abimelech kill the sons of Jerubbaal. The men of Shechem sided with Gaal against Abimelech, a son of Jerubbaal.

The sons of Jerubbaal were killed on one stone by the son of a servant. Abimelech was killed by a stone dropped on him by a woman.

29. There is a repeated behavior found in verses 31, 42, 47. What started Abimelech's fire and kept the fire raging?

In each case, Abimelech was told something. Someone reported a bit of news or gossip designed to inflame him.

APPLY THE PICTURE

James 3:5-6 says:

"Even so the tongue is a little member and boasts great things. See how great a forest a little fire kindles! And the tongue is a fire, a world of iniquity. The tongue is so set among our members that it defiles the whole body, and sets on fire the course of nature; and it is set on fire by hell." —James 3:5-6

What a perfectly apt description of Abimelech's experience. Mind your tongue when you speak to one another, knowing that your words have this power in them, and put away from yourself those people in your life who like to keep contentions stirred up. Remember, too, that the Zebuls in life who start that fire and set one person against another often get burned as a result.

LESSON 9

Oppression #5: Tola and Jair

READ

Judges 10:1-2, 3-5

BUILD THE PICTURE

Tola, Judges 10:1-2

1. What do we know about Tola?

He appeared on the scene in the wake of the devastation left by Abimelech and the men of Shechem. He was from Issachar, but he left Issachar to come to Shamir, where he lived and died. He was a *moshia* (deliverer) but also a judge. He judged Israel for 23 years.

The name, **Tola**, means "worm," **Puah** means "splendid," and **Dodo** means "beloved." Put together, Tola is the beloved, splendid worm. What a perfectly awful name to give a man, and yet what a perfectly splendid picture this worm embodies.

The *tola* worm is referenced in Scripture a number of times because it was the source of the scarlet dye used in the Tabernacle fabrics and priestly garments. Tola is often translated not as "worm" but as "scarlet." The scarlet from this worm was also used in offerings for cleansing from leprosy (Leviticus 14) and the defilement of death (Numbers 19:6).

On a less glorious note, the scarlet worm was symbolic of sin and a despised man.

> *"'Come now, and let us reason together,' says the LORD, 'Though your sins are like scarlet, They shall be as white as snow; Though they are red like crimson [tola], They shall be as wool.'"* —Isaiah 1:18

> *"How much less man, who is a maggot, and a son of man, who is a worm [tola]?"* —Job 25:6

Lesson 9: Walking a Winding Road | 189

> *"But I am a worm [tola], and no man; a reproach of men, and despised by the people."* —Psalm 22:6

THE PICTURE OF THE *TOLA* WORM AND CHRIST

The worm is identified as "coccus ilicis" and has a particular behavior that presents us with a poignant picture of Christ on the cross.

As the tola worm prepares to bring her children into life, she fixes herself permanently to the wood of a tree with her eggs deposited beneath her. She lives and dies there as her children begin to take life beneath her. As the mother dies, the scarlet fluid in her body stains the surrounding wood and covers her children in its crimson flow. In the same way, Christ allowed Himself to be fixed to that tree, shedding His own blood to bring many sons to glory (Hebrews 2:10). He died for us, that we might live through Him.

2. **From what oppressor did Tola save Israel?**

   The verse clearly says that after Abimelech, Tola arose to save [Hebrew: *yasha*] Israel, but there is no oppressor identified except perhaps Abimelech, but he was dead. Did the death of Abimelech relieve the oppression? Does the death of any tyrant end the oppression? No, not usually. There is always the fall-out from the overturn of power, and a vacuum where leadership had once been. What happens when no new leader steps into the place of leadership? Chaos reigns, or there is a renewed fight for the kingship.

   A new leader was clearly needed, and so God sent Tola to Shamir. But that doesn't answer the question of what oppressor is being represented in the narrative. To find that answer, we have to look at the picture behind the place name, Shamir.

3. **Why Shamir? What is the significance of Shamir?**

   Shamir is a town just opposite Shechem and within the vicinity of the devastation Abimelech wreaked. The name **Shamir** comes from the common word *shamir*, which means thorns in the sense of something sharp, hard, or flinty—that which pricks or cuts. It is used most often in Isaiah to describe the effects of the Lord's judgment against a nation—on Israel as a whole (Isaiah 5:5-7, 7:23-25), but also Samaria in particular (Isaiah 9:18), as well as Assyria (Isaiah 10:17).

Consider the following verses:

> *"For wickedness burns as the fire; It shall devour the briers [shamir] and thorns, and kindle in the thickets of the forest; They shall mount up like rising smoke. Through the wrath of the LORD of hosts the land is burned up, and the people shall be as fuel for the fire; no man shall spare his brother."* —Isaiah 9:18-19

This is exactly how Abimelech's wickedness played out. As a result of choosing the bramble king, the Land was overrun with his thorns and briers and had to be burned. But then the thorns and briers sprang up again in the wake of the devastation.

> *"And now, please let Me tell you what I will do to My vineyard: I will take away its hedge, and it shall be burned; and break down its wall, and it shall be trampled down. I will lay it waste; It shall not be pruned or dug, but there shall come up briers [shamir] and thorns. I will also command the clouds that they rain no rain on it. For the vineyard of the LORD of hosts is the house of Israel, and the men of Judah are His pleasant plant. He looked for justice, but behold, oppression; for righteousness, but behold, a cry for help."* —Isaiah 5:5-7

This is a picture of judgment against oppression and unrighteousness. Once God's vineyard (Israel) was laid waste, thorns and briers sprang up where there had once been gardens and fruitfulness.

> *"It shall happen in that day, that wherever there could be a thousand vines worth a thousand shekels of silver, it will be for briers [shamir] and thorns. With arrows and bows men will come there, because all the land will become briers [shamir] and thorns. And to any hill which could be dug with the hoe, you will not go there for fear of briers [shamir] and thorns; but it will become a range for oxen and a place for sheep to roam."* —Isaiah 7:23-25

Where the word *shamir* is used in the Old Testament, it is most often in reference to a place being laid to waste, where judgment has come. A fire has swept through the land, destroying all the good vineyards, and in their place, thorns and briers *[shamir]* spring up again. The land becomes a hard, thorny place that is unfruitful and difficult in which to live. And so begins the cycle where gardens are given over to thorns and briers, fire and devastation, only to grapple with thorns and briers again. It is a vicious cycle that all began when the people chose for themselves the bramble king with his crown of thorns and so incurred the curse. (While the place named Shamir may not actually be like this, this is the picture embodied in that name.)

PICTURE SUMMARY

Tola, God's judge and deliverer, left his home in Issachar to come to Shamir, the place of thorns, and dwell alongside those people recovering from a devastating judgment. He did not come to save them from an outside oppressor as the other judges had, but to save them from the devastation their own behavior had brought on them as a result of having chosen the cursed bramble king to rule over them. Tola ruled and judged Israel, dealing with their issues and providing instruction, for 23 years. He is a picture of Christ as Savior, but also the Holy Spirit as helper.

This judge embodies the hope of renewed fruitfulness and peace after the devastation—something we can experience in a small way when God brings us out of our oppressions and begins to restore our lives. But this rebuilding can only happen when we return to Him.

APPLY THE PICTURE

4. **There are two conditions that land God's people among the *shamir* and thorns. Read Isaiah 32:9-15 and Zechariah 7:12. How are the conditions of the people described?**

   Isaiah 32:9-15 describes a people at ease who have become complacent, upon whom judgment falls suddenly, and who are laid waste. They weep for the fruitful fields, which have turned to *shamir*.

   Zechariah 7:12 describes a people who have *"made their hearts like flint [shamir], refusing to hear the law and the words which the LORD of hosts had sent by His Spirit through the former prophets."* And so God's wrath burns against the unrepentant people, they fall under judgment, and their land is left desolate and given to brier and thorns.

   Complacent people. People whose lives are occupied with pursuits after pleasure or riches.

   Hardened people. People who are unrepentant and have hardened themselves to God, and as a result, suffer devastation in their lives, fall on hard times, and become occupied with difficulties and sorrows.

In His parable of the sower, Jesus talks about believers who fall into thorny places in life, whose lives get overgrown by *shamir*.

> *"And some fell among thorns, and the thorns sprang up with it and choked it . . . Now the ones that fell among thorns are those who, when they have heard, go out and are choked with cares, riches, and pleasures of life, and bring no fruit to maturity."* —Luke 8:7, 14

Knowing what we know about the *shamir* and how they came about for Israel, how does the seed in the parable end up among the thorns?

The brier and thorns are part of this cycle that began with complacency, unrepentance, unrighteousness, and pursuing wrong things by wrong ways (e.g., Abimelech pursuing the kingship by Canaanite ways).

Unrighteousness leads to oppression and cries for help (Jotham's cry that invoked the curse on Abimelech and the men of Shechem).

Oppression leads to devastation, and devastation is followed by the *shamir* and thorns overtaking what had once been fruitful fields. And then comes the weeping.

When you become occupied with things in this life that take you away from a walk with God, there are consequences. Life gets thorny. Life becomes oppressive, even when there is no actual oppressor in your life. You are your own worst enemy in this. Tola doesn't actually save anyone from an outside oppressor. This is an internal oppression that the people bring upon themselves.

5. **How do you deal with a land overgrown with *shamir* that seems unredeemable?**

The only way to deal with the brambles is to set them on fire and purge the land.

The fire in the land began as a problem with the people being disobedient and pursuing what was right in their own eyes. They had become preoccupied with pursuing things in this life by the Baal and Ashtoreth way and had no intention of returning to God or God's ways.

6. **How do you redeem a preoccupied and unrepentant people?**

Abimelech, the bramble king, and the men of Shechem stand as examples of those who are positionally in the Land and yet have fallen away and become so unrepentant that the only solution is for the LORD to consume them—or have them consume each other. He lets their carnal "Canaanite" side run itself out to the bitter end. The resulting overthrow is likened to a fire burning through the people.

The overthrow that these men experienced can become our experience as well if we follow the same path.

> *"For it is impossible for those who were once enlightened, and have tasted the heavenly gift, and have become partakers of the Holy Spirit, and have tasted the good word of God and the powers of the age to come, if they fall away, to renew them again to repentance, since they crucify again for themselves the Son of God, and put Him to an open shame. For the earth which drinks in the rain that often comes upon it, and bears herbs useful for those by whom it is cultivated, receives blessing from God; but if it bears thorns and briers, it is rejected and near to being cursed, whose end is to be burned."* —Hebrews 6:4-8

God must deal with our unrepentance, whether it comes from complacency or hardness of heart. He may need to set a fire in our lives to clear out the thorns that choke us, and it will be a devastating overthrow of our lives.

There are those who never repent, and God takes them out of the picture. But those who do repent, or are simply victims of the curse, often face the brier and thorns (cares and sorrows) that spring up as a consequence and overrun their devastated life. But God doesn't leave them to deal with the devastation alone. For those who turn to Him, He is also a Savior who comes to their place of thorns and helps break the cycle and rebuild.

PROFILE OF THIS OPPRESSION

Through this study of Judges, we have been talking about oppressions and how we get into them. There are oppressions that we cause by our own decisions and actions, and we can get caught up in the *shamir* and thorns for that reason.

But life can be thorny for those who are in the middle of an oppression not of their own making. Believers can get caught up and become collateral damage in the wake of other people's disobedience, like the people of Thebez in Abimelech's narrative.

Life can also be thorny for those who are faced with a life that has been devastated as a consequence of their own sin and are trying to get back on track with God and make something fruitful out of what has become a field of thorns. In the end, it takes an out-pouring of the Spirit to make that life fruitful again (Isaiah 32:12-18). It also takes the work of a Savior. Tola presents the picture of a particular experience of life—the return of a devastated people through the work of a savior and the beginning of hope for the future.

Questions for Reflection:

Consider the cycle of the *shamir*. Disobedience and unrepentant sin lead to oppression. Oppression leads to devastation, and devastation is followed by the *shamir* and thorns suddenly overtaking us so that we become unfruitful. And then comes the weeping. Do you feel you are caught somewhere in this pattern?

- If you are feeling oppressed, have you considered where the oppression began? Is there an issue you in your life that you need to address or a sin of which you should repent?

- Does the conflict involve something you have been pursuing? Have you diverted into pursuing an earthly gain or reward as opposed to a spiritual one?

- What effect is it having on your life and the lives of those around you?

    My thoughts: There are right ways and wrong ways to pursue the crown (reward). When Abimelech could not realize his desire by godly means, he pursued it by taking the Canaanite path. He took his crown by force, but did not keep it. In doing so, he brought the people into oppression.

- Oppression leads to devastation, which is a consequence of sin and judgment (whether on your part or another's). If you have experienced devastation in your life, did the Savior come to you in the wake of that devastation to offer comfort or guidance? If so, how?

- New thorns can begin to grow out of the devastation. Has life become thorny for you in the aftermath? If so, how?

- Is it worth it to you to suffer the devastation and deal with the thorns in order to get back on a godly path and find some peace and fruitfulness?

Or is it easier to live in a thorny place by finding your own ways to cope?

Remember the lesson of Deborah and Barak. The people took those winding byways of coping and compromise that only made the oppression last longer. Coping can become oppressive. It will not break the cycle. Getting back to the godly path is what will bring the peace, quietness, and righteousness you crave.

- For Israel in the days of the judges, the Savior, Jesus Christ, was yet to come. The hope of Him was embodied in the judges who were cast in the role as deliverers as well as helpers. Now that the Savior has been realized, how does He play a part in breaking this cycle of oppression?

Oppression doesn't happen only because of sin in a believer's life. We can suffer oppression for following a *godly* path in life, in which case we endure the hardship and are rewarded with crowns in the coming Kingdom. But we can get also sucked into the oppression caused by other people doing what is right in their eyes and falling into sin.

- Have you become occupied by someone else's oppression? If so, now that you are in this thorny place, how do you get out? Should you get out? Might there be a purpose in God's eyes for staying where you are?

God sent Tola to live and die in the place of Shamir for the sake of helping the people living in those conditions.

- Can you look beyond your own condition to help others suffering under the same conditions?

- How does being in that thorny place yourself make you more able to help those people? (Remember "Me" from Isaiah 50:4-10.)

BUILD THE PICTURE

Jair, Judges 10:3-5

7. What do we know about Jair?

Jair was a Gileadite, from the tribe of Manasseh.

His name means "he whom God enlightens."

He had thirty sons (a measure of personal fruitfulness), who ride thirty donkeys (a measure of prosperity), and they had thirty towns called Havoth Jair (a relative kingdom).

Thirty, in Jewish tradition, is associated with kingship. Thirty is also the number associated with the Hebrew letter *lamed*, which comes from the root *lamad*, meaning "to teach or enlighten." This reinforces the meaning of his name. The three sets of thirty paired with the meaning of Jair's name gives us a picture of a ruler who enlightens—brings judgment and understanding to—his people.

Unlike Tola, Jair was a judge only. He judged Israel for 22 years.

He died and was buried at Camon. Camon means "to be risen, raised up, or to stand," in the sense of being exalted and established.

THE GRAND PICTURE: ABIMELECH, TOLA, JAIR

Abimelech's disobedience brought on the curse that started the oppression and fire that led to the devastation.

God called Tola to the place of thorns to deal with a people who had come through that devastation.

Now we have a follow-on picture of a judge who has "risen"—become exalted and established—to reign over a veritable kingdom with many sons and vast wealth. His name suggests a picture of God's light that has come upon a man. The man embodied that light, and he ruled and judged in that light. This is a picture of the kingdom to come.

THE PICTURE OF CHRIST

Before His death, Christ became the picture of Abimelech, the bramble king with a crown of thorns.

Matthew 27:28-29 tells us:

> *"And they stripped Him and put a scarlet robe on Him. When they had twisted a crown of thorns, they put it on His head, and a reed in His right hand. And they bowed the knee before Him and mocked Him, saying, 'Hail, King of the Jews!'"* —Matthew 27:28-29

For Christ, the true King, to assume the picture of the inglorious Bramble King was a cruel irony and a mockery. Even so, He took upon his head that crown of thorns—that vicious circle of the *shamir*—and with it, the curse that initiated the never-ending cycle of oppression and devastation.

At His death, He then fulfiled the picture of Tola the worm who came to save a people under that curse and caught in a place of *shamir*. He shed His blood on the wood of the tree that He might free them once and for all from the curse and thorns and restore them to abundant life.

He died, yet arose to be exalted and established, to reign as king and judge in the picture of Jair. This is a picture of Christ and a kingdom to come.

We know that before this future kingdom comes, there must be a day of judgment and reckoning for believers, but also for the nations. Christ may have broken the curse for believers, but this world is not yet free from the effects of the curse, or the cycle of oppression and devastation. When He comes again, Christ will come not as the savior but as the judge, and there will be a reckoning,

> *"So the Light of Israel will be for a fire, and his Holy One for a flame; It will burn and devour His thorns and his briers* [shamir] *in one day."*
> —Isaiah 10:17

LESSON 10

Oppression #6: Jephthah, Ibzan, Elon, and Abdon

READ

Judges 10:6–12:7 (Jephthah) and 12:8-15 (Ibzan, Elon, Abdon)

BUILD THE PICTURE

The Oppression, Judges 10:6-16

1. **Who did Israel serve this time?**

    They served the Baals and Ashtoreths, but also the gods of Syria, Sidon, Moab, Ammon, and the Philistines. This was an all-out encroachment on Israel from every side.

2. **Who oppressed Israel, and how long did the oppression last?**

    There was a dual oppressor this time: the Ammonites and the Philistines. Note: the Philistines were on the western coast and classified as Canaanites; the Ammonites were on the eastern coast and outsiders. Israel was fighting an oppression on two fronts: east and west, internal and external. This went on for 18 years. The Ammonites take the forefront in Jephthah's narrative; Samson will deal with the Philistines.

3. **What tribes were affected?**

    Initially, all of the tribes east of the Jordan (in Gilead) were overrun, but then the Ammonites crossed over to fight Judah, Benjamin, and Ephraim as well.

4. **The pattern: What has been God's response to Israel's cries for relief until now?**

    - **Othniel and Ehud?** The children of Israel cried out, and God immediately sent a savior.

- **Deborah?** The children of Israel cried out, and God sent a prophetess who engaged a savior.

- **Gideon?** The children of Israel cried out, and God sent a prophet to tell them to do some self-reflection. Then God raised up a savior.

- **Here?** The children of Israel cried out, and this time, God said, "I will deliver you no more. Go plead with your many gods for deliverance."

5. **What caused God to relent?**

    The people put away their idols and served the LORD. God's love for His people was so great that His soul could not endure their misery. It is hard to imagine such a wayward people being loved like that, but that is how God loves them, even now. That is how He loves all His children.

Jephthah Deals with Family, Judges 10:7-11:11

6. **Where did the battle set up?**

    The people of Ammon gathered together and encamped at Gilead. Israel encamped at Mizpah. The leaders of Gilead sought the man who would lead the battle. That, in itself, was a deviation from the pattern. God was the one who chose all the other deliverers prior to this. This time the men of Gilead chose for themselves, and they chose Jephthah.

7. **What do we know about Jephthah?**

    He was a son of the patriarch Gilead by a harlot. He was driven out of the family and went to live in the Land of Tob (Ammonite territory), where worthless [empty] men gathered to him. He became their leader and went about the country raiding.

    He had a bad relationship with his family. His brothers disinherited him because he was born to a harlot, and they only treated him like family when they wanted something from him.

    The name **Jephthah** means "he who opens [a way]; he who sets free or lets loose." His brothers looked to him to set them free from the Ammonite oppressor.

8. **Jephthah and Abimelech have similar pictures in their narratives. How are they similar and different?**

   Similarities:

   - Both were stigmatized because their mothers were considered less than honorable. Abimelech was the son of a concubine (servant). Jephthah was the son of a harlot.

   - Both decamped from their father's house but retained their identity with their father.

   - Both gathered to themselves bands of reckless and worthless men (although they used these men differently).

   Differences:

   - Abimelech used his army to slay the brothers with whom he had a grievance. Jephthah didn't avenge himself against the brothers who wronged him, although he could have.

   - Both were offered a rulership of sorts, but it came about in different ways. Abimelech took a kingship by force. Jephthah was offered a lesser headship which he accepted.

   - Jephthah retained his identity with God, where Abimelech did not. Jephthah gave the LORD credit for the deliverance with which he was tasked.

     > "... 'If you take me back home to fight against the people of Ammon, and the LORD delivers them to me, shall I be your head?'"
     > —Judges 11:9

   - As he accepted the headship, Jephthah acknowledged that the LORD was the greater authority as judge and ruler of the people and he was accountable for his treatment of his brethren.

     > "... and Jephthah spoke all his words before the LORD in Mizpah." —Judges 11:11b

   Abimelech did not acknowledge any accountability.

9. **What reason did his brothers give for approaching Jephthah now?**

   The men of Gilead had a problem. The Ammonites had moved into the land and were oppressing the people. They needed a man with an army who would fight the enemy. (Funny that no one from their own ranks stepped up.) They didn't go to Jephthah because they felt bad about how they had treated him. It doesn't seem that they felt any conviction to make amends. They had a problem, they needed a solution, and they needed someone who was expendable and no great loss to the family if he failed. And they were willing to make some concessions to get it.

10. What did they offer him as compensation?

They offered him headship over Gilead. Headship (Hebrew: *rosh*) is not the same as kingship (Hebrew: *melech*). This was more like a chieftain or clan leader.

11. Jephthah agreed, but he went to Mizpah for the official contract-making. Why Mizpah?

To understand the significance of what was going on here with Jephthah and his brothers, we need to look back at Mizpah's origin. You can read the full account in Genesis 31:48-52, but I will summarize it here.

Summary of Genesis 31: Jacob had an uncle named Laban. Laban was family through Jacob's mother's line and by marriage, but he was a foreigner—a Syrian—who didn't serve Jacob's God.

Laban was an abusive father-in-law to Jacob. He tried to rob Jacob every chance he got. He dealt treacherously with his own daughter, Leah, and used his other daughter, Rachel, to extort more profit out of Jacob. Laban had this mentality of "what is mine is mine, and what is yours is mine." He was greedy and manipulative, and he yet demanded integrity from Jacob. (A lot like the world today when dealing with Christians.) When Jacob tried to get away from him, Laban came after him, and there was a confrontation at Mizpah.

Mizpah was the place where Jacob and Laban came to an agreement over how to separate and how family relations would work going forward.

Mizpah had two names—Galeed (from which the name Gilead was derived) and Mizpah. It was named Galeed for the heap of stones that the men set up as a memorial mound. **Galeed** actually means "heap of witnesses," suggesting that if the covenant wasn't honored, the stones would cry out to God as witnesses. In addition to the heap of stones, Jacob set up a stone pillar called a *mizpah* or "watchtower." The *mizpah* was the reminder of the boundary and covenant between Jacob and Laban. **Mizpah** became the official name of the site.

These were the two covenant conditions struck at Mizpah between Jacob and Laban:

1) God would watch over the children of Israel to see that they didn't deal treacherously with their own families by afflicting them. Laban demanded that Jacob not deal treacherously with Laban's daughters and grandchildren.

2) Jacob instituted a second condition that there should be a line which family was not allowed to cross to do each other harm or go to war with one another. Jacob added this to the covenant, establishing a boundary to separate himself and his treacherous father-in-law.

Mizpah became the place where grievances and family issues were resolved. It was a place where families made covenants before God in regards to how family relations would work going forward, how they treated one another, and where boundaries were.

Like Laban, the men of Gilead were claiming the familial relationship with Jephthah, but their intent was solely to use him. Like Jacob, Jephthah was faced with having to reconcile with this family who had treated him brutally in the past.

Jephthah took the elders back to Mizpah to speak his covenant before the Lord, solidifying his headship over all of them. He spoke before the *galeed* (the heap of witnesses) and the *mizpah* (watchtower). When all this was done, if his brothers dealt treacherously and denied his headship, the stones would cry out.

APPLY THE PICTURE

12. When family reconciliation is needed, what barriers have to be overcome?

Remember the stumbling blocks for return. They don't just apply to a return to God. They can apply in family reconciliations as well. Barriers to reconciliation include: despair, self-pity, and rejecting love; fear; shame and humiliation; destructive anger or silence; and all the other outworking of our sinful nature including a desire for personal vengeance and vindication.

In Jephthah's case, he might have felt self-pity, shame, and humiliation for having been cast out of the family over something about which he could do nothing. It would have been very tempting to lash back with destructive anger and seek revenge, or tell them to go deal with their problems themselves and withdraw into silence. Fear of being hurt again and a lack of trust could most certainly have been a stumbling block that prevents restoration in the family.

13. **Why do you think Jephthah agreed to their proposal, knowing that his family was using him when their hearts hadn't changed toward him?**

    Somehow, in spite of his circumstances, Jephthah grasped the understanding of God's power and sovereignty and a vision of what was important—preserving the kingdom. He valued the headship and was willing to fight to gain it. Clinging to God's sovereignty, power, and love, and keeping the kingdom goal in sight, is what keeps a person from stumbling in oppressive circumstances.

14. **Do we treat our Savior like this, wanting only a solution to the problems we get ourselves into without having a change of heart or even desiring to repair our relationship with Him first?**

Questions for Reflection:

- If you were in Jephthah's shoes, how would you have responded to family that had treated you poorly?

- Have you had to establish boundaries within your own family? If so, what kind?

BUILD THE PICTURE

Jephthah deals with the Ammonites, Judges 11:12-40

JEPHTHAH'S JUDGMENT

Jephthah sorted things out with his family, provisionally, and was established at Mizpah. Then he turned to deal with the Ammonites. Jephthah's dealing with the Ammonites resembled something like a court case as Jephthah stepped into his judge's shoes to deliberate the issue. He didn't address the king of Ammon personally; he sent messengers (as a superior would to an inferior).

15. What was Ammon's grievance against Israel?

> "Because Israel took away my land when they came up out of Egypt, from the Arnon as far as the Jabbok, and to the Jordan."
> —Judges 11:13

Ammon laid claim to the territories of Reuben and Gad that Moses and the children of Israel had taken from the Amorites (Numbers 21:24-26). This was the land that lay between the Arnon and Jabbok rivers, and from the Jordan as far east as the border of Ammon. They took the land from the Amorites, but didn't infringe on Ammonites. The Ammonites never really had a claim to this land.

16. What other territories had the Ammonites infringed on?

In addition to Reuben and Gad, the Ammonites had raided across the Jordan as far as Judah, Benjamin, and Ephraim.

17. How did Jephthah build his case? What were his three main arguments?

1) The credit for taking the land belonged to God; therefore, the land ultimately belong to God. This isn't a fight for territory between Ammon and Israel. It is a fight between Chemosh and God.

2) Jephthah brought up the point about Balak, who was king of Moab in the days when Israel took the land. Why bring up Balak?

Before the territories of Reuben and Gad belonged to the Amorites, they belonged to Balak, King of Moab. The Amorites took the land from Moab, so Moab would have had the greater claim, and yet Moab didn't dispute the territory.

3) How long had it been since Israel took over the disputed territory? Three hundred years had passed. While that was a generalized time span, it made the point that if this was such an issue, Ammon should have spoken up sooner.

18. What was Jephthah's conclusion?

> "Therefore I have not sinned against you, but you wronged me by fighting against me. May the LORD, the Judge, render judgment this day between the children of Israel and the people of Ammon."
> —Judges 11:27

Notice the word Jephthah used for judge: *shaphat*. Jephthah himself was a *shaphat* (chieftain-judge) over Gilead, but he deferred his own station to the greater authority of the LORD. The LORD was the one who had given the land to Israel, and He was the great Shaphat over this situation.

I think it is absolutely marvelous how Jephthah embraced his relationship with the LORD and gave glory to Him in this circumstance, when everyone in his life had conspired to disenfranchise him from that identity and place. He was the son of a harlot, and yet he recited Israel's history going back three hundred years. Who taught him that? Who taught him to have this understanding of God and relationship with Him? It really is astounding.

JEPHTHAH'S VOW AND VICTORY

19. What was Jephthah's vow and was it a rash vow?

In Judges 11:30-31, it is clear that Jephthah was devoting a person to death—the one who came out of his house would be a person and not an animal. He left the selection of that person open-ended. If the LORD was the one avenging Israel, then it was the LORD's right to choose the sacrifice befitting the act. It seemed rash, and yet he made this vow under the influence of the Holy Spirit.

Judges 11:39 says that Jephthah carried out his vow as he vowed, and offered his child as a burnt offering. That is the literal statement made in the text, but it is one that is difficult to accept. Without doubt,

God hates human sacrifice, and particularly child sacrifice. We feel compelled to explain how God's judge could perform something that goes against Mosaic Law and God's very character.

It can be argued that maybe Jephthah sent his daughter into a reclusive lifestyle as a way of devoting her to God. This might explain the emphasis on lamenting her virginity. While that makes for a more reasonable explanation of Jephthah's action, it is a construct not defined in the language of the text. The text is fairly unequivocal when it says he did what he vowed.

Perhaps Jephthah did not know the Mosaic Law's provision for redemption of humans since he had been expatriated from family and country? That seems odd, given that he knew so much of Israel's history and had retained such a strong identity with Israel's God.

Perhaps this episode was meant as an object lesson against making rash vows. It is possible.

But what about the prophetic picture of Christ that runs through Jephthah's account? That is something we cannot overlook. At some point, God must communicate, if only in picture models, that regardless of His abhorence of child sacrifice, He Himself would offer His only son as payment for delivering His people. If we explain away this text, saying that it does not mean what it says, do we risk leaving out a crucial part of the Messianic picture? Yes, we do.

The first rule of hermenuetics is to take the text for its literal meaning, unless a figurative meaning is clearly indicated by the surrounding context, e.g. Isaiah 5:7, *"For the vineyard of the LORD of hosts is the house of Israel..."* The Isaiah 5 passage has a figurative context indicated by the metaphor at its beginning. By contrast, Jephthah's narrative has no such figurative context. It has a literal context, and so, for the purpose of this study, I insist on letting the text say what it says. Jephthah vowed to offer as a burnt offering the person who came out of his house to greet him, and he did as he vowed, to his great anguish.

20. What made this episode with Jephthah's daughter so tragic?

Her innocence. The passage dwells very heavily on the emotion of the events as they played out. It belabors Jephthah's reaction to his daughter coming out the door to greet him, his daughter's response, and even the community's response.

21. The daughter submitted willingly. Why? What does her reaction tell us about her values and view of God?

The daughter's acceptance of her own impending death was astounding, but then there was something of the father in the daughter. Her father had raised her to understand the sovereignty of the LORD and the obligation to fulfill vows. She came out the door singing praise, and it is almost as if she offered herself as a sacrifice of praise for the LORD's avenging of Israel. She asked only for a two-month delay for her own lament.

Questions for Reflection:

- Why make the deliverance of a people conditional on the death of a person? Why would that death have to be part of the picture?

- It is a horrifying thought to think of an innocent young girl put to death over what appears to be a rash vow. Are we as equally horrified at the thought of God putting to death His own Son to set us free?

- Was the daughter's sacrifice worth the price? What would you sacrifice for God's glory and His purpose?

Jephthah deals with the Ephraimites, Judges 12:1-7

22. Of what did Ephraim accuse Jephthah?

Not calling them to battle.

23. The Ephraimites' threat to burn his house in vengeance seemed out of proportion with the grievance. What was driving this?

Their anger smacks of arrogance and is similar to Abimelech's irrational rage in going after his own brethren with fire.

This was the same charge the Ephraimites had once leveled at Gideon in the days of the Midianite oppression. Much like their experience under the Midianites, the men of Ephraim had been victimized by the Ammonites, and their reaction when coming out of that oppression was one of destructive anger—except their anger was misdirected at Jephthah. Does that happen to victims? Yes, I think it does. The transference of anger was unwarranted, but it was a very real reaction nevertheless.

There might be another issue motivating this extreme response. Consider the passing of time: 40 years of rest (under Gideon) + 3 years (Abimelech) + 23 years (Tola) + 22 years (Jair) + 18 years (Ammonite oppression) = 106 years total.

The men in Gideon's day took issue with Gideon and received a soft, placating answer that soothed their egos but did not deal with their arrogance. Those men went on to raise up succeeding generations with the same attitude, and each generation grew more arrogant, aggressive, and entitled than the previous generation. The Ammonite oppression didn't humble them. Instead, it fed their victim mentality and reinforced the attitude of entitlement.

Jephthah was forced to deal with this.

Jephthah did not give his accusers a soft answer. He got back up in their face with the truth, and he attacked the entitled attitude. God had appointed him judge over Israel, and he was modeling God in his judgment against the Ephraimites.

24. According to Jephthah, the Ephraimites' accusation was unfair. How did he see it?

He claimed that he called them to fight, but they did not respond; therefore, he took his life into his own hands and fought without them. And God delivered the enemy into his hands.

Didn't Jephthah have more right to be angry than the men of Ephraim? Keep in mind, Jephthah had vanquished the enemy at great cost to himself. He had just put his only daughter to death in honoring the vow he made to deliver his people from their oppressor. And now he faced this squabble with his brethren over who was greatest in the kingdom. I imagine he looked at them, thinking, "You have no idea what you ask for or the kind of sacrifice it demanded."

All the Ephraimites cared about was the glory. They scorned the cost. In response, Jephthah's own righteous anger broke out against the Ephraimites.

25. What did the Ephraimites imply when they said "You Gileadites are fugitives of Ephraim among the Ephraimites and Manassites"?

In essence, they were saying, "You belong to us. What is mine is mine, and what is yours is mine." They came at Jephthah with the same argument that the Ammonites had used (and the same attitude that Laban had used on Jacob). They came at him like the enemy, so Jephthah dealt with them as an enemy.

26. The covenant at Mizpah demanded a respect for boundaries. How did this theme of boundaries play out in Jephthah's narrative?

The Ephraimites crossed the physical boundary of the Jordan to invade Gilead's territory for harm. It was an act of war. The Ephraimites crossed the boundary in the family relationship by fighting their own brethren and treating them like fugitives who deserved to be killed.

Jephthah re-established the physical boundaries, and then treated those who escaped from the battle as fugitives to be killed in an eye-for-an-eye style justice.

The taunting test: There was something of a derisive taunt in the test that the Gileadites devised to identify the Ephraimite escapees. Whenever a man of Ephraim came to the Jordan to cross back over to Ephraim's territory, the Gileadites would tell him to say "shibboleth" which means "flowing water" in Hebrew. If they wanted to cross the flowing waters, they had to say "flowing water" and pronounce it correctly. The Ephraimites couldn't pronounce the "sh" sound because of their dialect and so were detected.

27. Jephthah delivered Israel from the oppressor, but did his effort bring rest to the land?

No. The *shaqat* rest (quietness) that Israel experienced in the days of Gideon was the last rest they would have under the judges.

APPLY THE PICTURE

PROFILE OF THIS OPPRESSION

Jephthah dealt with oppression on three levels:

1) Family level: He had to be reconciled with a family who had dealt with him cruelly in the past. In this case, some barriers had to be overcome before reconciliation could happen.

2) **National level:** He had to deal with the foreign Ammonite oppressor who claimed Israel had taken something from them and wanted it back. He had to re-establish physical boundaries with the outside world. It played out in a court-like picture of judgment being rendered, and then there was war.

3) **Congregational level:** He had to deal with the Ephraimites who were acting like Ammonites. They accused him of taking what should have been theirs and came at him with threats. He judged them, but because of their unrepentance, it ended in war.

We are faced with similar oppressions in regards to family, nation, and congregation.

In regards to family, we may face issues that require putting up boundaries, particularly when family is abusive. On the other hand, some issues might need barriers removed for reconciliation.

In regards to Ammonites, that is, the secular world, we do not battle over a physical kingdom as Jephthah did. In this age, we battle to hold the borders of a spiritual kingdom against an Enemy who would impose his own kingdom and values on us. Though the battle is spiritual, we often find ourselves facing physical, worldly combatants.

28. When we find ourselves in contention with this world over the right to physical things, do we fight?

In Matthew 5:38-42, Jesus says:

"You have heard that it was said, 'An eye for an eye and a tooth for a tooth.' But I tell you not to resist an evil person. But whoever slaps you on your right cheek, turn the other to him also. If anyone wants to sue you and take away your tunic, let him have your cloak also. And whoever compels you to go one mile, go with him two. Give to him who asks you, and from him who wants to borrow from you do not turn away." —Matthew 5:38-42

29. We may find ourselves fighting the secular world to maintain the right to practice our faith in regards to conscience. Where does the battle play out in this regard?

In courtrooms, through the judicial process.

30. **Sometimes we are called by national leaders to fight for a physical kingdom. Do we fight?**

    This is a very personal decision and driven by many factors, including worldview. I will leave this for you to answer for yourself.

In regards to the congregation, sometimes we are faced with co-laborers who treat us more like outsiders and enemies than fellow believers. Instead of joining us in the fight to hold the borders against the outside world, they begin to view the body of Christ (the congregation or ministry) as a physical kingdom to be fought over, or the fight between fellow believers may simply be over physical things. When this happens, we become no better than the secular world in our pursuits.

31. **What is the source of the fighting?**

    According to James 4:1-6:

    > "Where do wars and fights come from among you? Do they not come from your desires for pleasure that war in your members? You lust and do not have. You murder and covet and cannot obtain. You fight and war. Yet you do not have because you do not ask. You ask and do not receive, because you ask amiss, that you may spend it on your pleasures. Adulterers and adulteresses! Do you not know that friendship with the world is enmity with God? Whoever therefore wants to be a friend of the world makes himself an enemy of God. Or do you think that the Scripture says in vain, "The Spirit who dwells in us yearns jealously"? But He gives more grace. Therefore He says: "God resists the proud, But gives grace to the humble." —James 4:1-6

32. **Fights with foreigners are sorted out in courts of law, but is that how we sort out this kind of fight within the body?**

    Paul blasts the Corinthian church for this very thing:

    > "Dare any of you, having a matter against another, go to law before the unrighteous, and not before the saints? Do you not know that the saints will judge the world? And if the world will be judged by you, are you unworthy to judge the smallest matters? ... I say this to your shame. Is it so, that there is not a wise man among you, not even one, who will be able to judge between his brethren? But brother goes to law against brother, and that before unbelievers! Now therefore, it is already an utter failure for you that you go to law against one another. Why do you not rather accept wrong? Why

do you not rather let yourselves be cheated? No, you yourselves do wrong and cheat, and you do these things to your brethren!"
—1 Corinthians 6:1-2, 5-8

Why not let yourself be cheated? There is a novel thought. Is this thing over which you are fighting of any heavenly value, or is it something transient? Where are your values? Let issues between believers be sorted out between believers who discern the difference between what is of spiritual value and what is only of earthly value. And do not treat fellow believers like the enemy!

33. What should be our goal in any conflict with a fellow believer?

Peace, good-will, and the meeting of needs on both sides.

Questions for Reflection:

In regards to family . . .

- Have family members ever crossed boundaries with you? If so, in what way?

- Did you reset the boundaries? If so, how? If not, why not?

- How do you let family know when they have crossed a boundary?

- How does family let you know when you have crossed a boundary with them?

- Is a lack of reconciliation adding to the oppression in your life?

In regards to the secular world . . .

- What kind of borders or boundaries do you fight to maintain against the secular world? What does this fight look like for you?

In regards to community or fellow believers . . .

- When someone accused you wrongly of something, how did you react—like a Gideon or a Jephthah?

BUILD THE PICTURE

Ibzan, Elon, and Abdon, Judges 12:8-15

These three judges follow closely on the heels of Jephthah's narrative and wrap into the big picture of Christ in much the same way Tola and Jair wrapped into Abimelech's narrative. Jephthah parallels the picture of Abimelech to an extent, while Jephthah's daughter is the counterpart to Tola in portraying Christ's death on the cross. Now we have a three-fold picture of the kingdom embodied in Ibzan, Elon, and Abdon. Let's look at each one, and then consider their combined picture.

34. What do we know about Ibzan?

Ibzan means "whiteness" or having the whiteness of tin—a highly crystalline silvery-white metal. He lived and died in Bethlehem, but it isn't specified whether it was the Bethlehem in Zebulun or Judah. He judged Israel for seven years.

He had thirty sons, thirty daughters, and brought in thirty wives for his sons. (You couldn't walk around Bethlehem without tripping over one of his relatives.) This was a kingdom overflowing with an abundance of progeny.

35. What do we know about Elon?

Elon means "mighty" as an oak is mighty. The root word *ayil*, gives us examples of other things that are mighty—a ram, pillar, strong man, and mighty tree.

He came from Zebulun and died in Aijalon. **Zebulun** means "exalted dwelling place." **Aijalon** means "field of stags or rams" from the root word *ayal*, which is the intensive form of *ayil*, or "mighty ram."

He judged Israel for ten years.

36. What do we know about Abdon?

Unlike Ibzan and Elon, he is not identified with a place so much as with his fathers. He was Abdon, son of Hillel the Pirathonite.

Abdon means "servile" from the root word *abad*, meaning "to work or serve." This is the description of a servant.

Hillel means "singing, praising" from the root *halal*, meaning "to shine, praise, or boast" (as in hallelujah).

Pirathon means "princely" from the root word *parah*, meaning "leader or commander." Pirathon was assigned to the tribe of Ephraim. Ephraim means "doubly fruitful."

So, in other words, he is *a servant, son of praise, son of the king.*

He judged Israel for eight years and, much like Jair, he was known for his personal progeny in the form of forty sons and thirty grandsons, and a wealth of seventy donkeys.

ABOUT HEBREW NUMBERS

The narrative of these three judges dwells heavily on the use of numbers, which form much of the picture. The meaning of numbers in the Scripture is important, but their interpretation can go far afield, especially when studied from Jewish sources that incorporate elements of kabbalah and traditions. The best way to understand the meaning of numbers is to investigate them the way we look up Hebrew words; that is, look for where they are used in the biblical text and in what context, then draw some conclusions from that. I have summarized for you below the basic pictures behind the numbers in these judges' narratives.

Seven: Seven is the number of completeness and perfection (spiritual and physical). It marks the completion of creation week and is tied to the picture of sabbath rest.

Eight: Eight is one step beyond the completion represented by seven that marks a step into a new beginning. It is tied to the celebration of the Feast of Tabernacles, which is a seven-day feast held over for an eighth day. The Feast of Tabernacles is associated with Messiah's kingdom (Zechariah 14) and the eighth day, a new beginning after that.

Ten: Ten is one of the numbers representing completion, along with the number three, seven, and twelve. It represents testimony. In the book of Genesis, the phrase "God said" appears ten times which is testimony to His creative power. It represents the fullness of the law, in the giving of the ten commandments. It represents completeness of order, but also the fullness of judgment, as seen in the ten plagues on Egypt.

Note: *Any number times ten represents a fullness of that number.*

Thirty: Thirty (3 x 10) is associated with the Hebrew letter *lamed*, meaning teaching and enlightenment; it is also the redemption price of a bondservant, and beginning of ministry or service as priest or king (King David is an example).

Forty: Forty (4 x 10) represents the fullness of creation. It can represent a generation. For example, Israel spent forty years in the wilderness until that generation was dead. It can also represent the fullness and completion of time or action, as in "forty days and forty nights" or the land having rest for forty years.

Seventy: Seventy (7 x 10) is completion in its fullness. The number seventy brings to mind Daniel's seventy weeks as well as Jesus' command to forgive not just seven times, but seventy times seven.

APPLY THE PICTURE

THE PICTURE OF CHRIST IN JEPHTHAH, IBZAN, ELON, AND ABDON

Israel in Jesus' day was a lot like Israel in Jephthah's day. There was an outside oppressor, Rome, but there was also a tremendous amount of oppression within Israel itself at a congregational level. They understood obedience, but had no heart for God. Their spiritual shepherds fattened themselves on God's flock. They walked according to what was right in their own eyes, and they afflicted one another even as Rome afflicted them. And God was watching. Into this hotbed of oppression, Jesus, like Jephthah, was born.

Jephthah's mother was a harlot; Jesus' mother, Mary, would have been considered a harlot for having borne a son out of wedlock and not by Joseph. Jesus, like Jephthah, suffered rejection by his own people. Jesus lived in exile for a period of time to escape Herod; He left Judea for a ministry in Galilee when His own brothers rejected Him.

There is a shadow picture of Jesus' triumphal entry in Jephthah's return to Mizpah. Jephthah's name means "he who opens a way; he who sets free or turns loose." Inherent in the name was the expectation that Jephthah would be the one to free his people from their oppressor. There was the same expectation of Jesus. While His own people hailed him as king, their expectation of Jesus as king was that He would throw off the oppression of Rome as the Messiah and claim the physical kingdom—not that He would reconcile them to God through Himself. Jesus allowed Himself to be hailed as king, and when the Pharisees objected, He rebuked them, saying that if the people did not hail Him as king, the stones would cry out (Luke 19). Jesus' rebuke evokes that picture of the covenant made at Mizpah before the *galeel*—the heap of stones who were witnesses. His statement carried a warning to the Pharisees against crossing familial boundaries with the intent to do harm and not to afflict one another because God was watching.

Like the Ephraimites with Jephthah, the Pharisees contended with Jesus over His right to headship over His people at a national and congregational level. They charged him with horning in on territory that was rightfully theirs as spiritual leaders—that He and His followers were nothing more than renegades. They refused to acknowledge His messiahship as king over His people. They even raised the point of his less-than-honorable birth. The fight over words escalated to a physical fight as Jesus took up a whip of cords, and in righteous anger and judgment, drove them out of His Father's house, just as Jephthah drove the Ephraimites out of his father's territory. It was a moment of reestablishing the boundaries.

The Ephraimites came to Jephthah in the wake of his victory and his daughter's death, demanding a greater place in the kingdom. I imagine Jephthah looked at them wearily and wondered if they would make the same sacrifice he had made to claim the inheritance they presumed to take by force. Similarly, among Jesus' own disciples, we see the argument over who was the greatest in the kingdom. Jesus, knowing at what cost the kingdom would be delivered, questioned whether they were willing to pay the cost he would have to pay to achieve it.

The least addressed oppression in Jesus' narrative is the fight with the external oppressor, Rome. His confrontation with the Roman authorities was brief. The Gospels record him on trial before Pilate in a conversation over the right to rule the kingdom and by whose authority, very similar in form to Jephthah's own arguments with the Ammonites.

The picture of Christ's death is found in Jephthah's daughter, and Jephthah's anguish is the anguish of God the Father Himself over the sacrifice He had vowed to make. The salvation of God's people was conditional upon Jesus' death on the cross, and Jesus fulfilled his Father's vow to redeem His people by giving His life willingly.

If we do not allow that Jephthah did as he vowed he would do, then the picture of the cross is written out and we segue straight to the picture of the kingdom. (Skipping over the picture of the cross creates some theological difficulties, however. This is why I insisted that we allow the text to say what it literally says about Jephthah's vow, as hard as it is to reconcile.)

A picture of the Messianic kingdom with its fullness of all things is invested in this three-fold picture of the judges.

Ibzan is the judge, brilliant in whiteness and enlightenment, who reigns from the house of bread—a place of blessing and provision—with an abundance of sons and daughters. Thirty evokes a sense of a kingdom full of light and enlightenment, even the fullness of the Godhead, and his seven years of service evokes the picture of physical and spiritual completion and perfection associated with sabbath rest.

Elon is the judge who is mighty in strength like the oak, the ram, or the strong man. He comes from an exalted dwelling place, and his resting place is the field of stags or mighty rams (reinforcing the imagery of his strength and majesty, even in death). His ten years of service denotes a completion with the added fullness of testimony, law, order, and judgment.

Abdon is the judge who has a duality in him as a servant with a royal lineage. Though servile, he is a son of praise and of the king. His kingdom encompasses the fullness of creation, generation upon generation of abundant life and prosperity associated with a Messianic kingdom that is also a kingdom of light. The picture in Abdon is tempered with servant pictures. There is the remembrance of the redemption price of a servant, and the age that marks the beginning of service for priest and the (Davidic) king.

In their combined expression, these three judges portray an archetypal judge of majestic strength and wisdom and a kingdom in its fullest expression. Where Jephthah paints a picture of Christ in His first advent, the judges who follow paint a picture of Him in His second advent.

LESSON 11

Oppression #7: Samson

READ

Judges 13-16

BUILD THE PICTURE

The Oppression, Judges 13:1-2

1. Who were the Philistines and where were they generally located?

The Philistines were descendants of Noah's son Ham through the line of Mizraim (Egypt) who immigrated to the western seacoast of Canaan. They lived in Judah's territory, and occupied the five main cities of Gaza, Ashkelon, Ashdod, Ekron, and Gath.

The name Philistine means "immigrant."

2. How long did they oppress Israel?

Altogether they oppressed Israel since the days of Jephthah. Back in Judges 10:6-8, we see that Israel had given herself over in totality to the gods of all the surrounding nations. God sent the Philistines and the Ammonites against them in a two-fold oppression. Jephthah dealt with the Ammonite oppressors, but not the Philistines.

After the initial eighteen years of Ammonite rule, the Philistines continued to oppress Israel through the six years of Jephthah's rule, twenty-five collective years of Ibzan, Elon, and Abdon, and then ruled over Israel for an additional forty years. Add all that up and we see that the Philistines had been occupiers and combatants for roughly eighty-nine years total. Think of the generations that have passed. A person would have to be well over ninety years of age to even remember what life was like before the Philistine oppression. Philistine domination was the only thing this generation knew.

3. **There has been a pattern of Israel crying for help and God answering. What happened this time?**

   Israel didn't cry out for help this time. What does that tell you? They were no longer fighting their oppressors. They had given themselves over completely to what had become the new norm and accepted their oppression in silence (silence is one of our stumbling blocks).

   Did God quit fighting for Israel when Israel quit fighting for herself? No, He didn't.

4. **The narrative began at a place called Zorah. What is the picture behind this name?**

   The name **Zorah** (Hebrew *tsorah*) comes from the root word *tsirah*, meaning "hornet." The hornet only appears in a few verses but with a very specific context (Exodus 23:28, Deuteronomy 7:20, Joshua 24:12).

   > "And I will send hornets [tsirah] before you, which shall drive out the Hivite, the Canaanite, and the Hittite from before you."
   > —Exodus 23:28 (cf. Joshua 24:12)

   > "Moreover the LORD your God will send the hornet [tsirah] among them until those who are left, who hide themselves from you, are destroyed."—Deuteronomy 7:20

   Tsirah or hornets are God's agents for driving enemies, particularly hidden enemies, into the open where they can be addressed.

   Tsirah comes from the root word *tsarah*, which means "to be leprous." Leprosy is an affliction God sends on Old Testament Israel as a sign that there is serious sin within the person—a sin that is systemic and so deeply engrained as to be like a character flaw, very hard to put a finger on, and very hard to eradicate. The outward corruption pointed to the inward corruption.

   So, what is the connection between a hornet and leprosy?

   This Hebrew word family creates a picture of things that have similar purpose.

   > **The purpose of the hornet (*tsirah*)** is to drive out physical enemies and hidden enemies into the light. Hornets reveal external enemies.

> **The purpose of leprosy (*tsarah*)** is to drive hidden sin to the surface and make it known. Leprosy reveals internal sin that needs to be resolved.

5. **In what sense was Israel leprous at this point?**

   She had given herself over completely to idolatry and sin. The corruption had gone through and through the people. She had become numb and no longer cried out against her oppressors.

6. **The narrative begins with a man named Manoah. What does the meaning of the name Manoah lend to the picture?**

   Manoah means "rest," from the Hebrew word *nuach*. It is close to the name, Noah, and evokes that early picture of a time when the world was so given over to idolatry and wickedness that it faced divine judgment, much like Israel here in Manoah's day.

   Genesis 5:29 tells us that Lamech named his son Noah, saying, *"This one will comfort us concerning our work and the toil of our hands, because of the ground which the LORD has cursed."*

   Here in Judges, Manoah recalls that same sense of divine comfort and hope for a generation sunk in sin and defilement as a result of the curse. He is a reminder that while God judges, He is also merciful in not wiping out all of Israel but providing a remnant to carry forward.

   In Lesson 2, we talked about three kinds of rest: **Shabbath** (ceasing), **nuach** (sitting down), and **shaqat** (quietness). The judges have only provided the *shaqat* (quietness), and even that ended in the days of Gideon. The *nuach* rest, on the other hand, was charateristic of Joshua's work in giving Israel a "sitting down" place in the Land. The *nuach* rest is never mentioned in the Judges narrative until now in the name of this minor character in this final judge's account.

7. **Why would the author want to remind us at this point that Israel still had a "sitting down" place in the Land?**

   Because there was still hope for Israel, even in her degenerate condition. Even though she was spiritually dead at this point and had walked away from God, her place in the kingdom was still secure. She had not been put out of the kingdom.

APPLY THE PICTURE

So, let's project this picture of Israel into a New Testament context. We have a view of Israel coming to the end of an age, so to speak. What does the church look like at the end of this age?

8. **Which churches in Revelation 3 follow a similar model of leprous Israel pictured here?**

    The church of Sardis, for sure. Also, to a certain extent, the church of Laodicea, which was neither hot nor cold but what you might describe as almost numb to their conditiion.

9. **Why would we need a reminder that these churches still have a "sitting-down" place in the kingdom—a secure inheritance?**

    This is a reassurance for those of us who believe that salvation cannot be lost. As bad as they are, these churches still have a "sitting down" place in the kingdom, even as degenerate Israel had a "sitting down" place in the Land. Like Israel, the experience of those who have fallen away will be very different in the kingdom, and not without weeping and gnashing of teeth.

Obviously, God no longer afflicts us with physical leprosy as He did Israel in the Old Testament, but our spiritual "old man" can have a leprous quality about him. Paul says in Ephesians 4:17-19:

> *"This I say, therefore, and testify in the Lord, that you should no longer walk as the rest of the Gentiles walk, in the futility of their mind, having their understanding darkened, being alienated from the life of God, because of the ignorance that is in them, because of the blindness of their heart; who, being past feeling, have given themselves over to lewdness, to work all uncleanness with greediness."* —Ephesians 4:17-19

Blindness, being past feeling, being alienated from God—these are all "leprous" conditions.

Question for Reflection

- How does God drive hidden sin to light in our lives? What do our hornets look like?

BUILD THE PICTURE

The Promised Son, Judges 13:3-5

Manoah's wife was barren. The Angel of the LORD appeared to her to announce that she would have a son who would be a Nazirite from the womb and would begin to deliver Israel.

10. Who else in the Bible followed a similar pattern?

Hannah, mother of Samuel—who was a prophet and also a judge—and Elizabeth, mother of John the Baptist. Both women were barren, and both bore sons who were Nazirites from birth.

It is tempting to include Mary in this list. While she was not barren, her conception was no less miraculous. The angelic announcement was given to her directly, not to Joseph, and she bore a son who would deliver His people. Even though Jesus was not a Nazirite by vow, He was *nazir* or separated from his brothers in the likeness of Joseph who was exiled in Egypt (Gen. 49:26). He was separated for the purpose of saving them. There is this shadow picture of Christ in Samson.

11. What Nazirite rules was she required to follow?
- Do not drink wine or similar drink
- Do not to eat anything unclean

12. What is the significance of the word *chalal*, translated as "begin to" in Judges 13:5?

> "... he shall begin [chalal] to deliver Israel out of the hand of the Philistines."

"Shall begin" implies that Samson would not deliver Israel fully. That is the literal meaning of the statement, but there is a deeper nuance in the word *chalal*.

Chalal means to be "profaned, defiled, polluted, desecrated" by being "fatally wounded, pierced, or bored through."

In a literal sense, it is when something that was healthy and whole is pierced so that a hole is created (like a wound), and through that hole disease and corruption enter. The *chalal*-ing can be accomplished in a physical sense such as a wound in the body that lets in infection.

In a figurative sense, *chalal*-ing is a opening act that sets off a chain of events that lead to a person becoming weak, sick, diseased, grieved, or sorry. For this reason, it is often translated as "begin to" (do something.) The *chalal*-ing is the catalyst action that opens a way toward that end defilement.

If you look at how events play out, the initial act may be innocent, but it usually involves a loosening of restraint that then leads down the path to the person being corrupted or profaned or toward profaning God. The corruption or profaning can be of a spiritual or sexual nature.

In its most figurative sense, *chalal* means to play the flute for someone—a flute being an instrument bored through with holes and used as enticement toward a lack of restraint.

Look at how this word is used in these passages. Where do these beginnings lead?

Genesis 6:1-2: *"Now it came to pass, when men began to* [chalal] *multiply on the face of the earth, and daughters were born to them, that the sons of God saw the daughters of men, that they were beautiful . . ."*

Genesis 9:20: *"And Noah began to* [chalal] *be a farmer, and he planted a vineyard."*

Genesis 11:6: *"And the LORD said, 'Indeed the people are one and they all have one language, and this is what they begin to* [chalal] *do . . .'"*

Numbers 25:1: *"Now Israel remained in Acacia Grove, and the people began to* [chalal] *commit harlotry with the women of Moab."*

Isaiah 53:5: *"But He was wounded* [chalal] *for our transgressions, He was bruised for our iniquities."*

Does the Isaiah 53 verse strike a discordant note when lumped with the rest? It did for me. Isaiah 53 speaks of Christ's death, and it seems wrong somehow to think of Christ's actions defiling him the way that the rest of humanity profaned themselves. And yet, isn't that exactly what happened? From the day of His birth, Jesus was set upon a path that led to His *chalal*-ing. When He died on the cross, He fulfilled the concept of *chalal*-ing in both the literal and figurative forms. He was literally pierced in the hands, feet, and side with a mortal wound from which He died, but He was also *chalal*-ed in a sense of being defiled when He took our sin upon Himself in death.

The word *chalal* shows up four times in Samson's narrative (Judges 13:5, 25; 16:19, 22) and each time, there is a further descent toward a grievous end.

Questions for Reflection:

There can be times in our life when we groan to ourselves "how did I get into this mess?" Sometimes a decision and subsequent course of action that seemed right at the time may have started us down a path that didn't end so well. Or perhaps it is our children who have taken a path in life that we knew would not end well for them and yet we were powerless to stop them.

- What was the *chalal*-ing moment?
- What prompted your/their decision to start down that path?
- If you had to do it over again, would you make a different choice? (You might not. Jesus didn't.)

Conversation with the Angel of the LORD, Judges 13:3-24

The exchange between Manoah, his wife, and the Angel of the LORD is broken into two parts that follow a basic pattern.

Round 1: The Angel spoke to the wife (v3-5)

        The wife told Manoah (v6-7)

                Manoah prayed to the LORD (v8)

Round 2: The LORD heard Manoah; the Angel reappeared to the wife (v9)

        The wife called to Manoah (v10)

                Manoah addressed the Angel (v11)

There is an unusual reversal of cultural norms in this exchange. In Round 1, the Angel went to Manoah's wife first to announce the birth, not Manoah. In Round 2, the Angel reappears to the wife first, and Manoah trailed after his wife as she led him to see the Angel—defintely not the norm in Hebrew culture. Then there ensued a rather awkward conversation between Manoah and the Angel of the LORD. The Angel's responses to Manoah's questions appear almost stand-offish when we compare them to a similar conversation with Gideon.

Manoah was a bit of the odd man out in the narrative, while his wife's role was more pronounced and almost central. Looking forward, Manoah plays a very minor role in Samson's life, not unlike Joseph, Jesus' father. It seems that God was clearly taking charge of the raising and instruction of this child.

Let's work through the narrative.

Round 1:

13. Why didn't Manoah's wife ask the Man of God his name or from where he came?

She did not know, but she suspected He was the Angel of the LORD because of His awesome countenance.

14 How did the woman's account differ from what the Angel told her?

The Angel never made the stipulation that Samson would be a Nazirite to the day of his death. We could argue that one who was a Nazirite from birth would be a Nazirite for life until his death. Nevertheless, she added the statement, and it would come to pass. She also left out Samson's God-given commission, that he would begin to deliver his people. That seems a curious omission.

15. Why did Manoah ask God to send the Man of God to him?

Why didn't he take her word for it? He seemed to question his wife's account. I think he wanted to hear for himself.

Round 2:

16. How did the Angel respond to Manoah's questions?

- "Are You the Man who spoke to this woman?"

    "I am."

- "What will be the boy's rule of life, and his work?"

    "Of all that I said to the woman let her be careful." The Angel doesn't answer Manoah directly but refers him back to the wife. We get a curious sense here that Manoah will be left out of the loop when it comes to raising this child.

- "Please let us detain You, and we will prepare a young goat for You."

    "Though you detain Me, I will not eat your food. But if you offer a burnt offering, you must offer it to the LORD." The Angel refused the food but

suggested an offering to God. Manoah could thank God for this miraculous visitation . . . hint, hint. There was a little prompting as to who correctly deserved the glory.

- **"What is Your name, that when Your words come to pass we may honor You?"**

"Why do you ask My name, seeing it is wonderful?" That is a rather sharp rebuff.

In each case, the Angel's answers were brief, almost curt, and He deflected back to the woman in regards to the rules for the boy's life. It is almost as if the Angel were putting distance between Himself and Manoah.

17. At what point did Manoah realize he had been speaking to the Angel of the LORD? What was his reaction?

When he offered the burnt offering to God and "the man" disappeared in the flame, then he knew to whom he had been speaking and fell on his face. He panicked because he has seen God.

18. What was the reaction of Manoah's wife?

I have to chuckle at her presence of mind. She seemed to be the more rational of the two in pointing out the obvious: "We aren't going to die. We are having a baby!" This was joyous news to a barren woman.

> *"So the woman bore a son and called his name Samson; and the child grew, and the LORD blessed him."* —Judges 13:24

19. What do we know about Samson so far?
- His name, Samson or Shimshon, means "like the sun."
- His birth was announced to his mother first.
- He was a Nazirite from birth. What Nazarite rules did he have to follow? (Numbers 6)

As a Nazirite, a layman like Samson would be given a status like a priest since he was to be considered "holy to the Lord," and his restraints are actually higher than those required for the priests.[1]

o He was to separate himself from the vine—no grape or wine products. If Israel is likened to a vine, then this might be equated

---

1 Bard, Mitchell G. *Nazirite*, Jewish Virtual Library, 31 May 2021, www.jewishvirtuallibrary.org/nazirite.

to Samson separating himself from his brethren. He was being called out for a specific purpose.

- o He could not cut his hair. He was to let his locks grow unrestrained the way the untended grapevine was allowed to grow in the Sabbath year.

- o He could not go near a dead body so that he became defiled or unclean. If he became defiled, technically he had to shave his head and start over.

- He would experience a *chalal*-ing. His life would take him down a path that would lead to his defilement.

- We know nothing about his early years, up to the point where he stepped into his role as deliverer of Israel. There is only this summary phrase which is echoed in Luke's description of Jesus:

Judges 13:24: *"The child grew in stature, and the LORD blessed him."*

Luke 2:40: *"And the Child grew and became strong in spirit, filled with wisdom; and the grace of God was upon Him."*

- We know what was prophesied about Samson.

  - o **In Genesis 49:16-17:** *"Dan shall judge his people as one of the tribes of Israel. Dan shall be a serpent by the way, a viper by the path, that bites the horse's heels so that its rider shall fall backward."*

    Notice, the viper doesn't strike the rider. It strikes the horse which then brings down the rider. The downfall of the rider is accomplished by using an intermediary agent. Like the viper, Samson will be the provocateur. He will engage the enemy through a secondary agent or with outrageous, almost venemous, acts. These cause a reaction that then brings the enemy's downfall. It is a circuitous route but effective.

  - o **In Judges 5:2, 31 (the Song of Deborah).** Back in Lesson 6, we worked through the translation exercise of the first and last verses in the Song of Deborah.

    "When leaders lead in Israel, when the people willingly offer themselves, Bless the LORD! . . . Thus let all Your enemies perish, O LORD! But let those who love Him be as the sun when it comes out in full strength." — Judges 5:2, 31 (NKJV)

In verse 2, we discussed the different pictures that come out of the translations for *"when leaders lead"* and then brought all the possible variations together in an amplified version of the passage. Thus, the amplified verse might be rendered:

> *"When leaders lead in Israel* [When God raises up a leader who is under a Nazirite vow and without restraint and turns him loose on His enemies for vengeance], *when the people willingly offer themselves, Bless the LORD!*

In verse 31, we noted that *"as the sun when it comes out in full strength"* is another veiled reference to Samson, whose name means "like the sun."

Samson is not mentioned by name in the verses, but the picture of him is there: The imagery of a Nazarite leader being turned loose on an enemy for vengeance, combined with a lack of restraint and great strength. His lack of restraint will be a key element in the unfolding events. Like the sun, he will shed light on the condition of Israel and reveal the enemy's treachery.

This prophetic picture in the Song of Deborah is easily overlooked because it is veiled by translation difficulties and out of context with the immediate events recorded in the Song of Deborah. But then the pictures of Christ in the Old Testament prophets are equally veiled and seemingly out of context with the immediate events described in those passages. It wasn't until the man himself was realized that the ancient pictures could be identified.

20. Why would God choose to use someone who is without restraint to deal with an enemy?

There will be nothing civilized about the war that God waged against the Philistines. They were brute beasts without morals or conscience, and God sent a bigger and stronger brute beast to deal an eye-for-an-eye type of justice against them.

21. Why would God use someone who is without restraint to judge a rebellious, unrepentant people?

Samson was a mirror image of unrestrained Israel who did what was right in their own eyes. He horrified and appalled them with his lack of restraint, but in truth, he was a only reflection of themselves.

Samson provides an excellent illustration of the warning Paul gives us in Romans 2:1: *"O man, whoever you are who judge, for in whatever you judge another you condemn yourself; for you who judge practice the same things."*

APPLY THE PICTURE

From the day of his birth, Samson was separated from his idolatrous brethren and the Canaanites around him by a Nazirite vow, a vow which distinguished him as a man wholly devoted to the Lord's service. We do not take Nazirite vows like Old Testament Israel did, but we are called to be separated from the Canaanite elements in our lives, so that we, like a royal priesthood, might be sanctified for God's use.

22. How do we separate ourselves from the world?

The separation is not created by withdrawing from the world. That is an impossible thing, as Paul writes in 1 Corinthians 5:9-10, and it defies our commission to go out into the world. We need to be in the world, but not of it; that is, of its character.

Separation is achieved by creating a distinction between a holy lifestyle and a worldly, carnal lifestyle. The distinction is created by doing something opposite or different in nature. To give you an Old Testament example, there is the commandment to remember the Sabbath day and keep it holy. How is the Sabbath day kept holy? By doing something different on that day—rest instead of work. The reversal of activity and the contrast in its character is what creates the distinction and separates the Sabbath from the work week.

So, run with that thought. **What activities or behaviors do we as believers do that are opposite or different from the carnal world around us?** It can be as simple as telling the truth instead of a lie, or working for an honest wage instead of stealing. We can separate ourselves from the world in how we value things such as the sanctity of life, marriage, and family. What other ways can you imagine?

I should warn you, though. This practice of doing something different to create a distinction can easily slip into a legalistic practice of performing ritual acts. That is what happened in Judaism. A host of Jewish liturgical traditions and rules for lifestyle come out of the application of this idea of creating separation and distinction. To give you an extreme example, some orthodox Jews keep the law against boiling a young animal in its mother's milk (Exodus 24:36) by keeping dairy and meat in separate kitchens so that there can be absolutely no possiblity of mixing the two. We can look at that practice and say, yes, that creates separation, but it is so superficial and far removed from the law that inspired it that it loses its connection with the original intent. The physical practices can get caught up in the superficial, external appearance without communicating the internal, spiritual character or values, and we can revert to a lifestyle of works instead of grace. The separation and distinction must reflect the *character* of holiness, not simply the works.

That being said, we are called to be separate in how we conduct our lives as children of love and light and holiness (2 Corinthians 6).

23. How do we separate ourselves from the "Canaanite" inside us?

This topic is pretty much the sum of our New Testament teachings. It involves the battle to put off the old man and put on the new man (Ephesians 4:17-24, Colossians 3:10). Just as we make the distinction between ourselves and the outside world, we make a distinction between our old and new man characters in a similar fashion. The reversal of activity and the contrast in behavior and character is what creates the distinction between the two natures, so that we become children of light instead of darkness, love instead of hate, peacemaking instead of violent, others-focused instead of self-focused, etc. Two opposing natures cannot rule one body. Therefore, the objective is to become one vessel with one nature, holy and set apart for the Lord's service.

24. How do we separate ourselves from the believers who are acting like Canaanites? (1 Corinthians 5, 2 Thessalonians 3)

Paul addresses this with both the Corinthians and Thessalonians. If a believer is engaged in a sinful lifestyle and unrepentant of it, we are called to withdraw from fellowship with that believer.

Questions for Reflection:

- How well have you done with separating yourself from the world? Are there situations where you feel you have compromised too much? If so, what opposite actions can you take to create that separation?

- How well have you done at dealing with your "old man" nature? Are there some behaviors the LORD has driven to light in your life that need to be addressed?

- More and more, churches are beginning to experience inter-congregational division and separation when they adopt non-biblical stances on various issues. What are some issues that have brought about division in church bodies?

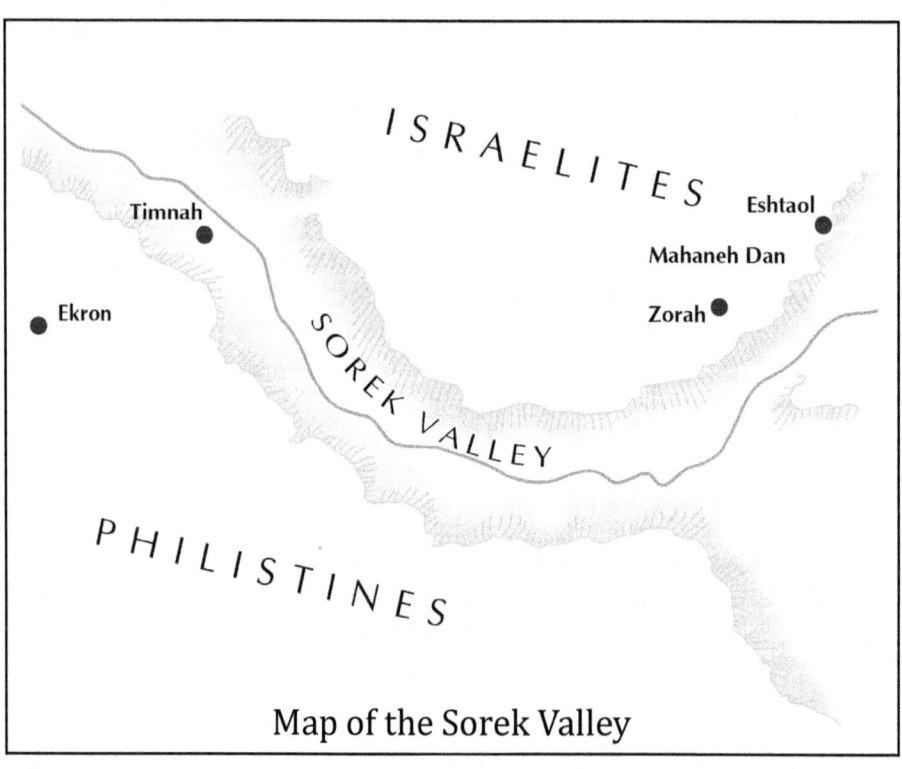

Map of the Sorek Valley

BUILD THE PICTURE

"And the Spirit of the LORD began to [chalal] move upon him at Mahaneh Dan between Zorah and Eshtaol." —Judges 13:25

25. Where did the narrative take place and how do the names of the places add to the narrative picture?

The narrative opens in the Sorek Valley, which lies on the border between the tribes of Dan and Judah. North of the valley are Israelite-held lands, and there we find Zorah, Eshtaol, and Mahaneh Dan mentioned in Judges 13:25. The Sorek Valley itself and the lands south are Philistine-controlled.

Sorek means "choice vines."

Mahaneh Dan means "camp of Dan," and was the site of an early Danite military encampment situated between Zorah and Eshtaol. **Zorah** means the "hornet," and **Eshtaol** means "entreaty."

PICTURE SUMMARY

Samson was a man living physically on the border, in a staging place for war. He also lived spiritually on the borderline between his "man of God" side and his "Canaanite" side, which was also on the verge of conflict.

Samson had an impetuous, hornet-like character that was very driven by his lusts and by what was right in his own eyes. He was not given much to entreaty—to asking permission, seeking advice, enquiring of the LORD. Given the choice, he acted instead of asking.

When the Spirit began to move on him—gave him that push to get him off the fence—Samson by nature headed toward Zorah and into the valley of choice vines on his way to Timnah. It was a *chalal*-ing moment.

Question for Reflection:

- Is it better to ask for permission before you act or ask for forgiveness afterwards?

Part 1: Samson and the Philistines, Judges 14:1-4

26. The narrative begins in Timnah. What do we know about Timnah?

Timnah means "portion" or a place where portions are reckoned. It was a place of reckoning, appropriate to the narrative. Historically, it was a stockyard where sheep-shearing took place (Genesis 38:12-14). It featured in the story of Judah and Tamar, in which Judah was taken in by a woman who sat beside the road and pleased his eye. He had relations with her and was fleeced, so to speak, when she took his signet and staff and disappeared.

Like Judah, Samson went down to Timnah and finds a woman along the way who pleased his eye.

27. There has been a theme through the Judges' narrative of doing what was right in your own eyes as opposed to what is right in God's eyes. Was Samson's request for a Philistine wife right or wrong . . .

- **. . . in his own eyes?**

    Right. The phrase "*. . . for she pleases me well*" in verse 3 is literally "she is right in my eyes" in the Hebrew.

- **. . . in his parents' eyes?**

    Wrong—according to the Law (Deuteronomy 7:3). The Philistines were Canaanite and therefore forbidden in marriage. Then again, if God's people had become indistinguishable from the Philistine in their idolatrous practices, what was the issue?

    Sometimes the path our children follow will go against everything we have tried to teach them, and it will appall us. And it will indeed be a *chalal*-ing moment for our children that will take them down a very tragic path. We have to trust that the Lord's purpose is in it.

- **. . . in God's eyes?**

    Right. God had purposely planned things this way.

The Lion in the Vineyard, Judges 14:5-9

28. What was troubling about Samson being near a vineyard?

Nazirites were supposed to stay away from anything having to do with the vine. He was flirting with defilement.

29. To have a lion come roaring out of the vineyard at him might be hinting that . . .?

Maybe he wasn't where he should be. It might be a warning. Yet his being here was part of the plan. God had sent him down this path, and when the Spirit came upon him, he killed the lion. Even so, he hid the fact from his parents.

30. Why would Samson not tell his parents he had killed a lion?

It was a defiling act for a Nazirite. He was supposed to keep himself away from carcasses and dead things, particularly those of unclean animals, including lions.

31. The young lion, the *kephir ari*, is a literal lion, but it is also used figuratively in Scripture. Of whom or what is the young lion figurative?

The *kephir ari* (young lion) is used figuratively in the Old Testament to describe an enemy of Israel with a particular lion-like character—young, fierce, always hungry, and on the prowl.

Here are a few examples:

"The roaring of the lion, the voice of the fierce lion, and the teeth of the young lions [kephir ari] are broken."—Job 4:10

"As a lion is eager to tear his prey, and like a young lion [kephir ari] lurking in secret places." —Psalm 17:12

"Their roaring will be like a lion, they will roar like young lions [kephir ari]; Yes, they will roar and lay hold of the prey; they will carry it away safely, and no one will deliver."—Isaiah 5:29

"She brought up one of her cubs, and he became a young lion [kephir ari]; He learned to catch prey, and he devoured men." —Ezekiel 19:3

This last passage describes Israel as the young lion who is taken to Babylon. The description is an echo of the picture of Samson.

32. Of whom/what is the vineyard figurative? (Isaiah 5:1-7)

Israel.

33. Put the pictures together. Of what is the young lion in the vineyard a picture?

The Philistines. God's vineyard—His people and His land—had been overrun by the young lions. The valley of choice vines had become the lions' hunting ground and hiding place, and Samson was sent to deal with them. His first act was the symbolic act of killing of this young lion, which he does through the power of the Spirit.

34. What is our reaction to the thought of a person eating something out of a carcass?

Ew, gross. Through human eyes, Samson's act was a defiling moment. To eat something out of a carcass is the act of a scavenger. That Samson would do such a thing without a second thought represented a descent into baseness and bestiality. It is a *chalal*-ing moment. He was becoming something of the character of the lions he was sent to remove. But it served God's purpose that he followed this path.

35. If the lion is symbolic of the enemy, then what is the sweetness that comes from seeing your enemy dead at your feet?

The honey—the sweetness—is vengeance. Samson partook of the sweetness and shared his victory over the enemy with his parents.

Inasmuch as they had gone along with God's program, they had become partakers with Samson in the vengeance that God was preparing to inflict on the Philistines.

Samson's Feast & Riddle, Judges 14:10-20

36. God sent Samson to deal with the young lions hiding in His vineyard. How did Samson draw them into the open?

With a feast. Nothing draws a meat-eater out of hiding faster than the smell of a nice, fat sheep or goat roasting on a spit, and the Philistines came with alacrity.

37. What kind of a feast is this? What is the occasion?

It was a seven-day wedding feast.

38. Who are Samson's "companions"?

It is understood from verse 20 that they were Philistines. It seems odd that Samson would be a groom without companions. Where were his own people? Hadn't they been called to the wedding feast? Surely they were called, but none came. For whatever reason, these thirty Philistines off the street were appointed to him companions to be with him at his wedding— probably something along the line of groomsmen. And there arose the question of garments.

39. What was Samson's riddle?

> *"Then Samson said to them, 'Let me pose a riddle to you. If you can correctly solve and explain it to me within the seven days of the feast, then I will give you thirty linen garments [cadeen] and thirty changes of clothing [beged].'"*—Judges 14:12

By way of entertainment, Samson posed a riddle and offered garments as a prize for solving the riddle. Why use clothing as a prize? Because it played into the picture of this particular oppression.

There are eight different Hebrew words translated as "garment" or "clothing," each with a different use, sense, or character. The particular ones emphasized here are *cadeen* and *beged*.

Cadeen are the sheets or wraps worn over the top of clothing. **Beged** are the clothes worn beneath the sheet, including underclothes.

Beged is a common word for garment and used extensively in Scripture, but most often in the following ways:

- A man is given a new *beged* when his status or condition changes (like a priest changing his garment before entering the Lord's Tabernacle).

- When a man is made unclean, he must wash his body and his *beged*.

- When a man is mourning, he rends his *beged*.

- *Beged* can be used as a disguise, particularly in war. *Beged* are taken among the spoils of war (as something taken from the enemy by force, treachery, or pillaging).

So we can see that, in general, these "under" garments often reflect the character or condition of the man. Figuratively, character, like clothing, becomes an outward expression and extension of the inner man. When a man's status or condition changes, there is often a change in his garment.

The *beged*'s hidden or under-the-sheet character is reflected in its root word, *bagad*.

Bagad means to act treacherously, deceitfully, unfaithfully, covertly, or fraudulently—all hidden acts that go on behind the scenes or beneath the sheets, so to speak. *Beged* can be treacherous when it is used to disguise or hide the man's character or intentions—when the outside clothing and inside man don't match.

Samson offers a riddle and this prize of clothing. If he wins, he collects thirty shirts (one from each companion). If he loses, he has to hand over thirty shirts (a princely sum). He takes upon himself an obligation that is thirty times greater than the rest. To the Philistines, Samson must have seemed an easy mark with nominal risk on their side. They agree to the riddle challenge and set out to fleece Samson.

And so, the *bagad*-ing began.

40. Who *bagad*-ed who—how did the treachery play out?

Note: in Judges 14:15, some translations (including the NKJV) read *"But it came to pass on the seventh day..."*. Other versions, including the Septuagint and Syriac, say it was the fourth day, which makes more sense with the timeline; however, the use of "seventh" may have been deliberate on the part of the author as a literary device. By rendering it "seventh," the author creates three repetitions of "seven" in the passage, similar to the repetition of the number thirty, thus evoking a sense of totality or completion.

The Philistines went to Samson's wife and threatened her to get her to work on Samson. The wife then went to Samson and nagged him until he told her (apparently the enticement angle didn't work so well). Then she relayed the answer to the Philistines, and the Philistines told Samson the answer.

Notice how all this played out through the wife who acted as an intermediary in this exchange, just as Manoah's wife was the intermediary character between Samson's father and the Angel of the LORD. In both cases, there is a degree of separation between the men, and the woman is the pivotal point around which the action revolved. This creates an intentional focus on the woman.

When the Philistines told Samson the answer, he replied:

> *"If you had not plowed* [charash] *with my heifer, you would not have solved my riddle!"* —Judges 14:18b

41. What does the word *charash* mean and how does it add to the understanding of the oppression's profile?

We studied this word in Lesson 6 when we talked about King Jabin carving out an empire in Israel using his general, Sisera, as a tool; Sisera's tools were iron chariots. Now we have another *charash*-ing going on, but with a different tool. Samson used the word *charash* figuratively of a heifer (his wife) being used as another man's tool for plowing. *Charash* doesn't actually mean to plow. Plowing illustrates what it means to *charash*, but it is only half the picture of this word.

Just to refresh your memory, *charash* has two definitions:

Definition #1: To cut in, plow, engrave, or otherwise devise. In a broad sense, it means to use a tool to fabricate something—to engrave, etch in, or dig out. It is the act of fabrication or devising something.

Definition #2: To keep silent, act deaf or dumb, hold one's peace. Schemes are working out behind the scenes, but everyone is acting like they don't see or hear what is taking place. They hold their peace.

The Philistines plowed with Samson's heifer. They needed something revealed, so they devised a way to get it. They laid the groundwork with their threats and lies, then sat back and kept quiet—held their peace—while Samson's wife did the dirty work for them.

The wife allowed herself to become their tool. She kept quiet and didn't tell Samson what the Philistines were doing to her. She sided with her oppressors in agreeing to dupe her husband—an act of unfaithfulness. She carved and plowed away at him until she finally dug up what was he had been hiding.

But Samson was keeping quiet about something, too. He hid the story of the lion and honey from everyone, including his parents. He revealed it to only one person—his wife. Something that was hidden, when it came to the light, also brought the treachery to light.

The key to unraveling the treachery lay in discovering who knew what and from whom they had heard it. When the answer surfaced, it pointed directly at the wife and revealed her unfaithfulness. It also revealed the Philistine's treachery.

The Philistines used Samson's wife as their tool for digging up and revealing the answer to the riddle, but God used Samson as His tool for digging up and revealing their hearts. God used the Philistines' own tactics on them.

42. Why didn't his wife tell Samson what was taking place?

Fear, certainly. But then she was Philistine at heart, and she came from a culture where this kind of treachery was the way things operated. She valued her own safety, but also the safety of her Philistine family. If she had gone to Samson, he might have protected her, but her father's house would still have been at the mercy of the Philistines. There was no good way out of this. And let's face it, all this *charash*-ing was over a stupid bet for some garments. If you were the wife, wouldn't your family's safety be more important than your husband having a new set of clothes that he really didn't need in the first place? The bet was foolish from the beginning.

43. How did Samson deal treacherously with the Philistines in return?

What is sweeter than honey? Vengeance.
What is stronger than a lion? Samson.

Samson said, "Okay, you win. I'll be right back with your prize," and he delivered their prize, but not out of his own closet. He went down to Ashkelon, murdered thirty Philistines, stripped them, and delivered the filthy, blood-stained garments to his companions. Garments are, after all, a reflection of the inner man, and the Philistines had not been dressed correctly.

44. If you were the Philistine receiving these garments, what would this communicate to you?

Personally, Samson would scare the living daylights out of me. He was brutal, without conscience or restraint, and thought nothing of killing men just to get some satisfaction over a lost bet. He was the big, bad beast who beat them all.

THE PICTURE OF THIS OPPRESSION

Judges 14:15 says: *"... they said to Samson's wife, 'Entice your husband, that he may explain the riddle to us, or else we will burn you and your father's house with fire. Have you invited us in order to take what is ours? Is that not so?'"*

45. Look at the verse above. What were some specific tactics of this oppressor?
- They don't attack directly. There is no direct confrontation.
- They seek leverage by using people close to the victim as tools.
- They threaten violence against the tool and/or the tool's family.
- They accuse the tool of treachery against them. False accusations are meant to create a false sense of guilt in the victim.
- They make themselves out to be victims when it suits their purpose through fraud and lies

---
APPLY THE PICTURE

THE PROFILE OF THIS OPPRESSION

This oppressor is very sophisticated. They never confront head on, but manipulate things behind the scenes. They use people as tools, thus removing themselves from the danger of exposure. They use threats, treachery, fraud, lies, and destructive violence. They wield guilt, false accusations, and make themselves out to be the victim when it suits their agenda.

There is usually a secondary oppressor in this scenario—the tool that is being used. Because of the pressure being brought to bear on them, they become oppressors themselves. Their actions are driven by fear, shame, humiliation, and guilt, and they often react with destructive anger and silence. Keeping one's mouth shut when you should speak up is an earmark of this kind of oppression, and perpetuates this oppression.

46. What are some scenarios where this kind of oppression might play out in our day (in personal, family, community, or even national contexts)?

> Questions for Reflection:
>
> - Have you ever been the victim of *charash*-ing like Samson?
> - Has anyone ever used you as a tool the way the Philistines used Samson's wife?
> - How might things have turned out differently if the wife had gone to her husband and explained what the Philistines were doing to her?
> - Have you ever been caught in the middle of a conflict between two warring parties where there was no way out without someone getting hurt? If so, how did you deal with it and how did it end?

BUILD THE PICTURE

Part 2: Samson and the Philistines, Judges 14:20–15:8

47. How did Samson deal with his wife's treachery?

The wife's treachery was an act of unfaithfulness against her husband. Samson uncovered the truth to find his wife had been used by another man, became enraged, left the wedding feast in his anger, and returned to his father's house without her. She was then given to the Philistine who was Samson's best man (the man who used her as a tool for his own purpose). So, technically, she became an adulteress.

Samson's Philistine wife is a reflection of Israel who had given herself over to her oppressors. Samson modeled how God would deal with unfaithful Israel at a future date by sending her into the Babylonian captivity. In the book of Lamentations, the author described how God, like an angry bridegroom, stormed out of the bridal chamber and left adulterous Israel in the hands of her oppressors. And yet, God did not forsake His Bride. He left her in exile for a time, but then returned for her, in much the same Samson returned for his bride in Judges 15:1.

48. Why did Samson's father-in-law give his wife to another man?

Think about the father-in-law's statement. What he had done was objectionable. He had no right to give Samson's wife to another man. He had no right to step in the middle of a husband and wife dispute and take control like that. If anything, he hindered Samson's effort at reconciliation. It broke all the boundaries, but more than that, it was a slap in the face to Samson that his father-in-law should deny him what was rightfully his.

But wasn't that what Samson had just done to the Philistines? He offered them a choice prize for solving the riddle, but when he lost, he delivered a less-than-choice prize. So, without actually saying it, the father-in-law intimated that it was Samson's loss this time. The choice prize was rightfully his, but now he was getting the consolation prize of the second daughter instead. He caused Samson to lose face the way Samson had caused the Philistines to lose face.

Taking Samson's wife from him was a very subtle form of domination and retaliation. The father-in-law's action fits with the profile of this oppressor. He went behind Samson's back to arrange things and used Samson's wife (indirectly this time) to get a dig at Samson. Then he deflected the blame onto Samson by implying Samson was the one who started it. "Don't blame me. I thought you hated her. It is your own fault things turned out this way." This was part of the enemy's tactic to place false guilt and blame on the victim.

49. What was Samson's response?

". . . This time I shall be blameless regarding the Philistines if I harm them!" You say I was to blame for what happened at the wedding? This time it's on you.

50. Samson's purpose was to drive hidden things to light. The first time, he drew the young lions out of hiding with a feast. How did he drive this new treachery to light?

He burned them out with fire. The Philistines denied Samson his wife who was the means of his personal fruitfulness, so Samson denied the Philistines the fruitfulness that they had enjoyed at the expense of Israel (God's bride). He tied three hundred foxes together in pairs, attached flaming torches to their tails, and turned them loose in the standing grain to shed a little light on things.

Three hundred foxes is a lot of foxes to be found in a relatively small area. Perhaps this is a testament to Israel being overrun with wild predatory beasts (and bestial men) as a result of their unfaithfulness. First lions, now foxes.

51. What time of year was it?

The time of the wheat harvest, which meant the fields were at their peak and their driest.

52. What burned?

All the grain, vineyards, and olive groves—totality of the year's harvest. The land was laid bare. There was no more vineyard for lions to hide and hunt in.

53. What did the burning reveal?

The father-in-law's treachery.

54. Treachery, once revealed, gave way to open warfare. What was the Philistines' response?

They burned the father-in-law for being the cause of the fire, but they also burned Samson's wife in an eye-for-an-eye type of vengeance. If they had stopped with the father-in-law, there might have been an end to it. But their renewed attack on Samson's bride brought on another round of retaliation.

55. What was Samson's response?

He laid into them and gave them a sound and thorough thrashing. Samson avenged his wife's death and then ceased.

The battle raged between Samson and the Philistines over Samson's Philistine bride. The bride was the central focus. The real battle was between God and the Philistines over Israel. Even though she was a Philistine, Samson's wife was a model of Israel in her unfaithfulness and her victimization. Samson remained faithful to her even when she was not faithful to him.

56. Samson settled at the rock of Etam (v8). The word for "settle" indicates a permanent dwelling. He was there to stay. What does the name "Rock of Etam" add to the picture?

The Hebrew word used for "rock" is *cela* which means an "exalted or high cliff or rock of refuge"—a place where you should be safe from enemies. David used it to describe God in Psalm 18:2:

> "The LORD is my rock [cela] and my fortress and my deliverer; My God, my strength, in whom I will trust; My shield and the horn of my salvation, my stronghold." —Psalm 18:2

Etam means "lair of wild, predatory birds or beasts" like eagles or lions. Would you want to climb a high cliff to reach the eagle's lair or go into this predator's den after him? I wouldn't.

APPLY THE PICTURE

Keep in mind, Samson was a man given over to his Canaanite side with little conscience or restraint, which makes him an ideal tool for the Lord's purposes. He was also the judge whom God has sent to execute judgment on the Philistines. He is not necessarily an example we should model in regards to taking vengeance and retaliating. If anything, he models the destructive path that retaliation takes when it is allowed to play out.

57. Once we begin down the path into cycles of retaliation, where does the path end? What stops the cycle?

Questions for Reflection

- *"Don't blame me. It's your own fault..."* Have you ever had someone do something hurtful to you and then make an excuse for their behavior by turning the blame back on you as if they were innocent?

    o If so, what was the reaction from your Canaanite side?

    o What should be our response as a child of God?

- *"Yeah, but he started it..."* Have you ever been called to act as judge between two people caught up in this cycle of retaliation? If so, how did you put an end to it and sort things out?

- What are some of the ways we can stumble in dealing with this kind of oppression? (Think of the stumbling blocks we have been studying.)

- Just because you quit fighting and seek a place of refuge, does that mean the enemy stops pursuing you?

BUILD THE PICTURE

Part 3: Samson and the Philistines, Judges 15:9-20

58. The Philistines used the same tactics as before: Find a tool to do your work for you and compel cooperation with the threat of violence. Who was their tool this time?

The men of Judah.

59. How did they compel cooperation?

They marched on Lehi and encamped there, then intimidated Judah with a show of force to deliver Samson. Notice that they didn't ask the men of Judah to deal with Samson. The Philistines wanted Samson delivered to them so that they could deal with him themselves.

60. How many men did it take to drag the lion out of his lair?

Three thousand men.

Samson, the judge, executed punishment on the Philistines, but they refused to accept it as an end to the matter. They told the men of Judah they wanted Samson in order to do to him what he had done to them (but they don't say what). Samson told the men of Judah the same thing—he only did to them what they had done to him and that what he did was fair. So there was a stalemate. Both sides were justified in their own eyes for what they had done and proposed to do.

61. The men of Judah were asked to judge between the Samson and the Philistines. How did they judge the matter?

The men of Judah judged in the Philistines' favor because the Philistines ruled over them. They wanted no fight with the Philistines, so they turned Samson, their deliverer, over to that brutal Gentile court to be killed.

62. Samson allowed the men of Judah to deliver him to the Philistines under what condition?

That they didn't kill him themselves. That wasn't part of the picture. Instead, they bound him with ropes and led him back to Lehi.

63. The confrontation played out at Lehi. What does the name Lehi add to the picture?

The name **Lehi** springs from the common word *lechi* meaning "jaw" or "cheek." If you open your mouth and press your fingers into hollow of your cheek between your grinders, that is your *lechi*.

Lechi is used in a very specific context in Scripture. Look at what happens to the *lechi* in the following verses:

> *"Now gather yourself in troops, O daughter of troops; He has laid siege against us; They will strike the judge of Israel with a rod on the cheek* [lechi]." —Micah 5:1

> *"Let him give his cheek* [lechi] *to the one who strikes him, and be full of reproach."* —Lamentations 3:30

> *"I gave My back to those who struck Me, and My cheeks* [lechi] *to those who plucked out the beard; I did not hide My face from shame and spitting."* —Isaiah 50:6

> *"They gape at me with their mouth, they strike me reproachfully on the cheek* [lechi], *they gather together against me."* —Job 16:10

Lechi is used most often in context of getting a slap in the face as an act of rebuke or scorn.

64. What slap in the face did Samson receive and from whom?

He got a slap from his own countrymen. Instead of fighting with him against the enemy, they came to arrest him and hand him over to be killed by the enemy. He also got a slap in the face from the Philistines, in that they had overcome him using his own people.

65. How did Samson return the slap in the face?

At Lehi, God let loose His own tool and armed him, appropriately, with a *lechi*—a jawbone—of a donkey. Samson returned the rebuke with a slap from the mouth of a donkey. (This was not the only time the mouth of a donkey delivered a rebuke. Remember Balaam?)

When he was finished, Samson sang this victory song:

> *"With the jawbone of a donkey, heaps upon heaps, with the jawbone of a donkey I have slain a thousand men!"* —Judges 15:16

There is a play on words in the Hebrew.

> Donkey, in Hebrew, is *chamor.*
> Heaps, in Hebrew, is *chamorah.*

Both words take their root from the word *chamar*, which means to boil, bubble, or froth up and yet come to nothing. It also carries the sense of being red—not just in color but figuratively from being troubled or in turmoil.

Donkeys are *chamar*-ish in color but also *chamar*-ish in nature. They are stubborn and tend to boil up suddenly in a fit of temper. A thousand Philistines have boiled up against Samson in donkey-like fashion, but their frothing came to nothing. Heaps upon heaps rose up but died away just as quickly.

66. Who fought with Samson?

Three thousand men delivered him into the hands of the Philistines, then stood around and watched without lifting a finger. Samson is a lot like Shamgar, who also took on the Philistines alone, only Shamgar did it with an oxgoad.

67. Compare Samson's victory cry in verse 16 with his cry for deliverance in verse 18. How does Samson relate to God?

> *"Then he became very thirsty; so he cried out to the LORD and said, 'You have given this great deliverance by the hand of Your servant; and now shall I die of thirst and fall into the hand of the uncircumcised?'"*—Judges 15:18

His cry for deliverance is a curious contrast to the victory cry. In his victory cry, Samson exalted himself without mention of the Lord's part in the battle. But then he turned and abased himself as a servant before the LORD, confessing that it was the LORD who gave the deliverance and he was just the tool. Though he was strong and overcame his enemies, his strength couldn't save him from death for the simple lack of water. He cried out to God for the life-giving water.

68. How did God respond?

In response, God split the hollow place that was in Lehi. Literally, He split the *maktesh*—the grinding bowl (a picturesque way of describing the hollow place in the jaw surrounded by grinders). God opened the mouth in response to Samson's cry, and water poured forth. And so Samson named the place En-Hakkore or "the spring of the caller."

Samson understood from whom deliverance came and the role God had given him. While he did not give Israel complete deliverance or rest, he was still established as their judge in the days of the Philistines. He judged Israel for 20 years.

69. Having dealt with the Philistines, how does he respond to his betrayal by the men of Judah?

That is a bit of a loose end. You would think that he would do something or say something to them, but he didn't.

Samson, the Harlot, and the Philistines, Judges 16:1-3

The text doesn't give us a sense of when the rest of the narrative takes place. It just opens with "Now." But we know the events of Chapter 16 took place within Samson's time as judge, not after, because of the narrative is bookended by the phrase "he judged Israel twenty years" (Judges 15:20, 16:31). The inclusio suggests the events happened within that time period.

God used Samson with his Canaanite proclivities to deal with a Canaanite enemy and create a picture. In terms of the big picture, the transitional episode with the harlot of Gaza is part of the previous picture but it also ties to the narrative with Delilah. So let's continue building the picture through this episode and then apply it.

70. The narrative opens in Gaza. What do we know about Gaza?

Gaza was a Philistine stronghold, a fortified city deep in enemy territory. Samson had to traverse the length of Philistine territory to get there from his home near Zorah.

Gaza or 'Azzah means "the strong," from root word *az*, meaning "strong, fierce, greedy, or cruel." Gaza was somewhat of an archetypal city in its strength and fortifications, like Jericho.

71. Why would Samson go all the way to Gaza? For what purpose?

In terms of following his Canaanite tendencies, Samson was going about as far down that road as he could go. By entering Gaza, he was making a statement that he could do what he wanted, when he wanted, where he wanted, and there was nothing that could hold him. While he was there he saw a harlot, and he took her. I don't think his purpose for going to Gaza was for the sake of visiting the harlot alone. I think she was part of the statement he was making. Not only did he penetrate the enemy's stronghold, he took one of their women to boot, simply because it pleased him to do so. It was an act of domination. It was an in-your-face provoking act that made the Philistines froth because of the sheer audacity of it.

Once again, a woman became the tool for his enemies to trap Samson.

72. **The text belabors the fact that this all happened at night. Look at the timing of events. How long did the Philistines wait for Samson to come out?**

All night. The Gazites were told that Samson was there and the *charash*-ing—the plotting behind the gate—began.

> "They were quiet [charash] all night, saying, 'In the morning, when it is daylight, we will kill him.'" —Judges 16:2

Why didn't the Philistines just go in and get Samson, if they knew where he was? Why stand guard all night? The guy was behind the gate, and he wasn't getting out. He may as well have been in the grave at that point. We can speculate that maybe they didn't fight at night, or maybe they couldn't get in because the gate was closed, or maybe they just wanted the pleasure of taking him down publicly and in broad daylight. But we don't know really. No reason is given.

73. **If Samson left at midnight (and took the gate with him), but the Philistines remained there all night until morning, then what does that tell us?**

That means he passed by without them seeing him—or hearing him even, it seems. He must have made some noise when he pulled the gate out of the wall, but it appears that they didn't hear anything either, in spite of their being quiet all night.

City gates are usually opened with the morning sun. It's a little funny to think that Samson, whose name means "like the sun," just opened the gates a bit early that morning.

74. The text isn't specific, but Jewish tradition holds that Samson actually hauled the gates to Hebron and planted them on the hill there. Why Hebron?

Hebron was a city in Judah, thirty-five miles away from Gaza. It was one of the first conquests mentioned in the book of Judges (Judges 1:10), the place where the Anakim giants had been defeated. Hebron was given to Caleb as a reward for his faithfulness to God. That was a long time ago.

The name **Hebron** means "association" from the root noun *heber*, which means associations and the root verb *habar*, meaning literally "to be united" or "joined together." When applied to human relationships, it means "to be in league with" any number of bad associations (charmers, robbers, murderers) or in alliances with wicked nations or idols. It is almost always used in a negative sense.

So, with whom have the men of Judah joined themselves? The Philistines, and it is a bad association. They have prostituted themselves to the Philistine gods, and they have let themselves be used as the Philistines' tool for bringing one of their own into bondage. The men of Judah are the harlot of Gaza.

Samson escaped the clutches of the Philistines. He also escaped the clutches of the harlot who would have been the accomplice in his capture.

75. If you were the children of Israel living in Hebron, and you woke up one morning to find a Philistine gate planted on a hill outside your city, what message would you take from that?

If you were one of the ones who betrayed Samson, it would be shocking and not just a little terrifying. In the Hebrew culture, gates were where the judges sat to render judgment. To others it might be a message of hope, that what had been an enemy stronghold had been overcome and their gates had been broken.

PICTURE SUMMARY (Judges 14:1–16:3)

Samson, the great deliverer, was born of miraculous birth (born to a barren woman) and was a Nazirite from birth. His mother was told that he will begin to save his people, but the path he would take to accomplish that would lead to his defilement (and death). Little is known about his early life until he steps into his ministry. Something is known of him through prophetic pictures, but it is veiled.

Samson stepped on the scene as a poser of riddles and a diviner of men's hearts. He was like the sun when it came out at full strength, shedding light on the condition of his people. He confronted the young lions who have been feeding themselves on God's flock and vineyard. First he drew them out by sitting down with them at a feast and posing a riddle aimed at revealing their treachery and true character. Twice he resorted to physical violence and gave them a thorough thrashing.

The Philistine lions dealt with Samson treacherously by using one of his own to betray him. He was arrested but went willingly on condition that his own people not kill him themselves. He was delivered a proverbial slap in the face and handed over to the Philistines to be killed. And when the act of deliverance was finished and he was near death, he cried out to God, "I thirst!" Though he was strong, he acknowledged that he could not save himself, nor did he seek deliverance from his own brothers standing by. His cry was to God alone. The LORD responded with an outpouring of life-giving waters that revived Samson and brought him back from near death.

The secondary picture: Samson found himself locked behind closed doors in an enemy stronghold in the dark with the enemy guard stationed outside the gate. The place should be his grave, and yet the fortress couldn't hold him. In spite of the guards, he passed out of the place in the night, taking with him the gates so that they might not be closed again. He planted the gates before his people as a message.

APPLY THE PICTURE

PICTURE OF CHRIST IN SAMSON

In the same way, Jesus Christ, the great deliverer of God's people, was born of a miraculous birth (to a virgin). Though He is not a Nazirite by vow, he is *nazir* or separated from his brothers in the same way Joseph was separated from his brothers when he was sent down to Egypt. He would be the Savior of His people, but the path He would take to accomplish this would lead to his defilement and death. Like Samson, little is known about His early life until He steps into His ministry. Something is known of Him through the prophetic pictures, but it is veiled.

Jesus stepped on the national scene as a poser of parables and dark sayings and a diviner of men's hearts. He was the Light, shedding light on the condition of his people who had been overrun by external and internal enemies. He confronted the Pharisees, the wolves in sheep's clothing who had been pasturing themselves on God's people and keeping them in bondage. The Pharisees were a lot like the Philistines in that the external appearance with which they clothed themselves hid a much different nature beneath the sheets. Jesus drew them out in various ways. He began by sitting down at meals and feasts and posing parables aimed at revealing their treachery. One such parable was even about a wedding feast where a guest was found wearing an unsuitable wedding garment. These parables riled Pharisaic lions, and they began plotting against Him in Philistine-like *charash*-ing. On two occasions Jesus resorted to physical violence and gave them a thorough thrashing.

The Pharisaic lions dealt with Jesus treacherously by using one of His own—an intimate friend—to betray him with a kiss. They went in force to the solitary place where He had taken refuge, and they arrested Him. They did not kill Him themselves—that was not part of the picture—but delivered Him a slap in the face literally and figuratively before handing Him over to a Gentile court to be put to death.

The act of deliverance in Jesus' case was through His death on the cross. Like Samson, at that moment of deliverance, Jesus also cries out, "I thirst!"

> *"After this, Jesus, knowing that all things were now accomplished, that the Scripture might be fulfilled, said, 'I thirst!'"* —John 19:28

Instead of life-giving water, he was offered sour wine.

> *"... when Jesus had received the sour wine, He said, "It is finished!" And bowing His head, He gave up His spirit."* —John 19:29

But His death was not permanent. The battle having been won, God the Father returned Him to life, and His spirit was revived on the day of resurrection.

In the follow-on picture, Jesus finds himself buried in the tomb—behind the barred door of the darkest of enemy strongholds—with the Roman guards stationed outside in the event that someone should come and steal away His body. Like Samson, the place that should have been His grave could not hold Him. In spite of the guard stationed at the door, He passed out of that place in the night, taking with Him the gates of death so that they might not be closed again. He appeared before His people in his resurrected form as a message. When considering the picture of that gate planted on the hill before the people, think about what Jesus said in John 10 about being the door for His sheep. I will leave you to ponder that.

So, how does Christ respond to those of His own people who betrayed Him? He doesn't. He let the evidence of His resurrection speak for itself and left them to sort it out for themselves. Having accomplished the salvation aspect, Jesus' next role is that of judge.

As for the Roman guards—like those Gazite Philistines who waited beside the closed gate all night and were confronted in the morning with the escape accomplished—they were *charash*-ed into keeping their mouths shut over the monumental loss of face that the Pharisees and Rome had suffered in Jesus' resurrection.

There is a limit to how closely the shadow images of Jesus' life and death play out in the lives of Old Testament characters, but you can see the gist of the picture.

BUILD THE PICTURE

Samson and Delilah, Judges 16:4-21

Samson was a child of God set aside for God's purpose, and yet he still contended with his own carnal Canaanite lusts. In Chapter 15, he was revived and given newness of life only to take the path back into a sinful lifestyle with tragic consequences in Chapter 16.

Even as God used Samson to deal with the Philistines, God also used the Philistines to deal with Samson. The narrative continues in the Valley of Sorek, with Samson and Delilah.

76. What do we know about Delilah?

> Samson's wife pleased his eye. For the harlot, he felt nothing. But Delilah he loved. For the first time, Samson expressed an emotion and the woman was named, unlike the other two who were nameless. That is all we really know about Delilah. She was simply the woman he loved. She may have been Philistine, but the text doesn't expressly say. She was certainly in league with them. When the Philistines approached Delilah with their proposal to capture Samson, she didn't

have to be coerced the way Samson's wife did. They simply bought her. Each lord offered Delilah 1,100 pieces of silver, and that was all it took to secure her cooperation. Again, note, a woman was the middle man. She was the tool that they used to trap Samson.

77. What does the meaning of Delilah's name add to the picture?

The name Delilah means "feeble" or "to make feeble" from the root verb *dalal,* meaning "to hang low or be brought low."

Job uses *dalal* to describe a man hanging by a rope over a mine shaft.

> "He breaks open a shaft away from people; In places forgotten by feet they hang far away from men [dalal]; they swing to and fro."
> —Job 28:4

It is the picture of a man who is brought low—to the end of his rope, so to speak—in pursuit of something he desires. He dangles in a precarious and vulnerable position at the end of a rope between light and darkness, the living and the grave. In the context of the passage in Job, this treasure-seeker is contrasted to the man seeking wisdom. Add to that picture the description of the seductress in Proverbs 23:27-28:

> "For a harlot is a deep pit, and a seductress is a narrow well. She also lies in wait as for a victim, and increases the unfaithful among men."
> —Proverbs 23:27-28

Here, Lady Wisdom is contrasted to the harlot and the seductress, who are described as deep wells down which a man unwisely lets his rope in pursuit of something for which he lusts.

Samson, God's deliverer and judge, was also the proverbial fool who turned aside to the seductress in pursuit of pleasure instead of seeking wisdom. As a result, he found himself in a very precarious, and vulnerable position that would cost him dearly.

Another variant of the root *dalal* is *dalla* (feminine noun) meaning "a bundle of hair" or "threads of warp" that hang down from a loom and get cut off. *Dalla* is used in Song of Solomon 7:5 to describe the hair of the Shulamite bride who holds a king captive because of his love for her, a foreshadowing of Samson's destiny in Delilah's hands.

The picture element of the warp of thread in a loom also comes into play as the narrative progresses. It might be that Samson played off Delilah's name as he teased her with false answers.

The narrative develops in a three-and-four verse structure similar to Jotham and Abimelech's narrative. There are three false answers and one truth that ends climatically.

78. As we outline the conversation between Samson and Delilah, consider the tone Delilah took with Samson, and how his answers revealed his descent down the proverbial rope.

Delilah's first ask: *"Please tell me..."*
Samson: *"If they bind me with seven fresh bowstrings..."*

Delilah begins with a tease, playing to Samson's vanity perhaps. Oh, you big, strong man...

In Samson's reply, the Hebrew word for "bowstring" is an atypical use of the word *yether*, which literally means a length of rope or cord that is cut off, but is figurative of the excellency or abundance of man's life that comes to an end sooner or later. This is the same word as the name of Gideon's son, Jether, who was the end of Gideon's excellency and legacy. To give you the flavor of Samson's word choice, here are a few other examples:

> *"Does not their own excellence* [yether] *go away? They die, even without wisdom."* — Job 4:21

> *"I said in the cutting off of my days, I shall go to the gates of the grave: I am deprived of the residue* [yether] *of my years."* —Isaiah 38:10

Delilah's second ask: *"You have mocked me and told me lies. Please tell me..."*
Samson: *"If they bind me securely with new ropes..."*

Delilah's tone becomes a little more demanding upon discovering Samson had lied to her.

Again, Samson used the rope theme. But the ropes didn't work at Lehi. Why would they work this time? Note that the Philistines who had been hiding in Delilah's room up until then left at this point. It was clear that Samson was toying with her. Their presence is not noted in the third round of questioning.

Delilah's third ask: *"You have mocked me and told me lies. Tell me..."*
Samson: *"If you weave the seven locks of my head into the web of the loom—"* (the conditional statement is unfinished)

Note Delilah's imperious tone this time. She was growing stronger as Samson's will was weakening.

This time, Samson mentioned his hair, hedging at the truth without saying it. His remark about the seven locks of his head may indicate that the long, unshorn hair had been braided into seven locks and bundled together.

Delilah's final demand: *"How can you say 'I love you'..."*
Samson: Cut my hair.

This was a full frontal assault of feminine outrage. Funny that Delilah should demand proof of love from Samson, when she herself didn't love him. Like Samson's wife, Delilah pestered him until he was vexed to death, and then he caved. Notice that she had to send for the Philistine lords this time. They weren't waiting in the wings as before.

79. Samson told Delilah that his hair was the source of his strength. Was that a true statement?

No, actually, it wasn't. His strength was in God, not his hair. Leaving his hair uncut was a condition of the Nazirite vow, but so was abstaining from grape products and avoiding defilement from unclean things. There is no power in any of these things. They are only outward indications of an internal relationship.

80. *"... Then she began to [chalal] torment him, and his strength left him."* Where does this *chalal*-ing moment lead?

Remember: *Chalal* means to be "profaned or defiled" by being "fatally wounded, pierced, or bored through." When the Philistines took him, the Hebrew text says that they literally bored out his eyes. He is *chalal*-ed physically and figuratively.

81. What does the shaving of Samson's head reveal?

The enemy and Delilah's true heart. It also revealed that Samson had become complacent in thinking himself unconquerable. He didn't even realize the Spirit had gone from him. There is a notable absence of the Spirit at work in Samson from this point until the end.

82. The Philistines capture Samson in the Sorek Valley. Why take him back to Gaza?

For the humiliation factor. They marched him back the length of the territory so that all would see that Samson had been subdued. Gaza was where he had penetrated their stronghold, then escaped under their noses, taking the fortress gate with him. It was a monumental coup to subdue Samson and return on him all the humiliation they had suffered.

83. Why make him a grinder?

The Philistines made him a tool to be used for their pleasure, and in doing so reduced him to the status of a woman, literally. Grain grinding was the job of the women servants (concubines) as Job describes rather explicitly:

> "If my heart has been enticed by a woman, or if I have lurked at my neighbor's door, then let my wife grind for another, and let others bow down over her." —Job 31:9-10

Samson had made a point of taking Philistine women for his pleasure. Who's the woman now ... The Philistines were an enemy that really pushed the humiliation factor in their oppression.

The way out of all oppressions is a return to God, and the return begins with the man. Like Abimelech, God let Samson's behavior run its course until it had brought Samson to the end of his rope. Samson had broken the conditions of his vow, but more than that, he had sold himself into bondage to a foreign master and his godly purpose had been lost. The shaving of a Nazirite's head was a sign that he must start over in performing his vow to God. As Samson's hair began to grow, there was a renewal of his purpose.

84. There is a fourth and final *chalal*-ing moment in verse 22 when Samson's hair began to grow. Where did this *chalal*-ing lead?

Ultimately, to Samson's death. The four repetitions of *chalal* in the narrative suggest the completion and fullness of the journey.

Samson's Death, Judges 16:22-31

85. What was the occasion for the Philistine's revelry?

The celebration of Samson's capture. Samson had been reduced to a sideshow performer. Meanwhile Dagon was getting praise for bringing down Jehovah God's man.

86. Overall, the passage is presented in a timeline order, yet it seems like verses 23-25 don't quite follow the logical progression. What is the author's intent in deviating from the timeline structure?

There is a switching of verses 24 and 25. If the narrative was being written in a timeline flow, then the verses would flow in this order:

(v23) They gathered together to offer sacrifice to Dagon and rejoice.
(v25) They called Samson to perform.
(v24) When they saw him, they praised their god.

Instead, the author purposely switched verses 24 and 25 to emphasize the praise being heaped on Dagon.

(v23) They gathered together to offer sacrifice to Dagon and rejoice.
(v24) When they saw him, they praised their god.
(v25) They called Samson to perform.

This was the reason for which God sent Samson one last time—to deal a death blow to the Philistines and their god. The battle was not just one man against a bunch of Philistines. It was really a battle being waged on a spiritual level between God and Dagon, and Samson's work would not be done until he had taken down God's rival.

87. In a literal sense, Samson was weak and had to physically lean on the pillars of Dagon's temple for support. But on whom was Samson leaning in the figurative sense?

Even though Samson's hair had grown, it doesn't seem that the fullness of physical strength returned with it, but then the strength was never really in his hair. The hair was only symbolic of his relationship with God.

Samson was blind and powerless, standing in the middle of a heathen temple surrounded by heathen tormentors. It was a moment of darkness and utter defeat for him. In the midst of his wretched condition, Samson had a very personal moment with God. For the second time in the entire narrative, he called out to God with a request. This time he asked before acting.

88. What was Samson's request?

To be remembered by God. To be strengthened. To let him avenge himself for his two eyes. God's judge asked for an eye-for-an-eye justice, and then he asked to die.

The completion of a Nazirite vow required a comprehensive sacrifice—burnt offering, sin offering, peace offering, grain and drink offering. Samson offered his own life as the sacrifice for God granting him victory over his enemies. And so Deborah's prophecy is fulfilled.

> *"Thus let all Your enemies perish, O LORD! But let those who love Him be as the sun when it comes out in full strength."* —Judges 5:31

APPLY THE PICTURE

Samson grappled with three physical enemies, and one spiritual Enemy who continually *charash*-ed things behind the scenes.

1) **The spiritual Enemy,** Satan (& Dagon)

2) **The external enemy,** the Philistines

3) **The intimate enemy,** the Canaanite women in his life. The companions at his wedding might also be included in this category.

4) **The internal enemy,** his own lustful desires.

Samson did pretty well in dealing with the external oppressors with the Spirit's help. He didn't do so well with the intimate enemies. In the end, he failed miserably at dealing with his own carnal desires. His name meant "like the sun," but that light became sunk in darkness in the end.

When Samson lost the battle with his inner lusts, he suffered defeat on *all* enemy fronts. Consider that for a moment. When we lose the battle with our internal, carnal side, we also lose the battle on other fronts. We lose our credibility and effectiveness in dealing with sin in our immediate sphere of influence as well as our witness to the outside world. And Satan uses it as a way to bring us back into bondage.

We face the same enemies in our own context:

1) **The spiritual Enemy,** Satan

2) **The external enemy,** that is, the unbelieving, carnal, Canaanite world

3) **The intimate enemy.** This may be family, other believers, or those posing as the "bride" or "companions" at the Lamb's wedding feast who have no right to be there. These take the form of apostates, false

apostles, and false teachers. They comport themselves with Philistine-like tactics such as treachery, fraud, deceit (including hypocrisy, where their *beged* doesn't match the true character underneath), intimidation, and a pursuit of lusts and "gain" by the world's standard.

4) The internal enemy, that is, our carnal "dark" side

The New Testament verses addressing our battles with these are extensive, but I have pulled out a few passages that use imagery similar to the Samson narrative to describe these enemies.

> *"Be sober, be vigilant; because your adversary <u>the devil walks about like a roaring lion, seeking whom he may devour.</u> Resist him, steadfast in the faith, knowing that the same sufferings are experienced by your brotherhood in the world."* —1 Peter 5:8-9 (emphasis added).

> *"You are of your father the devil, and the desires of your father you want to do. <u>He was a murderer from the beginning, and does not stand in the truth, because there is no truth in him. When he speaks a lie, he speaks from his own resources, for he is a liar and the father of it.</u>"* — John 8:44 (emphasis added).

> *"Beware of false prophets, who come to you in sheep's clothing, but inwardly they are ravenous wolves."* —Matthew 7:15

> *"For such are false apostles, deceitful workers, transforming themselves into apostles of Christ. And no wonder! For Satan himself transforms himself into an angel of light. Therefore it is no great thing if his ministers also transform themselves into ministers of righteousness, whose end will be according to their works."* —2 Corinthians 11:13-15

> *"But there were also <u>false prophets</u> among the people, even as there will be false teachers among you, who will secretly bring in destructive heresies, even denying the Lord who bought them, and bring on themselves swift destruction. And many will follow their destructive ways, because of whom the way of truth will be blasphemed. <u>By covetousness they will exploit you with deceptive words</u>; for a long time their judgment has not been idle, and their destruction does not slumber."* —2 Peter 2:1-3 (emphasis added).

> <u>*But these, like natural brute beasts made to be caught and destroyed, speak evil of the things they do not understand, and will utterly perish*</u>

in their own corruption, and will receive the wages of unrighteousness, as those who count it pleasure to carouse in the daytime. They are spots and blemishes, carousing in their own deceptions while they feast with you, having eyes full of adultery and that cannot cease from sin, enticing unstable souls. They have a heart trained in covetous practices, and are accursed children. They have forsaken the right way and gone astray, following the way of Balaam the son of Beor, who loved the wages of unrighteousness; but he was *rebuked for his iniquity: a dumb donkey speaking with a man's voice restrained the madness of the prophet.*"
—2 Peter 2:12-16 (emphasis added). This passage draws heavily on the imagery of Samson's wedding feast and the victory at Lehi.

"For when they speak great swelling words of emptiness, they allure through the lusts of the flesh, through lewdness, the ones who have actually escaped from those who live in error. *While they promise them liberty, they themselves are slaves of corruption; for by whom a person is overcome, by him also he is brought into bondage. For if, after they have escaped the pollutions of the world through the knowledge of the Lord and Savior Jesus Christ, they are again entangled in them and overcome, the latter end is worse for them than the beginning.* For it would have been better for them not to have known the way of righteousness, than having known it, to turn from the holy commandment delivered to them." —2 Peter 2:18-21 (emphasis added). This passage echoes Delilah's allurement and Samson's downfall.

These are spots in your love feasts, while they feast with you without fear, serving only themselves. They are clouds without water, carried about by the winds; late autumn trees without fruit, twice dead, pulled up by the roots; raging waves of the sea, *foaming up their own shame*; wandering stars for whom is reserved the blackness of darkness forever." —Jude 1:3-4, 12-13 (emphasis added)

"For you were once darkness, but now you are light in the Lord. Walk as children of light (for the fruit of the Spirit is in all goodness, righteousness, and truth), finding out what is acceptable to the Lord. And have no fellowship with the unfruitful works of darkness, but rather expose them. For it is shameful even to speak of those things which are done by them in secret. But all things that are exposed are made manifest by the light, for whatever makes manifest is light."
—Ephesians 5:8-13

> *"The night is far spent, the day is at hand. Therefore let us cast off the works of darkness, and let us put on the armor of light. Let us walk properly, as in the day, not in revelry and drunkenness, not in lewdness and lust, not in strife and envy. But put on the Lord Jesus Christ, and make no provision for the flesh, to fulfill its lusts."* —Romans 13:12-14

> *"I say then: Walk in the Spirit, and you shall not fulfill the lust of the flesh. For the flesh lusts against the Spirit, and the Spirit against the flesh; and these are contrary to one another, so that you do not do the things that you wish."* —Galatians 5:16-17

> *"Therefore, since Christ suffered for us in the flesh, arm yourselves also with the same mind, for he who has suffered in the flesh has ceased from sin, that he no longer should live the rest of his time in the flesh for the lusts of men, but for the will of God."* —1 Peter 4:1-2

> *"Do not love the world or the things in the world. If anyone loves the world, the love of the Father is not in him. For all that is in the world—the lust of the flesh, the lust of the eyes, and the pride of life—is not of the Father but is of the world."* —1 John 2:15-16

God used Samson as a tool to exact vengeance on His enemies, but Samson got off track in his personal life before the job was done.

89. What did God have to do to get Samson back on track and remember where his true strength was?

He took away the sight of his eyes. Samson was always one to launch into action without asking first, according to what was right in his own eyes. Without his eyes, Samson had to ask for direction and submit to being led.

God also took His strength from Samson and humbled him at the hands of enemies who were as weak as Samson had been strong.

God did all that so that Samson would understand where his weakness was. It didn't matter how strong he was physically. He had a weakness, and his eyes were his downfall.

Jesus taught this lesson:

> *"You have heard that it was said to those of old, 'You shall not commit adultery.' But I say to you that whoever looks at a woman to lust for her has already committed adultery with her in his heart. If your right eye causes you to sin, pluck it out and cast it from you; for*

> *it is more profitable for you that one of your members perish, than for your whole body to be cast into hell." - Matthew 5:27-29*

We understand Jesus is using extreme hyperbole—obviously we are not called to pluck out our own eye—and yet this is exactly what Samson illustrates for us in a very literal way. The only way God was going to get His servant back on track was to remove that thing in his life that was causing him to sin.

Samson presents us with this incongruent picture of a man who pursued his carnal lusts to his own death, and a man who achieved God's purpose even in death. In our eyes, his actions are appalling, provoking, seemingly without conscience or restraint, and deserving of judgment. But we cannot forget that Samson was also a judge, invested with God's authority to execute eye-for-an-eye judgment on God's enemies. The man and his actions appear very differently depending on what lens you are viewing them through.

Samson's marriage to a Philistine woman was wrong in his parents' eyes, even according to the Law, but right in God's eyes because it suited God's purpose. Was Samson's taking of the harlot of Gaza or his affair with Delilah part of God's plan as well?

90. Do we model Samson's behavior in pursuing our carnal lusts, thinking that God's purpose will be accomplished regardless of what we do?

No, of course not. This is not a behavior to be modeled. We should not think for one moment that just because God used Samson's pursuit of women for His divine purposes—even to paint those pictures for us of Christ—that we should let our Canaanite side run wild and expect God to work His will through it. In Romans 6, Paul refutes this idea that just because we have been justified in Christ and freed of the law, we can continue to live in sin and expect grace to abound.

> *"Therefore do not let sin reign in your mortal body, that you should obey it in its lusts. And do not present your members as instruments of unrighteousness to sin, but present yourselves to God as being alive from the dead, and your members as instruments of righteousness to God. For sin shall not have dominion over you, for you are not under law but under grace."* —Romans 6:12-14

91. Second Peter 2:18-22 describes how a believer gets entangled again in sin. How do Samson and Delilah model a picture of this for us?

Delilah was an intimate enemy—one who professed to be joined with Samson but in her heart was not. She is similar in character profile to the false teachers that Peter describes—those who profess to be believers and yet are wolves in sheep's clothing. She allured Samson through the lust of the flesh after he had already escaped the Philistine enemy.

> *"For when they speak great swelling words of emptiness, they allure through the lusts of the flesh, through lewdness, the ones who have actually escaped from those who live in error. While they promise them liberty, they themselves are slaves of corruption; for by whom a person is overcome, by him also he is brought into bondage."* —2 Peter 2:18-19

Delilah represented a certain kind of liberty to Samson—a liberty to pursue his lusts. For Samson it was sex, but for believers it may be any kind of freedom or gain we wish to pursue. The false teachers promote a message of freedom and lack of restraint, but they themselves are corrupted by the same message and slaves to it.

Delilah had an appetite for money the way Samson had an appetite for women. Whatever love she might have felt for Samson was overcome by her greed, and through her greed, she brought Samson into bondage. She was, after all, only the middle man—the slave who brought another into slavery. She was in bondage to her own lusts, and when she overcame Samson, she brought him into bondage, too.

> *"For if, after they have escaped the pollutions of the world through the knowledge of the Lord and Savior Jesus Christ, they are again entangled in them and overcome, the latter end is worse for them than the beginning. For it would have been better for them not to have known the way of righteousness, than having known it, to turn from the holy commandment delivered to them."* —2 Peter 2:20-21

Samson is the ideal model of this. He escaped the Philistine enemy, only to be entangled again, and his latter end was worse than his beginning.

92. What does it take to free a believer who has been caught back up in bondage (what did it take for Samson to be freed)?

When we start down that winding road away from God, we often wake up to find ourselves enslaved and in the proverbial grinder. God lets us go through that experience of torment and buffeting by the enemy to teach us where our true strength is. And He reminds us:

> *"My grace is sufficient for you, for My strength is made perfect in weakness."* —2 Corinthians 12:9

93. Why is Samson remembered in the Hebrews hall of faith? (Hebrews 11:32-34)

Do you think it was his overall performance that won him a mention in the Hebrews hall of faith, or was it just that last step of faith when he returned to God after being broken? I wonder.

94. Samson's purpose was to shed light on things. We, too, are called to be children of light. What are some ways we model Samson in this?

Was Samson really a holy instrument for God's purpose, or is he just a man given over to his lust that God used in spite of his failings? We have discussed a number of stumbling blocks that people in oppression deal with, but I think the greatest stumbling block for Samson was letting his dark side rule him. He was supposed to be "like the sun" in revealing the truth of the Philistines character and Israel's condition, and he was. Even so, his pursuit of his Canaanite lusts are what drove him. We can model Samson in this for better or worse. We are called to be children of light, and yet we often fail to achieve that picture in its purity and completeness. And so we become this odd hybrid expression that can leave people scratching their heads. Is the man who declares himself a believer and yet lives a questionable lifestyle really a believer? Is that ministry leader really that impeccably righteous pillar of the community or is there another character hiding behind the facade? We should not have this duality about us, but we do. Overcoming that duality is part of pursuing our inheritance in the kingdom. We are to be one holy vessel with one godly nature, clothed in the garment of a godly character.

> Questions for Reflection:
>
> - How have you done with battling the various "enemies" in your life? Which one do you struggle with the most (personal, intimate, external)?
> - Have you or someone you know fallen victim to a wolf in sheep's clothing?
>   - If so, how did it happen?
>   - Are you still in their bondage? If not, how did you get out?
>   - What were some warning signs you should have heeded?
> - How do you guard yourself from falling for the Delilahs of this world, whether they take the form of carnal lusts or wolves in sheep's clothing?

Samson is the twelfth and final judge named in the book of Judges, and his narrative brings to an end the second part of the book. Part 2 focused on the oppressions and wars brought on by external enemies. There was some general in-fighting, such as the confrontations with the men of Ephraim from time to time, but that was not the primary focus.

Now, we segue to Part 3, in which the focus will be purely on the internal issues plaguing Israel. In terms of the timeline, we return back to the beginning of the time of the judges and follow the priesthood this time instead of the judges.

JUDGES, PART 3: NATION WITHOUT A KING

Judges 17:1–21:25

LESSON 12

Micah and the Danites

READ

Judges 17-18

PART 3 OVERVIEW

Chapter 17 begins the third and final section of the book of Judges. Part 3 covers chapters 17 through 21 and differs significantly from Part 2 in its focus, flavor, and narrative style. Here are some chief differences:

- Where Part 2 focused heavily on individuals and names, only three names are mentioned in the whole of Part 3, namely Micah, Phinehas, and Jonathan. Instead, the narrative speaks in generalities, identifying people by tribe or location, such as the Levite, the Danites, the men of Gibeah, the old man from the hills of Ephraim, the father-in-law, etc. This change in narrative style forces the reader's attention on the relationship aspect between the characters. Part 3 is all about relationships—broken relationships—between people and God.

- Where Part 2 focuses on the judges without mention of the priesthood, Part 3 now focuses on the priesthood without mention of the judges.

- Where Part 2 emphasizes Israel's worship of Baals and Ashtoreth specifically, Part 3 only presents general cultic practices with the critical comment that "everyone did what was right in their own eyes."

- Where Part 2 focuses on oppressions from external enemies, Part 3 doesn't describe any oppressions from outside invaders. All the action happens within the congregational dynamics, with the exception of Dan's campaign against Laish which we will talk about in this chapter.

- Where Part 2 presents Israel as being scattered, with the judges and oppressions localized in various parts of Israel, Part 3 presents the picture of Israel as a unified nation for the first time.

In regards to literary structure, Part 3 is framed in an inclusio.

> *"In those days there was no king in Israel; everyone did what was right in his own eyes."* —Judges 17:6, 21:25

This critical comment marks the beginning and end of the narrative of Part 3 and gives us the theme.

- The phrase *"everyone did what was right in his own eyes"* evokes a sense of returning to the wilderness existence that Israel had experienced when they wandered for forty years in the Exodus journey. As they prepared to enter the Land, Moses told them,

   > *"You shall not at all do as we are doing here today—every man doing whatever is right in his own eyes—for as yet you have not come to the rest and the inheritance which the LORD your God is giving you."* —Deuteronomy 12:8-9

   Entering the Land was meant to be an inherently different experience. When Israel returned to doing what was right in their own eyes, they began to relive the wilderness experience as a result. An unsettled character marks the narrative events in Part 3—a lack of vision and purpose, a dissatisfaction and bitterness, and subsequent rootlessness and fruitlessness.

- The phrase *"there was no king"* is repeated four times (Judges 17:6, 18:1, 19:1, 21:25), suggesting that the remedy for Israel's condition is the establishment of a king over the people. This sets the reader up for the transition from theocracy into monarchy as Israel enters the age of the kings in 1 Samuel.

Where in the timeline does Part 3 take place?

There are only two time markers in the narrative that anchor us to the timeline. The first is the account of the Dan's resettling in Laish, which is also mentioned in Joshua 19:47, thus placing that event very early in the Judges' narrative, perhaps even before the beginning of the oppressions.

The other is the parenthetical statement in Judges 20:27-28 noting that Phinehas, the son of Eleazar, the son of Aaron, stood before the Tabernacle in these days. Phinehas becames high priest after his father's death at the end of the book of Joshua; thus he was the presiding high priest at the start of the Judges' narrative. (He is not to be confused with the wicked son of Eli who comes after this time. That Phinehas was never high priest and died young because of his wickedness.)

Both time references place the events of Part 3 at the start of the judges' era, from which we can conclude that the narratives of Part 2 and 3 run concurrently, but follow a different trail of events.

As we have worked our way through the accounts of the judges in Part 2, we saw Israel slipping farther and farther into a Canaanite identity. They become more wicked with each passing judge and cry out less and less against their oppressors. Things won't get better as time progresses. Part 3 begins with a view of pervasive idolatrous practices and ends with the near self-destruction of the tribe of Benjamin over their alliance with the perverted men of Gibeah. It will seem like a continuation of Israel's descent into idolatry and wickedness, but it is not. These events do not happen at the end of the time of the judges as a follow-on to Samson. These events happen at the beginning. It is a staggering thought to consider that Israel was this way from their very beginning in the Land.

This is the overview of Part 3 which covers Chapters 17–21. For this lesson, we will only be covering Chapters 17–18, which detail Micah's idolatry and the Danites' settlement of Laish. Chapters 19–21 will be covered in the next lesson.

Let's begin.

BUILD THE PICTURE

Micah's Idolatry, Judges 17:1-13

1. **What do we know about Micah?**

    The narrative opens with the introduction of a man named Micah. There is no identification with a family line or even a specific tribe, which makes him a model for every man.

    Micah is associated only with a location vaguely referred to as the mountains of Ephraim, which may be in Ephraim or not. In actuality, this mountain range blends into the tribal holdings of Benjamin to the south and Manasseh to the north as far as Shamir (Judges 10:1). The mountains of Ephraim have been central to the Judges' narrative, mentioned thirteen times throughout, and would later become the seat of the idolatrous kingdom of Israel opposed to the southern kingdom of Judah. The kingdom lines are already being drawn here in the book of Judges.

Micah's name means "Who is like God?" which is the over-arching theme of Part 3. Who is like God? Depending on what voice inflection you use, the question can be expressed reverently with awe, as David uses it in Psalms:

> "Who is like the LORD our God, who dwells on high," —Psalm 113:5

> "Also Your righteousness, O God, is very high, You who have done great things; O God, who is like You?" —Psalm 71:19

Or it can be said with strength, as Isaiah relates in Isaiah 40. This was the first passage we studied when we talked about the stumbling blocks of oppression. Isaiah 40:18-25 answers this very question with a picture of God in His power compared to the inferiority of gods fashioned by the hands of men.

> "To whom then will you liken God? Or what likeness will you compare to Him?

> "The workman molds an image, the goldsmith overspreads it with gold, And the silversmith casts silver chains. Whoever is too impoverished for such a contribution chooses a tree that will not rot; he seeks for himself a skillful workman to prepare a carved image that will not totter.

> "Have you not known? Have you not heard? Has it not been told you from the beginning? Have you not understood from the foundations of the earth? It is He who sits above the circle of the earth, and its inhabitants are like grasshoppers, who stretches out the heavens like a curtain, and spreads them out like a tent to dwell in. He brings the princes to nothing; He makes the judges of the earth useless. Scarcely shall they be planted, scarcely shall they be sown, scarcely shall their stock take root in the earth, when He will also blow on them, and they will wither, and the whirlwind will take them away like stubble.

> "To whom then will you liken Me, or to whom shall I be equal?' says the Holy One." —Isaiah 40:18, 22-25

That would be the correct answer to "who is like God?"

But the same question can also be asked in a derisive or scornful tone, suggesting that anyone or anything can be God. This is the picture that Micah presents in Chapter 17. He has thrown off the God of power in pursuit of prosperity that he thinks he will get from idols of silver.

Consider the actions of Micah and his mother in verses 1-6. What is wrong with this picture?

2. **Why did Micah return the stolen money?**

    His mother's curse is obviously the catalyst that spurs Micah to return the stolen silver, and it may just have been a superstitous fear driving his actions. But the thrust of this passage highlights the hybridizing of godly and heathen practices, so we might also consider how Micah's actions are a twisted version of Mosaic Law.

    He steals, disobeying the eighth great commandment, but then, upon hearing his mother's curse, he owns up to the theft, as if the hearing of her curse or oath is the primary factor. So, what does Mosaic Law say about hearing a curse or oath? Leviticus 5:1 says:

    > *"If a person sins in hearing the utterance of an oath, and is a witness, whether he has seen or known of the matter—if he does not tell it, he bears guilt."*

    This law is about incurring guilt by withholding information—keeping quiet when you know very well what is wrong and who the culprit is. Micah heard his mother's oath—her curse. He knew what happened to the money, and he came out with an abrupt confession as if from a sudden pricking of conscience. Then, having confessed, he received his mother's blessing with no further repercussions, and everything is all right, apparently. He absolved himself of the sin of withholding information and is relieved of guilt on that count. But what of the sin of stealing? Would he have returned the money if there hadn't been a curse put on it? Of course not. Otherwise he wouldn't have stolen it initially.

    Here in Micah's actions, we see a skewed practice of keeping God's laws. The greater commandment is overlooked, while the lesser commandment is obeyed. But this is just the beginning.

3. **What was wrong with his mother's response?**

   To begin with, she receives the cursed money back happily, and instead of punishing her thieving son, she blesses him. Out of the same mouth have come cursing and blessing. This should not be.

   Then we find out she had devoted the money to the LORD, but the method of devotion was not to give it to the priesthood as prescribed by Mosaic Law for their sustanence, but to give it to the silversmith to make into idols. She devoted a cursed thing to the LORD for a cursed purpose, then compounds her sin by withholding the full amount of her vow. She vowed to return the 1,100 pieces of silver to her son in the form of idols, but in reality, she gave only 200 pieces to the silversmith and kept the rest. (This is like the sin of Anaias and Sapphira in Acts 5.)

4. **How did Micah get into the practice of idolatry?**

   It wasn't hard. He just built himself a shrine, made an ephod and some household idols, and consecrated one of his sons. He set up the physical things that made him feel like he was having a religious experience, then did what was right in his own eyes. And that was all it took.

5. **What do we know about the young Levite, and what is wrong with this picture? (Judges 17:7-13)**

   He isn't named but rather identified by his place of origin. He was from Bethlehem in Judah, of the family of Judah. How can he be a Levite and of the family of Judah? Aren't they separate tribes?

   I should explain briefly about Levites in the Land so that you will understand what is wrong with this picture. The Levites were never given any inheritance in the Land. Instead, they were alloted a number of cities scattered among the tribes. As a result, the Levites became attached to whatever tribe possessed their assigned city and were regarded as belonging to that tribe. And so we find here in the narrative that this young Levite came from Bethlehem and was attached to the tribe of Judah. That he came from Bethlehem is a little odd since Bethlehem was not a levitical city. His true origin is a bit of a loose end.

   He had been given an allotted inheritance and an allotted place in God's ministry, so why was he wandering about, looking for a place to stay? Instead of taking his bread and meat out of the offerings reserved for Levites, he was willing to hire himself out to another master for food, clothing, and ten shekels a year. To only offer ten shekels a year is a bit of an irony, considering Micah's mother had 1,100 shekels of silver to devote to the LORD—silver that should have gone to men like this young Levite instead of the silversmith. The very money that should have provided for the Levite had been turned into an idol that he served while he himself lived on a pittance.

Micah offered the young Levite an exalted place in his household as an honorary "father" and priest. But which is better—to be priest to a tribe of Israel, or priest to one man's house? You would think there would be more status in being a priest to a tribe, but the Levite was content to take the offer. The text even belabors the Levite's contentment with his new arrangement, though it was short-lived.

6. **What is the identity of the young Levite? (Judges 18:30)**

   I am going to skip ahead to Judges 18:30 and give you the identity of the priest because it ties into the imagery that plays out from here and will explain a few details.

   > *"Then the children of Dan set up for themselves the carved image; and Jonathan the son of Gershom, the son of **Manasseh [or Moses]**, and his sons were priests to the tribe of Dan until the day of the captivity of the land."* —Judges 18:30 NKJV

   Jonathan, the son of Gershom, was the young Levite who ended up serving in Micah's house before he decamped to the tribe of Dan. In the KJV, NKJV, and NASB Bibles, Jonathan is called the grandson of Manasseh, but in the NIV, ESV, RSV, and others, he is called the grandson of Moses. Why the descrepancy?

   In the name Manasseh, the "n" is suspended, kind of like a superscript character. This suspended letter happens only four times in the Old Testament and suggests that the word can be read with or without the letter. Thus, the name can be read as MNSH (Menashe or Manasseh) or MSH (Moshe or Moses).

   Either way, there are problems with Jonathan's lineage as it is recorded here.

   He was a Levite, and a Levite could not be a blood descendant of Manasseh, obviously. Manasseh and Levi are two separate tribes, and

Manasseh never had a son named Gershom, at least none recorded. So that lineage is suspect.

However, the Levite could be a descendant of Moses, who did have a son named Gershom (1 Chronicles 23:15), but Scriptural genealogies do not record Gershom having a son named Jonathan. So that lineage is unverified.

If Jonathan was, indeed, the grandson of Moses, that would have some significance. It would give him a distinction above other Levites by association with such an exalted figure, but even so, he would still not be a priest since the priesthood is through Aaron's line. Jewish scholars suggest that the suspended "n" was a subtle way of disassociating the apostate grandson from the godly patriarch to avoid the scandal of having a grandson of Moses figure as an apostate priest.

But why connect Jonathan with Manasseh instead? Jewish scholars propose that Jonathan was called the "grandson of Manasseh" not because he was of blood tie to that tribe, but because he was of the *character* of that tribe. Manasseh was known for their wicked practices and idolatry which this young Levite had adopted. This kind of relationship, where a son is identified with a father not by blood but by character or condition, is also found in other places in Scripture, such as the formulaic "son of man" statements. Here are some examples:

> *"God is not a man, that He should lie, nor a son of man, that He should repent..."* —Numbers 23:19a

> *"How much less man, who is a maggot, and a son of man, who is a worm?"* —Job 25:6

> *"Your wickedness affects a man such as you, and your righteousness a son of man."* —Job 35:8

> *"What is man that You are mindful of him, and the son of man that You visit him?"* —Psalm 8:4

> *"Blessed is the man who does this, and the son of man who lays hold on it..."* —Isaiah 56:2a

In all these cases, the relationship between man and son is based on their character, condition, or actions. And so, it might be argued that the author used the same precedent in calling Jonathan the son of Manasseh instead of Moses.

Throughout this study we have been adding the meanings of names to the pictures, so let's do that here.

Jonathan means "whom God has given."
Gershom means "I have been a stranger in a foreign land" (Exodus 2:22).
Manasseh means "one who forgets." (*"For God has made me forget all my toil and all my father's house"* Genesis 41:51.)

The association with Manasseh is very poignant in light of the meanings of this lineage of names. Jonathan became not just a foreigner in regards to being out of his appointed place, but he forgot his appointed work and even his father's house. How fitting.

7. **What is wrong with Micah's assumption in verse 13?**

   He thought that just having a bonafide Levite—the grandson of Moses, no less—performing the priestly service, however idolatrous, guaranteed God's blessing. Not only did Micah make an idol out of silver, he made an idol out of Jonathan as well.

APPLY THE PICTURE

In Chapter 17, we are presented with a picture of this odd hybrid of faith and idolatry. While Micah and his mother retain their identity with God to a certain degree, they work out their faith in idolatrous practices that are poor mimics of the God-ordained ones. They worship idols and expect to be blessed by God for their worship. That seems odd, doesn't it? Why not ask for the blessing from the idol? What purpose did these trappings of religion serve?

In my varied career, I once worked as a picture framer, and I remember the day a young man brought in a religious relic to be framed. He had paid a remarkable sum for a bit of wood someone had told him was a piece of the cross, and it was precious to him. He was loath to part with it even for the necessity of framing it, and tried to impress upon me with utter gravity my responsibility for treating this relic reverently. I felt a revulsion at the young man's fervor over this fraudulent bit of wood, because he had clearly made an idol out of it. And I felt a little like that silversmith being given a quantity of silver with which to make a household idol—like I was somehow facilitating that idolatry—but that was the business, and I was required to comply with the customer's wishes if he was willing to pay. I wanted to say something to him, to dissuade him from the lie, but I knew it would be futile. He was too heavily invested in the item to give up his worship of it.

In another job, I worked with a young man who had been raised Catholic but was no longer practicing that faith. He told me adamantly that he didn't believe in God, and yet he would still go religiously to church every Easter. I asked him why. If he didn't believe any of it, why go at all? What purpose did his attendance serve? He wouldn't, or couldn't, tell me. He seemed to think that showing up at church on Easter—performing that ritual activity—counted for something in God's book.

There are Micahs all around us. We come in contact with them where we work, where we shop—everywhere, really. They may not serve Baals and Asthoreth specifically, but they adopt these ritualistic practices that seem driven by an almost superstitious fear of who knows what. We see the lie that is at the heart of their actions—the belief that somehow a passing nod to God through their works counts for something in the heavenly realm. There are others that think a relationship with God is somehow embodied in the physical trappings of religion. By interacting with these things, they think they are interacting with God, when God is really out of the picture frame altogether.

What do we say to these people? What could I have said to the young man who worshipped a relic? As for the ex-Catholic, I am still hoping the salvation message gets through to him one of these Easters.

Micah is an example of how easy it is to slip into a focus on the external trappings of our worship practices, as if those are what make the experience. I think the temptation is there, however much we may cringe at the thought. It may begin with something as simple as a yearning for "old time" worship. Over the years, I have heard a number of Christians express a dissatisfaction with modern and increasingly contemporary church services. They say something along the lines of "It just doesn't feel like worship without _____ (fill in the blank)." What is worship supposed to feel like? What do we need to make us feel like we have connected with God and each other in fellowship?

What if we are stuck at home in isolation because of a pandemic? What if we can't meet at a church building for fellowship, and corporate worship is suddenly limited to households? How do you recreate the Sunday experience for your own household at home?

We know how Micah did it.

BUILD THE PICTURE

The Danites Send Out Spies, Judges 18:1-9

8. **Why begin the chapter with the statement *"In those days there was no king in Israel"*?**

   This is a critical comment on the narrative to follow. It suggests that if there had been a king, the following events might not have happened.

   The narrative opens with the tribe of Dan seeking a place for themselves because their inheritance hadn't fallen to them yet.

9. **If the Danites' tribal holdings have already been established by Joshua, why does it say their inheritance hasn't fallen to them?**

   Joshua took the Land in the sense that he broke the back of the political and military forces that had the power to push Israel out of the Land, but he did not thoroughly expel the common people still dwelling there. Thus, he gave Israel that "sitting down" rest in the Land, but left them with work to finish. It was the job of each individual tribe to drive out the Canaanites who remained.

   While the Canaanite powers could not dispossess Israel from the Land, they put up a good fight in holding onto what they had. Some of the Canaanites still had small forces with chariots of iron that were formidable to tackle. Such was the case of the Amorites living in the coastal lowlands of Dan's tribal lands. Judges 1:34 tells us:

   > *"And the Amorites forced the children of Dan into the mountains, for they would not allow them to come down to the valley."*

   This is corroborated by the account in the book of Joshua:

   > *"When the territory of the people of Dan was lost to them, the people of Dan went up and fought against Leshem [Laish]..."*
   > Joshua 19:47 ESV

In Joshua 19:47, the phrasing in the Hebrew says, *"When the territory of the people of Dan 'went out' from them."* "Went out" has been translated in a number of ways. The Jewish texts translate this as "slipped from their grasp" or went out of their hand. This implies wrongly that Dan lost all their territory.

Other translations render the phrase *"And the border of the children of Dan went beyond these."* This implies that they took their territory plus additional territory—also wrong.

The passage in Judges clarifies that Dan took the mountainous portion of their inheritance but could not take the lowlands. Having decided to abandon the lowlands, a portion of the children of Dan set out to look for a new inheritance. They began by sending spies out to assess the land.

10. Didn't Moses already send out spies to search the land?

In Numbers 13, Moses sent out twelve men (from the first generation) to assess the land and the people. Because of a faithless report by ten of the spies, the first generation refused to enter the Land and wandered in the wilderness until they died.

The Land was taken by Joshua, Caleb, and the second generation, and the tribes' inheritances were apportioned. Here, the second/third generation of the tribe of Dan persisted in the first generation's lack of faith and failed to press on and finish the job. They were stopped by the Amorite enemy they couldn't overcome by their own strength, and decided to forfeit their inheritance and seek another. They sent out spies in something like a replay of what Moses did.

Let's compare the two accounts:

- **Both generations spied out the length of the Land.** Moses' spies ended up at Rehob; the Danite spies ended up at Laish, which is just across the valley from Rehob. So, they both covered the same territory.

- **Moses' spies ran into the giants and fortified cities, but the Danites found a people who dwelt in safety and quietness.** There were no rulers in Laish or even fortified cities nearby to threaten the Danites. The people of Laish were isolated and made easy targets.

- **Both sets of spies report back.**

  When the first generation of spies reported to Moses, Caleb and Joshua said: *"Let us go up at once and take possession, for we are well able to overcome it... The land we passed through to spy out is an exceedingly good land. If the LORD delights in us, then He will bring us into this land and give it to us, a land which flows with milk and honey. Only do not rebel against the LORD, nor fear the people of the land, for they are our bread; their protection has departed from them, and the LORD is with us. Do not fear them."* The Danite spy sided with the other ten in saying, "We can't take them."

  When the second generation of Danite spies reported back, this time they brought an opposite report: *"Arise, let us go up against them. For we have seen the land, and indeed it is very good. Would you do nothing? Do not hesitate to go, and enter to possess the land. When you go, you will come to a secure people and a large land. For God has given it into your hands, a place where there is no lack of anything that is on the earth."* —Judges 18:9-10

  This report appears to be almost a verbatim quoting of Caleb and Joshua's assessment. They certainly changed their tune.

11. Why have this replay of sending out the spies?

I think it is interesting how generations repeat the actions of their predecessors, even when the outcome wasn't satisfactory in their eyes. Having no idea how to proceed and no leader to guide them (for there was no king in these days), this generation of Danites revisited Moses' playbook on how to take the Land. The faithlessness of the first generation of Danites that caused them to lose their inheritance and die wandering in the wilderness expressed itself in the next generation who have returned to the wilderness experience and are reliving it.

12. Where did the Danite spies begin their journey?

They began at Zorah and Eshtaol, where Samson would begin his ministry many years after this. If we had not established where in the timeline these events took place, it would be easy to think they are a continuation of Samson's narrative, because we are still dealing with the same people and places. This is why it is important to look at the who, what, where, *and* when of the picture.

13. **When they came to Micah's house, the Danite spies asked the Levite to inquire of God for what purpose?**

    This is a fine point but important. They only wanted to know if their journey would be prosperous, not if they should leave their inheritance or not. They had already rejected the LORD's inheritance and made the decision to abandon it, and yet they expect a blessing from God for it. Why bother to inquire of the LORD at all?

14. **What did the Levite tell them was God's response?**

    Moses' grandson echoes Moses' words in telling them *". . . Go in peace. The presence of the LORD be with you on your way."* Literally in the Hebrew: "The Lord is before the way in which you go." But it was a lie. The LORD was not going before them in this endeavor.

15. **The Danites chose Laish for their new settlement. What does the name add to the picture?**

    Laish means "lion" in the sense of an old lion—one that is strong and settled—from the root word *luwsh*, in the sense of kneading and crushing underfoot. It is a the picture of a lion established in his kingdom who is no longer challenged and, therefore, at ease. This is a continuation of the lion theme from Samson.

The Laish Campaign, Judges 18:11-31

16. **Where and how did the Danite refugees begin?**

    Their first staging point was at Mahaneh Dan, the encampment of Dan. Six hundred armed men of war gathered with their families and set out for Laish. Their first stop was at the house of Micah in the mountains of Ephraim, where they decided to provision themselves with Micah's household idols and priest—but not just any priest. This is the grandson of Moses. They are recreating the scene from the wilderness, complete with their own version of Moses.

17. **When the Levite priest questioned them, the Danites told him to *charash*. *Charash*-ing is a Philistine tactic that we studied in Samson. What Philistine tactics do the Danites use?**

    - They showed up in military strength at Micah's house. They didn't threaten him openly, but the implied threat was apparent, kind of like the Philistines showing up at Lehi in Samson's narrative and picking a fight with the men of Judah. It was the intimidation factor.

- They told the priest to keep quiet and go along with the program. There was this same kind of behind-the-scenes scheming as in Samson's narrative.

- They offered him a more prestigious place. Isn't it better to be the priest of an entire tribe than the priest of one man's house? (Funny how the Levite suddenly decided he wasn't so content with the arrangements he once welcomed.)

18. What was Micah's response when he found he had been robbed?

The text says that his neighbors gathered together and went after the Danites to retrieve the stolen possessions, but it is clear that Micah was among the number. There is an irony in that the silver idols that Micah complained had been stolen from him were made of the silver he himself once stole.

There was a bitterness in Micah's complaint over having lost his belongings, but it fell on deaf ears. If Micah had had a relationship with God, he might have had an advocate to bring justice on his behalf. But these idols and apostate priest are powerless and mute.

The Danites responded to Micah with the warning, *"Do not let your voice be heard among us, lest angry men fall upon you . . ."* The Hebrew word for "angry" actually means "bitter of soul."

19. Why were the Danites bitter of soul, and how did the bitterness influence their actions?

They came into the Land with certain expectations that weren't realistic. Maybe they thought that the experience would be easy, that life would be nothing but blessing, and the enemy was already conquered for them.

Wrong expectations led to frustration, a failing in faith, and a failure to overcome the enemy. In their eyes, God had not upheld His promise to give them their inheritance, so they sought another way to take another inheritance that seemed good in their own eye—mostly because it was easier to take.

Their bitterness over having to leave their inheritance is the same bitterness that marked the previous generation's wilderness wandering, along with the desire to throw off God's authority and choose their own leadership, priesthood, and direction in life.

As a result of their bitterness, the children of Dan became base and brutal. They were violent, angry, merciless, opportunistic, and mercenary. They marched the breadth of the Land to possess a dwelling place that was not their own and resettled there without a backward glance.

20. How did the Danites take Laish?

The author's description is decidedly brief and to the point. They struck it with the sword and set the city on fire, then rebuilt the city and lived there. There are no details of the battle, except the remark that the there was no deliverer for the people living in Laish. Reading the account, I almost feel sorry for the inhabitants. They were a quiet people, isolated, and far from help. Granted, they were Canaanites and destined to be driven from the Land by one of the tribes, and yet there was no glory in the way the Danites went about it.

The author notes that the children of Dan set up idolatrous practices there that would remain until the day of the captivity of the Land. The city of Dan is mentioned as late as 1 Kings 12, when Jeroboam, king of the northern Kingdom of Israel, set up a golden calf in Dan for the people to worship. The city of Dan becomes a center for cultic practices in the north during the age of the kings, and will be the first to go into captivity. They will be taken by the Chaldeans, who Habakkuk described very much like the Danites.

> *"For indeed I am raising up the Chaldeans, a bitter and hasty nation which marches through the breadth of the earth, to possess dwelling places that are not theirs. They are terrible and dreadful; Their judgment and their dignity proceed from themselves. . . . They all come for violence; Their faces are set like the east wind. They gather captives like sand."* —Habakkuk 1:6-7, 9

Just because God let them go didn't mean He forgot their faithlessness.

APPLY THE PICTURE

In our own way, we are pursuing an inheritance and a reward. Like Israel, we live and battle among the Canaanites of our day, and the enemy is strong. But just as God left the Canaanites in the Land to test Israel and teach them to fight, so He does with us.

Let's face it. No one goes into these trials willingly; given the option, we would avoid the trials altogether. And so, we can begin to rationalize a reason for escape.

When we are faced with a severe trial, oppression, or just a very strong enemy in our journey, how easy is it to convince ourselves that the roadblock in our way is really a sign from the Lord that maybe we shouldn't be where we are? Maybe the reason we aren't experiencing victory in the battle is because it isn't a battle we were called to fight. Maybe we should just stop fighting and take another path—take another job, cut ourselves off from a difficult family situation, find a quieter place to live.

That's what the Danites did. The fight that the Lord put before them was more than they felt they could overcome, so they went seeking an easier enemy to tackle. They settled for an isolated outpost where there were no enemies around and the people lived at ease. It was an ideal setting, but it wasn't where God wanted them. God wanted them in the struggle. He wanted them to value the inheritance enough to fight mightily for it. Instead, they walked away from Him and the inheritance.

When we are faced with trials, should we seek escape from the struggle or slog through it and let it refine us?

When we make that decision to escape, do we first ask the Lord if this is something we should do, or do we simply ask for His blessing on the way, the way the Danites did?

What do we lose in our relationship with God when we do this?

The Danites went into a land that was already prepared for them with established vineyards, olive and fruit groves, and fields golden with grain, all for the taking when the Lord drove their enemies out before them. They expected to experience prosperity, peace, and rest, but instead found themselves in a pitched battle with strong enemies.

The Danites saw the Land stretched before them and forgot about the relationship with God. But then, that is what usually happens. When we find ourselves in a comfortable situation or with the promise of prosperity on the horizon, the relationship with God quickly fades back to a distant horizon.

The relationship with God is what must be pursued first and foremost. The whole purpose in being faced with trials that are beyond our ability to conquer is that they drive us to God. We wouldn't pursue the Lord with nearly as much vigor if it wasn't for the conflict in our lives. And, yes, we go through the trials and battle the enemy for the Kingdom rewards, but how much better to go through the trials simply for the experience of engaging the Lord in our lives?

The Danites looked at their situation from their own eyes and not God's eyes. They went into the experience with an expectation of God but without understanding what God expected of them. When they discovered that they couldn't oust the enemies and claim the inheritance in their own strength, instead of turning to God, they became frustrated and bitter and abandoned the effort and the relationship.

When we begin a relationship with God with the expectation that the Christian journey is going to be a cake walk, frustation and bitterness will set in quickly, and we will stumble as the tribe of Dan stumbled.

> ## Questions for Reflection:
>
> - Are you frustrated over the difficulties you are having in life right now and seeking a way of escape?
>
> - If so, what do you expect God to do?
>
> - What does God expect you to do?
>
> - What if this trial you are going through isn't for your sake, but someone else's? What if it is shaping you to meet a need in someone else's life down the road? Would you press on through the struggle if that were the case?

LESSON 13

The Redemption of Benjamin

READ

Judges 19–21

OVERVIEW

The Inclusio and Chiastic Structure of Chapters 19–21

These final chapters of the book of Judges are heavily structured in both an inclusio and chiastic format that set the reader up for Israel's transition to a monarchy.

They are encapsulated in the critical comment, *"there was no king in Israel,"* suggesting that the lack of national leadership is responsible for the tragedy unfolding. If only there had been a king, things might have turned out differently.

There is also a chiastic structure in Chapters 19–21 that reinforces the theme of a coming monarchy. The narrative action begins with the individual and builds out in increasing social circles to family, city, and tribe until finally the entire nation comes together as one united front to deal with the crisis.

The apex of the chiasm is Israel's national unification, which sets up a logical argument of a need for a monarchy as the people's attempt at self-governance failed miserably.

Chiastic Structure of Chapters 19-21:

Levite	Individual
Concubine/father-in-law	Family
Men of Gibeah	City
Tribe of Benjamin	Tribe
Congregation of Israel	**Nation**
Remnant of Benjamin	Tribe
Men of Jabesh Gilead	City
Daughters of Shiloh	Family
Every man to his inheritance	Individual

From this apex, the action then resolves back to the individual in reverse order with the statement:

> "So the children of Israel departed from there at that time, every man to his tribe and family; they went out from there, every man to his inheritance." —Judges 21:24

The Chiastic Progression

The narrative begins with the individual. There are four main individuals mentioned: the Levite from the hills of Ephraim, his concubine, her father in Bethlehem, and the old man in Gibeah who is also from the hills of Ephraim. They are not known by name, only by the place where they live.

The narrative begins with conflict between a husband and wife. As a result of her sin, both she and her husband end up in places where they should not be. The husband is detained by his overly-hospitable father-in-law in Bethlehem beyond what is prudent, which creates a new dilemma over where to stay the night. A bad decision is made at the end of the day, and they end up at inhospitable Gibeah.

At Gibeah, the narrative then expands from the individual interaction to group interaction as the perverted men of Gibeah get involved and the crime is committed. The concubine is given to the men of Gibeah and dies after their abuse. The conflict then escalates to the national scene as the Levite reacts to the death of his concubine by cutting her up and sending her body parts out to the tribes. Chapter 19 ends with the call to Israel to gather as a congregation.

With the exception of the Levite's questioning in Chapter 20, the individual characters disappear from the narrative at this point. Instead, the conflict circle enlarges to the city, tribe, and national levels. The congregation of Israel confronts the tribe of Benjamin, who take the side of the perverted men of Gibeah; and the incident ends with judgment being determined against Benjamin and war.

In the aftermath of judgment, Chapter 21 opens with wailing and gnashing of teeth as Israel grapples with the unreconcilable dilemma of how to provide wives for the remnant of Benjamin so that their inheritance might not be lost. The turmoil finally settles when a solution is found at Shiloh. The remnant of Benjamin are provided wives and everyone returns to their family and inheritance. Thus the chiasm is resolved back to the individual level.

No one character is featured as the narrative resolves. Instead, the focus is on the building conflict that begins with one woman's act of unfaithfulness and spirals out to engulf the nation in a crisis.

As we work through the narrative, I want to approach the text as a case study of handling conflict within the congregational body. We will look at the actions, reactions, and attitudes of the various parties, consider the consequences of each, and derive some do's and don'ts from Israel's tragic example.

BUILD THE PICTURE

The Levite's Journey, Judges 19

1. **Who or what is the focus of chapter 19?**

    While the concubine provides the catalyst for the action, the narrative of Chapter 19 focuses rather on the Levite and his physical journey to Bethlehem and then to Gibeah, with a heavy emphasis on his experience of hospitality in both places.

2. **What was the Levite's experience in Bethlehem?**

    At Bethlehem, he was greeted by his father-in-law with an excessive display of hospitality. The man pressed him to stay for five days, but on the fifth day he departs.

3. **What was wrong with the father-in-law's response?**

    It seemed odd to me that a man would harbor his wayward daughter without conscience or consequence for four months and without making an effort to send her back to her husband. He left it to the husband to come and get her, and when the husband showed up on his doorstep, he ushered him in to a joyous feast. Hospitality rules are strictly adhered to in middle eastern culture, and the father-in-law is exemplary in this—to the point that his actions seem almost obsequious and in bad taste. If my son-in-law had showed up on my doorstep to collect my harlot of a daughter, as much as I might ingratiate myself to him, I don't know that I would press him to stay for six days. He did not come to visit for his pleasure.

The man of Bethlehem excels in hospitality and good works, but in dealing with the sin in his family, he appears tolerant and ineffectual. A man can be generous to a fault.

4. **Why did the Levite choose Gibeah over Jebus (Jerusalem)?**

    The servant implored the Levite to turn in at Jebus, but he didn't want to because Jebus was a city of foreigners. Jebus was still under Jebusite control at the time (Judges 1:21), whereas Gibeah belonged to the Benjaminites. Gibeah represents family, where Jebus doesn't.

5. **What was the Levite's experience in Gibeah?**

    Interestingly, the name Gibeah comes from the word *gebiyah*, meaning "a hill" in the sense of being rounded like a bowl turned upside-down—an empty bowl.

> **Side note:**
>
> In keeping with the theme of a coming monarchy, we should note that Bethlehem was the city of King David, whereas Gibeah was of King Saul. The contrast between the two cities here is a reflection on the contrast between the kings. David, like the man of Bethlehem, was exceedingly generous of heart, but also tolerant and ineffectual at dealing with sin in his family. Like Gibeah to Bethlehem, King Saul was inferior and found lacking in every way compared to King David.

   The empty bowl is an apt picture of the kind of hospitality the Levite received in Gibeah. Where the man of Bethlehem offered him the overflowing bowl, the people of Gibeah offered him no hospitality. It wasn't like the Levite needed anything. He had enough provisions for his servants and animals. All he needed was a place to lodge.

   The only hospitality he received was from a foreigner, an old man living in Gibeah who was himself from the mountains of Ephraim.

6. **What is wrong with this picture?**

    The lack of hospitality in itself pointed to hostile intent. While not obvious in the daylight, the dark side of Gibeah came out at night when the perverted men make their appearance. Just as the concubine's father harbored sin in his house, the town of Gibeah was also a sanctuary for sin on a larger scale. The men of Gibeah were completely without hospitality, and not only tolerated sin but participated in it.

7. **The incident at Gibeah is patterned after the account of Sodom (Genesis 19:1-11). What makes the difference between the two accounts?**

   Where Lot harbored angels in Sodom, the old man in Judges harbored humans. What plays out in Gibeah is the course that events take when there is no divine intervention.

   The concubine makes a curious counterpoint to Lot's wife. Both episodes reveal a turning of heart in each woman. Lot's wife went with her husband out of Sodom, but turned away from him at the last minute. Her heart remained loyal to the people of Sodom, and she died as a result. By contrast, the Levite's concubine turned away from her husband initially and was not spared her fate at the hands of the perverted men of Gibeah, but she turned back to him in the end. The text belabors her posture to a point, describing her vividly as dying on the steps of the house where her master was, with an arm outstretched in supplication toward the threshold. She, too, died, but with a different heart, it seems.

8. **What seems odd about the Levite's treatment of his concubine?**

   In Judges 19:3, the Levite went after his wayward concubine to speak kindly to her and bring her back to him. In the Hebrew, it says he went to speak "to her heart." After his initial show of kindness and forebearance, the Levite gave his concubine up almost heartlessly to the men of Gibeah. Even when he found her lying on the threshold the next morning, he didn't seem to notice that she was dead until he received no answer from her. But then, the text says that he picked her up himself and put her body on the donkey to take home. This may seem a minor point, but for a Levite to handle a dead body personally was a defiling thing. He sacrificed her to the men of Gibeah to keep himself from being defiled, but then defiled himself voluntarily for her sake. He could have simply abandoned her or had the servant load her on the donkey, but the fact that he did it himself tells us he still had a heart for his concubine. This is further reinforced by the strength of his outrage over her death.

   If he loved her so much, why give her up to the men of Gibeah to be abused like that?

   To answer that question, I think we have to consider what picture the scenario is painting for us. It is very much a picture of God and Israel.

PICTURE SUMMARY

The concubine's unfaithfulness in playing the harlot against her husband took them down a long road into places where they shouldn't have been. The Levite husband made the initial effort to retrieve her and appealed to her heart to return to him. She went with him, but there was no indication that her heart had changed or that she would be faithful to him going forward.

At the end of the day, the husband and concubine found themselves in a very dark place, and a bad situation developed into a crisis where a difficult decision had to be made. The Levite could not let himself be defiled by the perverted men, and so thrust his unfaithful concubine outside the door to be used as a harlot, at the cost of her life. It was her own harlotry that brought them to this place, and so it is not unjust for her to bear the consequences of her unfaithfulness, however brutal the judgment may be. Though it cost her her life, in the end the concubine returned to her husband humbled and with an attitude of seeking mercy. Perhaps her end fit her sin, or perhaps that is what it took to turn her heart so that she returned to her husband of her own accord.

When the Levite found his concubine on the threshold, abused to death, he made no outcry against the wicked men at first, but the lull was misleading. He did indeed feel something in his heart for his concubine, enough to defile himself for her, and when his outrage finally vented, it heralded a judgment that would be devastating in its scope and character.

APPLY THE PICTURE

PROFILE OF GOD AND ISRAEL

The Levite and his concubine are very much the picture of God and Israel. As we have seen throughout the Judges' narrative, time and again Israel played the harlot, to the point where, in Samson's day, God had to take the initiative to retrieve her when she no longer cried out against her oppressors. But Israel's heart didn't change, even after being brought back time and again.

There came a point in their relationship where Israel's wickedness and unfaithfulness required God to separate Himself from His servant or else risk being defiled Himself. And so, He thrust her outside the Land and into the arms of the Assyrians and Babylonians to be used and abused as the harlot and adulteress she was. The Captivity was an act of tough love, but that is what it took to bring Israel back to Him of her own will, seeking mercy. The books of Hosea, Isaiah, Jeremiah, and Lamentations portray God's dealing with Israel in much the same way as the Levite dealt with his concubine here in Judges.

Even though He put her through that exile that devastated her, God had—and still has—a heart for Israel, and His rage against the nations who abused and killed His people is beyond words. He has judged—and will judge, at a future date—those nations who have done this with a fury poured out in appalling measures. Not only the nations but those of His own people who side with those nations will also suffer catastrophically.

Chapter 19 ends with the call to the congregation to consider, confer, and speak up. Where do we as the Church stand in regards to Israel, unfaithful as she may be—with God or Gibeah?

When we look at this episode of the Levite and his concubine, we should make some observations for our own application.

9. **What does the concubine model for us?**

    Sin begins at an individual level. When we get off the path and onto those winding roads that take us away from God, we end up in places where we should not be. There may be no consequences at first. The concubine stayed at her father's house for four months with seeming impunity. That lull of time between the sin and the consequence can create a false sense of security and an outward appearance that nothing is wrong. But the consequences are far from complete. Even when we are on a path of return, bad decisions can land us in an even darker situation, where we can find ourselves outside the door and the mercy of the godless world. The scenario does not end well.

    Sin that we pursue on an individual level inevitably involves others and takes them with us down that path—our spouse, our families, even our community. Our actions cause collateral damage that radiates out to greater and greater social circles, and then other people's sin begins to interact with our own.

10. **What does the Levite model for us?**

    Having begun down this road as a consequence of another's sin, we can find ourselves at a crossroad of indecision over to how to act and react. Even as we are trying to address sin in the person's life, we are pitted against others whose hospitable accommodation of sin make our task of extricating the wanderer and getting them back on the return path that much more difficult.

When we get into these compromised situations, making good decisions over which path to take going forward can become increasingly difficult, and at the end of the day, what we thought were good decisions can turn out to be bad ones that land us in an even more difficult situation. In spite of our best effort, we can find ourselves faced with hard decisions and unsolvable dilemmas where there is no good solution without someone getting hurt. And then we resort to tough love, which the outside world will think is brutal and unfeeling, but it is necessary to keep ourselves from becoming compromised by sin.

Questions for Reflection

- How far down that path do we go in pursuit of that sinning brother or sister, or spouse?
- How do we react when we become innocent victims of their sin?

Here are some things to think about . . .

- The Levite left Gibeah without raising a cry over the murder of his concubine. What if this was one of us or even someone in the ministry?
    - Why might we opt to leave a situation rather than confront the people who victimized us? Why would a member opt to leave a ministry rather than raise an objection?

Reactions to feeling powerless include remaining silent or acting with destructive anger. The Levite reacted both ways, and his response will have some negative consequences going forward.

- How should a victim respond . . .
    - Should he/she retaliate with some equally outrageous act to express his outrage?
    - Should he/she try to enflame the greater congregation and whip up public opinion?

> - What is the protocol Jesus established in Matthew 18:15-17?
> - Did the Levite follow this protocol? If not, what did he do differently and why?

BUILD THE PICTURE

The Congregation's Response, Judges 20:1-17

11. What message was the Levite sending when he divided up his dead concubine and sent her out to the territories?

We get a clue from a similar act in 1 Samuel 11:7, where Saul cut up a yoke of oxen and sent the pieces out to the territories with the message that whoever didn't join him in battle, this would be done to his cattle. This was the message that this kind of act communicated, except that Saul did it with cattle whereas the Levite did it with a human being.

Receiving a decomposing body part would have been outrageous enough. But if the message implied that this would be done to the women of those who refused to come to the Levite's aid, then that might have been a reason for all of Israel to be up in arms.

12. What was the congregation's response?

All of Israel united for the first time in the book of Judges. Four hundred thousand fighting men from one end of the Land to the other gathered at Mizpah to hear the matter.

The parenthetical statement in verse 3 was added to show that the tribe of Benjamin was identified separately from the children of Israel and was not represented in the assembly.

Does it seem odd that the entire nation geared up for war before even investigating the matter? I think that was a misstep.

13. Why gather at Mizpah?

This Mizpah is not the same Mizpah that we studied in the narrative of Jephthah. That was east of the Jordan in Gilead. This Mizpah is in Benjamin's territory, notably placed between idolatrous Gibeah and

Bethel ("house of God"). It was very near the Palm of Deborah, which was located between Ramah and Bethel.

While the location is different this time, the meaning of the name and purpose of the place remain the same and add to the picture. You will remember that Mizpah means the "watchtower" and evokes the picture of the covenant Jacob made with Laban to: 1) not cross the established family boundaries to do each other evil; and 2) that Jacob would not afflict the daughters of Laban (namely Leah and Rachel, from whom all the daughters of Israel sprang). The watchtower was a reminder that God was watching over Israel to see that they did not deal treacherously with their own.

14. There was a trial, of sorts. What was lacking in the proceedings?

The congregation hears the Levite's story.

> *"So the Levite, the husband of the woman who was murdered, answered and said, "My concubine and I went into Gibeah, which belongs to Benjamin, to spend the night. And the men of Gibeah rose against me, and surrounded the house at night because of me. They intended to kill me, but instead they ravished my concubine so that she died. So I took hold of my concubine, cut her in pieces, and sent her throughout all the territory of the inheritance of Israel, because they committed lewdness and outrage in Israel." —Judges 20:4-6*

Upon hearing this, the text says that Israel rose as one man and immediately declared war on Benjamin.

Interestingly, several things are missing:

- The Levite's explanation of how they ended up in Gibeah was a little sketchy. He didn't relate the problems he was having with his concubine or the fact that she had played the harlot against him. From the way he described it, she seemed a completely innocent victim when, in fact, the outworking of her sin is what brought them to that place. It was not a pleasure trip.

- It is clear the Levite felt completely justified in making an equally obscene and objectionable gesture in response to the lewdness of the men of Gibeah.

- There was no investigation of the truth of his statement. Though the servant and the old man witnessed the events, neither are called as witnesses. According to Mosaic Law, two or three witnesses must testify before a verdict of guilt is rendered, particularly if the punishment involves a death penalty.

- Did Israel decide to go to war before or after they talked with Benjamin? Before. In fact, the tribe of Benjamin wasn't even represented at the trial, let alone the guilty parties.

Israel's decision to go to war against Benjamin appeared hasty, emotion-driven, and backed by only one man's sketchy account of the events. Granted, the victim was a Levite and, thus, a man of status in Israel, and it was clear that a crime had been committed. But there was a lack of orderliness and deliberation about the way the investigation was handled that somehow crossed a boundary.

15. When Israel showed up on Benjamin's doorstep with an ultimatum to hand over their men or else, how did the tribe of Benjamin react?

Benjamin armed for war. I wonder if the men of Benjamin were really that loyal to Gibeah, or if it was just the bullying attitude that Israel adopted that made them stiff-necked. The attitude with which we approach people can make or break a situation.

Benjamin mustered twenty-six thousand fighting men in addition to Gibeah's seven hundred select men, for a total of twenty-six thousand seven hundred men.[1] The text makes a point of mentioning that seven hundred of the men of Benjamin were left-handed and highly skilled at slinging stones. Their left-handedness was caused by the same condition that affected the judge, Ehud, who was also a Benjamite. These men had defects in their right hands that caused the hands to be closed and impeded. There are other mentions of left-handed men in Scripture, but the book of Judges is the only place where this left-handed defect is mentioned.

So the sides were drawn—four hundred thousand men of Israel against twenty-six thousand seven hundred men of Benjamin. It doesn't seem like Benjamin would have chance.

---

[1] The numbering is problematic. Verse 15 gives a total of 26,700 men of Benjamin. Verse 35 says that 25,100 Benjamites were slain. Verse 46 says that 25,000 were slain (a difference of 100). Add 600 to that number for the remnant of escapees, and you get a total of either 25,700 or 25,600 total men, which doesn't match the original count of 26,700.

The Battle, Judges 20:18-48

The battle sequence begins with nearly the same phrasing with which the book of Judges began. Compare the two verses:

> **Judges 1:1-2:** *"Now after the death of Joshua it came to pass that the children of Israel asked the LORD, saying, 'Who shall be first to go up for us against the Canaanites to fight against them?' And the LORD said, 'Judah shall go up. Indeed I have delivered the land into his hand.'"*

> **Judges 20:18:** *"Then the children of Israel arose and went up to the house of God to inquire of God. They said, 'Which of us shall go up first to battle against the children of Benjamin?' The LORD said, 'Judah first!'"*

In the beginning, Israel was facing the Canaanites. Here they faced their own brethren who they are treating like the enemy, but then the Benjamites are acting like Canaanites. There is a minor omission in that the LORD did not say at this time that He had delivered the enemy into Judah's hands. We will come back to that point in a moment.

Having been given what appeared to be the go-ahead, Judah launched itself at Benjamin and immediately lost twenty-two thousand men. Israel regrouped and launched a second time, only to lose another eighteen thousand men. Benjamin, on the other hand, had no casualties.

16. Why would the LORD cause Judah to suffer loss in this battle with Benjamin?

> Look very closely at the action sequence:
>
> - (v18-21) Israel set itself for war, then inquired of the LORD; the LORD gave the go-ahead, and Judah lost twenty-two thousand men.
> - (v22-25) Israel set itself for war again, then wept and inquired of the LORD; the LORD gave the go-ahead, and lost another eighteen thousand men.
> - (v26-35) Israel wept before the LORD and inquired of Him, the LORD gave the go-ahead, *then* they set themselves for battle, and *then* Benjamin was delivered to them.

The first time, Israel had already made the decision to go to war with Benjamin without inquiring of the LORD. They didn't ask *if* they should go to war, only who should go first. So, the LORD sent Judah, the largest of their forces, to be trounced by an inferior force. The second time around, Israel acted before asking again, and they lost again.

What did they do differently the last time? They *asked* before *acting*. Not only that, but there is a distinct attitude change at this point. They humbled themselves before the LORD with weeping, fasting, and offerings first, then waited for the LORD's decision. This time, the LORD told them He would deliver Benjamin into their hands, and it was done. But we should note that while Israel went out to fight, the text says that it was the LORD who defeated Benjamin before Israel. Verse 35 says that Benjamin lost twenty-five thousand one hundred men to Israel's thirty men.

17. What was the outcome of the battle?

The battle was won by an ambush tactic that Joshua had once used in the taking of Ai (Joshua 7). The ambush is mentioned as part of the battle sequence in Judges 20:29–33, but related again in greater detail in verses 37–46. The detailed account is housed within an inclusio bookended by the reference to twenty-five thousand men of Benjamin falling that day. As footnoted on page 283, there is an unexplained discrepancy between verses 35 and 46, but the discrepancy does not change the fact that it was a complete rout for Benjamin.

Verses 44-45 describe the thoroughness of the attack, focusing on the eye-for-an-eye aspect of the punishment with the use of the Hebrew word *alal* in verse 45:

> *"And eighteen thousand men of Benjamin fell; all these were men of valor. Then they turned and fled toward the wilderness to the rock of Rimmon; and they cut down [alal] five thousand of them on the highways. Then they pursued them relentlessly up to Gidom, and killed two thousand of them."* —Judges 20:44-45

The word *alal* has two meanings in the Hebrew.

The first usage of the word is "to glean," as in, to leave nothing behind in terms of a harvest.

> For example: *"When you gather the grapes of your vineyard, you shall not glean [alal] it afterward; it shall be for the stranger, the fatherless, and the widow."* —Deuteronomy 24:21 (cf. Leviticus 19:10)

You would harvest your field in one pass. If you gleaned or *alal*-ed your field, you would make a second pass to pick up the remnant.

The remnant of harvest was to be left for those in remnant status—orphans, widows, and the ex-patriated. To take the whole of your harvest was to treat the remnant among you with contempt and abuse them. Gleaning a field, therefore, was an act of severity against those who were defenseless and at your mercy, which leads to the second definition of *alal*.

The second usage of the word *alal* means "to abuse, deal severely with, make a fool of someone, satisfy your desire by vexing or making sport of, abuse (by thrusting through)."

> For example: "... So the man took his concubine and brought her out to them. And they knew her and abused [alal] her all night until morning; and when the day began to break, they let her go..."
> —Judges 19:25

In this usage, the word *alal* is almost always used in reference to people, and always in the context of excessive judgment or abuse being rendered. The Levite's concubine was *alal*-ed, and that treatment of her was revisited on the men of Gibeah and Benjamin in an eye-for-an-eye fashion. From the beginning, it was Israel's desire to abuse, humiliate, and ultimately destroy the men of Gibeah and Benjamin in retaliation for the concubine's death.

> "And the men of Israel turned back against the children of Benjamin, and struck them down with the edge of the sword—from every city, men and beasts, all who were found. They also set fire to all the cities they came to." —Judges 20:48

They intended to thoroughly cut off the tribe of Benjamin the way a man takes all of the harvest, leaving nothing for the widows, fatherless, and expatriated. But it was not God's intent.

Israel is God's vineyard. It is not often that God thoroughly *alals* or gleans His vineyard, and in this case, He orchestrated events so that a remnant was left. Six hundred Benjamite men took refuge among the pomegranate groves at the Rock of Rimmon. And yet, Benjamin had been so gleaned as to leave no wives for the widowers, which created a dilemma that we will see in the next chapter.

It is a small point, but the text says that the refugees of Benjamin stayed at the Rock of Rimmon for four months. Curiously, this is the same amount of time the concubine remained apart from her husband after fleeing from him. The number four may have been used to indicate a fullness of time, but it also has the effect of projecting the image of an unfaithful concubine onto the men of Benjamin.

APPLY THE PICTURE

Any time the LORD sends Israel into battle and they lose, there is something wrong with Israel's handling of the situation.

Yes, the men of Gibeah should have been handed over, and they might have been handed over if not for the bullying attitude and intimidating show of force with which Israel delivered their ultimatum. Once the defensive reaction set in, the battle then escalated to a new level and a new issue. The localized issue with one group suddenly created a schism within the congregation and multiplied to more ungodliness.

Bullying and aggression have this universal effect.

Yes, Gibeah's crime and Benjamin's lack of cooperation needed to be dealt with, but Israel came out of their places armed for war, eager to take down not just the guilty party, but the entire tribe, based on one man's say-so and before they had even investigated the matter. The men of Benjamin were their brethren, and yet Israel treated them like Canaanite enemies to be utterly destroyed.

Do we do this? Just because a sin has been committed and we are justified in delivering punishment, does that mean we come out of our corners swinging enthusiastically with lashing tongues, ready to slay our brother or sister in Christ as if they were the enemy? Does our judgment then become an *alal*-ing—do we use vindictive words that abuse and humiliate the person? To what end?

It wasn't so much what Israel did, but the heart with which they did it. It is worth noting that God dealt first with those who presumed to be judges before He dealt with the offenders. The attitude with which God's people approached the serious task of judging one another had to be done with an attitude of humility, self-assessment, sorrow, and seeking the LORD's will in the matter. Only when that was achieved did He allow them to deliver the punishment. Persisting in a wrong attitude lost the battle for them each time.

It loses the battle for us as well. How many relationships can we afford to lose before we learn how to judge each other rightly?

When God finally dealt with the offenders, He didn't take out the entire tribe as Israel had planned. He orchestrated the conflict to render right judgment and yet left a remnant through which the tribe of Benjamin might be restored.

It is always God's desire to see the sinner repent and be reconciled to Himself and His people, but that is not always our desire. Our revulsion over the sin and our desire for justice for a victim can drive us to take harsh, even radical, actions. And while we may be justified in dealing harshly with grievous sin within the body of believers, we can do it in a way that goes beyond beneficial punishment, almost to the point of vindictiveness and abusiveness. Instead of removing stumbling blocks that allow a return to God, we can throw up barriers that prevent any hope of reconciliation. We may not put the sinner to death physically, but our actions will cause the death of the relationship. This is not God's desire. This is us acting on what seems right in our own eyes.

Why would the LORD cause Judah to suffer loss in this battle along with Benjamin?

What obligation do we have toward one another as members of one body? When one suffers, do we not all suffer? When one is lost, do we not all grieve? Often times we don't, to our own condemnation.

The behavior in Gibeah didn't happen overnight. This entire incident, including the death of the concubine, might have been avoided if the behavior had been dealt with at its beginnings.

If we see a brother or sister in Christ sinning, and there is something we could say to prevent or turn them from it, should we not speak before the sin reaches the point where they must be put out of the congregation?

If we don't take action or at least warn them, and this is how it ends, should we bear some responsibility as a result? Yes, I think we should. We are never justified in taking a self-righeous stance when the judgment is handed down.

Leviticus 19:17-18 tell us:

> *"You shall not hate your brother in your heart. You shall surely rebuke your neighbor, and not bear sin because of him. You shall not take*

vengeance, nor bear any grudge against the children of your people, but you shall love your neighbor as yourself: I am the LORD." — Leviticus 19:17-18

Loving your neighbor is the second greatest commandment, and it has much to do with how we deal with offenses. Loving your neighbor means rebuking them at times when they are sinning. In fact, to withhold rebuke when it is needed is actually an act of hate, or at least unbrotherliness. But the key is the attitude and the motivation with which it is done. We can look to the Pharisees as a case in point. The Pharisees were zealous in rebuking people, not because they had any genuine concern with restoring a sinning person to a right relationship with God, but because they didn't want to be found guilty of breaking the law against not rebuking and hating. Do you see the self-centeredness and hypocrisy in that? Their actions were actually hate clothed in a self-righteous attitude.

You can rebuke out of a desire to distance yourself from the sin and the offender as if a he was not your brother, or you can rebuke the offender with an attitude that desires his restoration and a continuing relationship. The desire for restoration is at the heart of the command to love our neighbors as ourselves.

There is an echo of Jesus' teachings in how God dealt with Israel's excessive enthusiasm for delivering punishment on their brethren:

"Judge not, that you be not judged. For with what judgment you judge, you will be judged; and with the measure you use, it will be measured back to you. And why do you look at the speck in your brother's eye, but do not consider the plank in your own eye? Or how can you say to your brother, 'Let me remove the speck from your eye'; and look, a plank is in your own eye? Hypocrite! First remove the plank from your own eye, and then you will see clearly to remove the speck from your brother's eye." —Matthew 7:1-5

When this important step isn't accomplished on the part of the judges before exacting punishment, judgment falls on the judge and offender alike, and both experience loss. Even when the right attitude is finally achieved, the fall-out from having begun with the wrong attitude will have some consequences.

BUILD THE PICTURE

The Repercussions of Judgment, Judges 21:1-17

Once the dust settled in the aftermath of the battle, a few more details about what went on in the trial phase came to light. To begin with, there was an issue of an oath that Israel took that now must be honored.

> *"Now the men of Israel had sworn an oath at Mizpah, saying, 'None of us shall give his daughter to Benjamin as a wife.'"* —Judges 21:1

We are warned against taking oaths for a reason. When we are walking by the sight of our own eyes and not God's eyes, we make hasty and ill-advised decisions that run at cross-purposes to God's plan, and He has a way of turning the tables on us to confront us with our missteps.

As their oath attested, it was Israel's desire to see the tribe of Benjamin removed from the assembly—a decision over which they grieved bitterly after the fact, as we see in verses 2-3. But it was not God's desire, and so He orchestrated events to leave this loose end for a little divine comeuppance. He purposely preserved a remnant of Benjamin, which posed Israel with the unsolvable dilemma over how to restore the remnant for whom they had left no provision without breaking their oath. Oaths were binding and incurred judgment when broken.

When you pass judgment on your brother, you had better do it with an attitude that desires reconciliation and makes provision for his restoration, or else that person you laid waste in your abusive dispensing of justice might end up being the person you have to welcome back again.

18. What problem did the oath cause and what was Israel's solution?

> In their zeal to *alal* Gibeah and Benjamin, Israel went so far as to punish not just the guilty parties but completely lay waste all the marriageable women. Even though a remnant of the men were left, there was no way of rebuilding the tribe.
>
> So, the problem became how to find marriageable women when everyone is bound by this oath not to provide wives. So, how else can a man get a wife? One way was by taking them in war. If an enemy was killed, then the marriageble women in his family could be taken as prizes and married off to the victor.

So run with that thought. What enemy could Israel legitimately kill in battle in order to take their women?

19. Who didn't come up to Mizpah?

The question is appalling in its implications. Israel's first inclination is not to seek an enemy outside of the congregation to bear the brunt of its hasty oath, but to make an enemy from among its members. They proposed to kill their own just to get themselves out of this dilemma caused by the Benjamin debacle. But in their eyes, this is a win-win solution. Not only will they be providing wives for Benjamin, but they will be making good on a second oath they had taken.

> *"The children of Israel said, 'Who is there among all the tribes of Israel who did not come up with the assembly to the LORD?' For they had made a great oath concerning anyone who had not come up to the LORD at Mizpah, saying, 'He shall surely be put to death.'"*
> —Judges 21:5

When a count is taken, it turns out that the inhabitants of Jabesh Gilead (east of Jordan) did not appear.

This is a testament to how fine the wheels of judgment grind when these issues begin to resolve.

Jabesh Gilead's absence from the assembly might have passed unnoticed if it hadn't been for this dilemma caused by Israel's first oath. It would seem that redemption for the misstep of the first oath is now found in the execution of the second oath. And, indeed, the judgment against Jabesh Gilead is rather richly deserved. You will remember the name Gilead or *galeed*, from the original agreement between Jacob and Laban at the original Mizpah east of the Jordan in which Jacob agreed not to afflict a daughter of Israel (Genesis 31:50). Now a daughter of Jacob has been afflicted by one of their own, and the men of Gilead do not honor the covenant their father Jacob made before the *galeed* at Mizpah in seeing justice done on behalf of the Levite's concubine. So, as horrifying as Israel's solution is, the judgment against Jabesh Gilead isn't entirely untoward.

It is tragic, however, that Israel's only way out of their oath is to take more lives. Gibeah died for their sin. Benjamin died for their own sin, but also indirectly as a result of Israel's sin. The salvation of the tribe of Benjamin then depended upon the death of the inhabitants of Jabesh Gilead. The consequence of sin is death upon death upon death.

A side note: Though the inhabitants of Jabesh Gilead died, Jabesh Gilead did not disappear from Scriptural history. There remained a particular bond between Jabesh Gilead and the tribe of Benjamin because of this intermarriage, as we see in 1 Samuel 11, where King Saul, a Benjaminite of Gibeah, saved Jabesh Gilead from the Ammonites.

20. What was Israel's final solution when not enough women were taken from Jabesh Gilead?

The death of Jabesh Gilead seemed the ideal solution, until it was discovered that not enough women were taken for all the Benjamites.

There is no other solution except an act of *charash*-ing. A treacherous act of deception is hatched behind the scenes among Israel's leadership as they send the wifeless Benjamites into the vineyard of Shiloh in the days of the harvest feast. In God's vineyard, the remnant of Benjamin would be allowed to glean wives for themselves from among the young women who came to the feast. It had to be done without the families of the young women knowing about it, so that the men might be absolved of complicity and violating their oaths. And so wives were provided for the men of Benjamin from the daughters of Shiloh. It was accomplished by fraud, lies, and thievery, but it was accomplished in a way that resolved the situation with only the elders of Israel to bear the residual burden of guilt.

> *"So the children of Israel departed from there at that time, every man to his tribe and family; they went out from there, every man to his inheritance."* —Judges 21:24

As the turmoil settled in Israel, the book of Judges ends with the critical comment:

> *In those days there was no king in Israel; everyone did what was right in his own eyes."* —Judges 21:25

21. What does the picture of Shiloh add to the final picture in the book of Judges?

Tragic as it was, how appropriate that Israel should look to the vineyards of Shiloh for the answer to their unsolvable dilemma. We were told back in Judges 20:27-28, in a little parenthetical note, that Shiloh was where the Tabernacle of the LORD stood in these days. Mizpah was the place of judgment; Bethel was the place of weeping;

but Shiloh, where God dwelt in His Tabernacle, became the place of final hope for redemption, grace, and the restoration of Benjamin. Israel was God's vineyard and He didn't want it utterly *alal*-ed just yet. He left a remnant and provided a means of restoration and return for the remnant out of His own vineyard at Shiloh.

The name Shiloh means "place of rest" from the root word *shalah*, meaning "rest" in the sense of being happy, safe, secure, and prosperous. The root word carries the idea of being drawn out of turmoil, bondage, or toil.

The imagery of Shiloh here focuses on the nation being drawing out of turmoil—the turmoil of bad decisions and unsolvable dilemmas, the repercussions of sin, hopelessness of loss and separation—and being brought back into a place of tranquility, prosperity, and longevity.

Shiloh has a second usage, though. It also means "that which belongs to him," specifically in reference to a coming king in Genesis 49:10:

> *"The scepter shall not depart from Judah, nor a lawgiver from between his feet, until Shiloh comes; and to Him shall be the obedience of the people."* —Genesis 49:10

When added to the Judges' narrative here, particularly in light of the final critical comment, there is the sense that a king is coming who will set things right and restore Israel. Shiloh anticipates that.

22. What famous Benjamites would have been lost to history without this provision at Shiloh?

King Saul of Gibeah, for one. More significantly for us, the apostle Paul.

APPLY THE PICTURE

Think for a moment what our New Testament understanding would be without Paul's letters to the churches. Many of these churches might not have been born except by his evangelistic efforts and continuing ministry, including the Corinthian church.

The Corinthian church with its many issues and seemingly constant congregational strife could not have been a more suitable challenge for Paul the Benjamite, given his tribe's deplorable family history with its near self-destruction here in the days of the judges. Consider his reaction when he learned of the sexual sin that had taken place in the Corinthian church—sin over which the congregation was puffed up instead of being appalled (1 Cornithians 5). That had been Benjamin's response to the sexual sin of Gibeah. Paul was appalled, to say the least, and he came down on the church members with all the force he could muster. A people could be too hospitable in dealing with sin in their house, and this kind of sin had to be dealt with immediately before it could gain a foothold as it had in long-ago Gibeah.

To their credit, the Corinthian church put the sinning man from their midst, but with all the fervor of Israel in their dealing with Gibeah and Benjamin. The shut-out was completely devastating. Imagine Paul's horror at hearing this. It is like his own family's demise playing out again, right in his own church and at his own instigation. He quickly sent a second letter, urging them to forgive and allow for restoration.

> "But if anyone has caused grief, he has not grieved me, but all of you to some extent—not to be too severe. This punishment which was inflicted by the majority is sufficient for such a man, so that, on the contrary, you ought rather to forgive and comfort him, lest perhaps such a one be swallowed up with too much sorrow. Therefore I urge you to reaffirm your love to him. For to this end I also wrote, that I might put you to the test, whether you are obedient in all things." —2 Corinthians 2:5-9

Paul knew all too well the consequences of not providing for restoration and return of a sinning believer. How little we take his words to heart in dealing with our own members at times.

Questions for Reflection

Have you ever been in a situation where a conflict between yourself and another person was handled wrongly? Boy, I have. Sometimes I have been on the receiving end of it, and sometimes, I am ashamed to say, I have been the one swinging. How about you?

- Have you ever been admittedly in the wrong, even when it was a simple misunderstanding, and had the other person come out of their corner swinging to deliver your rebuke?

- Was the fault entirely on your side, or were they also to blame in part? If so, for what did they deserve judgment?
- Did they use humiliation to deliver the rebuke?
- Did they enflame others to their side so that you didn't feel you could be part of the fellowship anymore?

• Reverse the situation and put yourself in the right (like Israel). How was the issue resolved with your sinning brother?
  - Was the person on whom you passed judgment reconciled to you, or do they avoid you like the plague?
  - If fellowship was not restored, were you partly to blame for it, as Israel was? Might your attitude or aggressiveness have cost you that relationship?
  - Do you feel any sense of loss over the death of that relationship?
  - Punishment can be delivered with constructive rebuke or destructive vindication in taking back your own. Were you more concerned with your own integrity and vindication or with restoring fellowship?
  - To whom else have you spoken of the issue and how? Did you share the story in a way that would humiliate the offender?
  - What if the believer with whom you dealt harshly came back into your life? Would you be able to live/work with them again?

• Have you ever been in a situation where a conflict between yourself and another person was handled correctly and there was a reconciliation? What made the difference?

Conclusion

The book of Judges began with God's people being given a positional "sitting down" in the Land, and it was an inheritance that they would never lose. Not once in all the Judges' narrative was Israel sent from the Land, in spite of their idolatry and unfaithfulness. Yet, despite having this assurance, the inheritance was never fully realized in the days of Joshua. While some tribes did better than others at pressing on to claim the reward of their full inheritance, all of them failed to a degree. As a consequence, they had to live among the Canaanites they had failed to remove and deal with the resulting oppressions that overtook them. And so, Israel began to walk this winding road that led them down paths of coping and compromise into unsolvable dilemmas and deep spiritual darkness.

As believers in Jesus Christ, we, too, have been given a positional "sitting down" place in His kingdom to come, and are faced with the task of pursuing the full reward in that kingdom. Like Israel, we find ourselves living with Canaanites, not as a result of disobedience but obedience to the mandate to go out into the world to be the salt and light among its people. While we do not battle for a physical kingdom in this age, we have that Canaanite within us—our spiritual "old man"—with whom we struggle and are tasked with evicting. The degree to which we battle our inner Canaanite and hold the boundaries with the external Canaanite world defines our success in pursuing the full reward in the Kingdom.

In the book of Judges, Israel modeled for us the consequences of not pursuing our inheritance. We examined the eroding factor of the Canaanite element with whom Israel lived and the oppressions they fell into as a result of adopting Canaanite practices. We talked about the difficulties inherent in those oppressions and the points of stumbling that kept Israel in oppression. In the darkest days when Israel cried out against her oppressors, we saw the work of the Savior and Helper prefigured in the judges who intervened at times to restrain the enemy and bring the people back to God.

Like Israel, we, too, walk a winding road. Israel's journey was given for our admonition, that we might see the pitfalls, failures, and consequences before they ensnare us. Though our oppressions take different forms, they are of the same character and profile as those that beset Israel, and are, therefore, predictable. The book of Judges is a study relevant for us today.

I hope this study has equipped you with some foresight and skills in recognizing places where you might be losing the struggle with your Canaanites. The study of Israel's oppressions and their dynamics were meant to help you get off the winding roads of coping and compromise and over those stumbling blocks that keep you from returning to God.

If you are struggling, I encourage you to follow God's three-step process for getting out of oppression. Begin with yourself. Work through the stumbling blocks of Chapter 3 and consider where you have gotten off track, first in your personal relationship with God and then in your relationships with family, coworkers, etc.

Learn to see Christ as King in your life. This is the first and most important step.

Learn what is right in God's eyes and the truth of His Word. Know what "gain" you are pursuing—what is God's definition of freedom, wealth, and where contentment lies. Hold material wealth lightly.

Learn how (and when and who) to fight. Know the Enemy and his tactics. Equip yourself by a study of God's Word to strengthen yourself with the right mindset when you are under oppression. Understand the dynamics of oppression and what is needed to deal with it. Do not treat your fellow believers as the enemy when sin has to be addressed. That is a point at which you can stumble with horrible consequences.

Hold the borders. Guard the places where spiritual battles have already been fought and won. Maintain the borders in your personal life, family, and sphere of authority or influence where the world seeks entrance and control. Resist the eroding presence of the world around you.

Finally, live the faith openly and fruitfully. Get yourself back on the highway, and then begin helping others get past the same stumbling stones in their lives. The process was never meant to end with you.

Keep up the good fight, and pursue that inheritance!

See you in the Kingdom!

www.ingramcontent.com/pod-product-compliance
Lightning Source LLC
Chambersburg PA
CBHW060418010526
44118CB00017B/2264